C-473 CAREER EXAMINATION SERIES

This is your
PASSBOOK for...

Mason

Test Preparation Study Guide
Questions & Answers

NATIONAL LEARNING CORPORATION®

COPYRIGHT NOTICE

This book is SOLELY intended for, is sold ONLY to, and its use is RESTRICTED to individual, bona fide applicants or candidates who qualify by virtue of having seriously filed applications for appropriate license, certificate, professional and/or promotional advancement, higher school matriculation, scholarship, or other legitimate requirements of education and/or governmental authorities.

This book is NOT intended for use, class instruction, tutoring, training, duplication, copying, reprinting, excerption, or adaptation, etc., by:

1) Other publishers
2) Proprietors and/or Instructors of "Coaching" and/or Preparatory Courses
3) Personnel and/or Training Divisions of commercial, industrial, and governmental organizations
4) Schools, colleges, or universities and/or their departments and staffs, including teachers and other personnel
5) Testing Agencies or Bureaus
6) Study groups which seek by the purchase of a single volume to copy and/or duplicate and/or adapt this material for use by the group as a whole without having purchased individual volumes for each of the members of the group
7) Et al.

Such persons would be in violation of appropriate Federal and State statutes.

PROVISION OF LICENSING AGREEMENTS – Recognized educational, commercial, industrial, and governmental institutions and organizations, and others legitimately engaged in educational pursuits, including training, testing, and measurement activities, may address request for a licensing agreement to the copyright owners, who will determine whether, and under what conditions, including fees and charges, the materials in this book may be used them. In other words, a licensing facility exists for the legitimate use of the material in this book on other than an individual basis. However, it is asseverated and affirmed here that the material in this book CANNOT be used without the receipt of the express permission of such a licensing agreement from the Publishers. Inquiries re licensing should be addressed to the company, attention rights and permissions department.

All rights reserved, including the right of reproduction in whole or in part, in any form or by any means, electronic or mechanical, including photocopying, recording, or by any information storage and retrieval system, without permission in writing from the Publisher.

Copyright © 2025 by
National Learning Corporation

212 Michael Drive, Syosset, NY 11791
(516) 921-8888 • www.passbooks.com
E-mail: info@passbooks.com

PASSBOOK® SERIES

THE *PASSBOOK® SERIES* has been created to prepare applicants and candidates for the ultimate academic battlefield – the examination room.

At some time in our lives, each and every one of us may be required to take an examination – for validation, matriculation, admission, qualification, registration, certification, or licensure.

Based on the assumption that every applicant or candidate has met the basic formal educational standards, has taken the required number of courses, and read the necessary texts, the *PASSBOOK® SERIES* furnishes the one special preparation which may assure passing with confidence, instead of failing with insecurity. Examination questions – together with answers – are furnished as the basic vehicle for study so that the mysteries of the examination and its compounding difficulties may be eliminated or diminished by a sure method.

This book is meant to help you pass your examination provided that you qualify and are serious in your objective.

The entire field is reviewed through the huge store of content information which is succinctly presented through a provocative and challenging approach – the question-and-answer method.

A climate of success is established by furnishing the correct answers at the end of each test.

You soon learn to recognize types of questions, forms of questions, and patterns of questioning. You may even begin to anticipate expected outcomes.

You perceive that many questions are repeated or adapted so that you can gain acute insights, which may enable you to score many sure points.

You learn how to confront new questions, or types of questions, and to attack them confidently and work out the correct answers.

You note objectives and emphases, and recognize pitfalls and dangers, so that you may make positive educational adjustments.

Moreover, you are kept fully informed in relation to new concepts, methods, practices, and directions in the field.

You discover that you are actually taking the examination all the time: you are preparing for the examination by "taking" an examination, not by reading extraneous and/or supererogatory textbooks.

In short, this PASSBOOK®, used directedly, should be an important factor in helping you to pass your test.

MASON

DUTIES

Works along bricklayers and cement masons in the preparation and finishing of cement, concrete, brick, tile and other masonry work to grade and contour; performs related work. This classification covers the installation, with or without the use of mortar or adhesives, of the following: brick, concrete block, gypsum partition tile, pumice block or other lightweight and facsimile units and products common to the masonry industry; fire clay products and refractory construction; rough cut and dressed stone, marble panels, and state units, and installation of structural glazed tile or block, glass brick or block, and solar screen tile or block.

SCOPE OF THE EXAMINATION

The written multiple-choice test may include questions on scaffolding and related rigging; mixing of materials used by masons, bricklayers and cement masons; usage of manual and power tools employed in bricklaying and cement masonry; recognition of hazardous situations and implementation of safety measures; concrete block, brick, specialty masonry, mortar and grout, general building code requirements; and other related areas.

HOW TO TAKE A TEST

I. YOU MUST PASS AN EXAMINATION

A. *WHAT EVERY CANDIDATE SHOULD KNOW*

Examination applicants often ask us for help in preparing for the written test. What can I study in advance? What kinds of questions will be asked? How will the test be given? How will the papers be graded?

As an applicant for a civil service examination, you may be wondering about some of these things. Our purpose here is to suggest effective methods of advance study and to describe civil service examinations.

Your chances for success on this examination can be increased if you know how to prepare. Those "pre-examination jitters" can be reduced if you know what to expect. You can even experience an adventure in good citizenship if you know why civil service exams are given.

B. *WHY ARE CIVIL SERVICE EXAMINATIONS GIVEN?*

Civil service examinations are important to you in two ways. As a citizen, you want public jobs filled by employees who know how to do their work. As a job seeker, you want a fair chance to compete for that job on an equal footing with other candidates. The best-known means of accomplishing this two-fold goal is the competitive examination.

Exams are widely publicized throughout the nation. They may be administered for jobs in federal, state, city, municipal, town or village governments or agencies.

Any citizen may apply, with some limitations, such as the age or residence of applicants. Your experience and education may be reviewed to see whether you meet the requirements for the particular examination. When these requirements exist, they are reasonable and applied consistently to all applicants. Thus, a competitive examination may cause you some uneasiness now, but it is your privilege and safeguard.

C. *HOW ARE CIVIL SERVICE EXAMS DEVELOPED?*

Examinations are carefully written by trained technicians who are specialists in the field known as "psychological measurement," in consultation with recognized authorities in the field of work that the test will cover. These experts recommend the subject matter areas or skills to be tested; only those knowledges or skills important to your success on the job are included. The most reliable books and source materials available are used as references. Together, the experts and technicians judge the difficulty level of the questions.

Test technicians know how to phrase questions so that the problem is clearly stated. Their ethics do not permit "trick" or "catch" questions. Questions may have been tried out on sample groups, or subjected to statistical analysis, to determine their usefulness.

Written tests are often used in combination with performance tests, ratings of training and experience, and oral interviews. All of these measures combine to form the best-known means of finding the right person for the right job.

II. HOW TO PASS THE WRITTEN TEST

A. NATURE OF THE EXAMINATION

To prepare intelligently for civil service examinations, you should know how they differ from school examinations you have taken. In school you were assigned certain definite pages to read or subjects to cover. The examination questions were quite detailed and usually emphasized memory. Civil service exams, on the other hand, try to discover your present ability to perform the duties of a position, plus your potentiality to learn these duties. In other words, a civil service exam attempts to predict how successful you will be. Questions cover such a broad area that they cannot be as minute and detailed as school exam questions.

In the public service similar kinds of work, or positions, are grouped together in one "class." This process is known as *position-classification*. All the positions in a class are paid according to the salary range for that class. One class title covers all of these positions, and they are all tested by the same examination.

B. FOUR BASIC STEPS

1) Study the announcement

How, then, can you know what subjects to study? Our best answer is: "Learn as much as possible about the class of positions for which you've applied." The exam will test the knowledge, skills and abilities needed to do the work.

Your most valuable source of information about the position you want is the official exam announcement. This announcement lists the training and experience qualifications. Check these standards and apply only if you come reasonably close to meeting them.

The brief description of the position in the examination announcement offers some clues to the subjects which will be tested. Think about the job itself. Review the duties in your mind. Can you perform them, or are there some in which you are rusty? Fill in the blank spots in your preparation.

Many jurisdictions preview the written test in the exam announcement by including a section called "Knowledge and Abilities Required," "Scope of the Examination," or some similar heading. Here you will find out specifically what fields will be tested.

2) Review your own background

Once you learn in general what the position is all about, and what you need to know to do the work, ask yourself which subjects you already know fairly well and which need improvement. You may wonder whether to concentrate on improving your strong areas or on building some background in your fields of weakness. When the announcement has specified "some knowledge" or "considerable knowledge," or has used adjectives like "beginning principles of…" or "advanced … methods," you can get a clue as to the number and difficulty of questions to be asked in any given field. More questions, and hence broader coverage, would be included for those subjects which are more important in the work. Now weigh your strengths and weaknesses against the job requirements and prepare accordingly.

3) Determine the level of the position

Another way to tell how intensively you should prepare is to understand the level of the job for which you are applying. Is it the entering level? In other words, is this the position in which beginners in a field of work are hired? Or is it an intermediate or advanced level? Sometimes this is indicated by such words as "Junior" or "Senior" in the class title. Other jurisdictions use Roman numerals to designate the level – Clerk I, Clerk II, for example. The word "Supervisor" sometimes appears in the title. If the level is not indicated by the title, check the description of duties. Will you be working under very close supervision, or will you have responsibility for independent decisions in this work?

4) Choose appropriate study materials

Now that you know the subjects to be examined and the relative amount of each subject to be covered, you can choose suitable study materials. For beginning level jobs, or even advanced ones, if you have a pronounced weakness in some aspect of your training, read a modern, standard textbook in that field. Be sure it is up to date and has general coverage. Such books are normally available at your library, and the librarian will be glad to help you locate one. For entry-level positions, questions of appropriate difficulty are chosen – neither highly advanced questions, nor those too simple. Such questions require careful thought but not advanced training.

If the position for which you are applying is technical or advanced, you will read more advanced, specialized material. If you are already familiar with the basic principles of your field, elementary textbooks would waste your time. Concentrate on advanced textbooks and technical periodicals. Think through the concepts and review difficult problems in your field.

These are all general sources. You can get more ideas on your own initiative, following these leads. For example, training manuals and publications of the government agency which employs workers in your field can be useful, particularly for technical and professional positions. A letter or visit to the government department involved may result in more specific study suggestions, and certainly will provide you with a more definite idea of the exact nature of the position you are seeking.

III. KINDS OF TESTS

Tests are used for purposes other than measuring knowledge and ability to perform specified duties. For some positions, it is equally important to test ability to make adjustments to new situations or to profit from training. In others, basic mental abilities not dependent on information are essential. Questions which test these things may not appear as pertinent to the duties of the position as those which test for knowledge and information. Yet they are often highly important parts of a fair examination. For very general questions, it is almost impossible to help you direct your study efforts. What we can do is to point out some of the more common of these general abilities needed in public service positions and describe some typical questions.

1) General information

Broad, general information has been found useful for predicting job success in some kinds of work. This is tested in a variety of ways, from vocabulary lists to questions about current events. Basic background in some field of work, such as sociology or economics, may be sampled in a group of questions. Often these are principles which have become familiar to most persons through exposure rather than through formal training. It is difficult to advise you how to study for these questions; being alert to the world around you is our best suggestion.

2) Verbal ability

An example of an ability needed in many positions is verbal or language ability. Verbal ability is, in brief, the ability to use and understand words. Vocabulary and grammar tests are typical measures of this ability. Reading comprehension or paragraph interpretation questions are common in many kinds of civil service tests. You are given a paragraph of written material and asked to find its central meaning.

3) Numerical ability

Number skills can be tested by the familiar arithmetic problem, by checking paired lists of numbers to see which are alike and which are different, or by interpreting charts and graphs. In the latter test, a graph may be printed in the test booklet which you are asked to use as the basis for answering questions.

4) Observation

A popular test for law-enforcement positions is the observation test. A picture is shown to you for several minutes, then taken away. Questions about the picture test your ability to observe both details and larger elements.

5) Following directions

In many positions in the public service, the employee must be able to carry out written instructions dependably and accurately. You may be given a chart with several columns, each column listing a variety of information. The questions require you to carry out directions involving the information given in the chart.

6) Skills and aptitudes

Performance tests effectively measure some manual skills and aptitudes. When the skill is one in which you are trained, such as typing or shorthand, you can practice. These tests are often very much like those given in business school or high school courses. For many of the other skills and aptitudes, however, no short-time preparation can be made. Skills and abilities natural to you or that you have developed throughout your lifetime are being tested.

Many of the general questions just described provide all the data needed to answer the questions and ask you to use your reasoning ability to find the answers. Your best preparation for these tests, as well as for tests of facts and ideas, is to be at your physical and mental best. You, no doubt, have your own methods of getting into an exam-taking mood and keeping "in shape." The next section lists some ideas on this subject.

IV. KINDS OF QUESTIONS

Only rarely is the "essay" question, which you answer in narrative form, used in civil service tests. Civil service tests are usually of the short-answer type. Full instructions for answering these questions will be given to you at the examination. But in case this is your first experience with short-answer questions and separate answer sheets, here is what you need to know:

1) Multiple-choice Questions

Most popular of the short-answer questions is the "multiple choice" or "best answer" question. It can be used, for example, to test for factual knowledge, ability to solve problems or judgment in meeting situations found at work.

A multiple-choice question is normally one of three types—
- It can begin with an incomplete statement followed by several possible endings. You are to find the one ending which *best* completes the statement, although some of the others may not be entirely wrong.
- It can also be a complete statement in the form of a question which is answered by choosing one of the statements listed.

- It can be in the form of a problem – again you select the best answer.

Here is an example of a multiple-choice question with a discussion which should give you some clues as to the method for choosing the right answer:

When an employee has a complaint about his assignment, the action which will *best* help him overcome his difficulty is to
- A. discuss his difficulty with his coworkers
- B. take the problem to the head of the organization
- C. take the problem to the person who gave him the assignment
- D. say nothing to anyone about his complaint

In answering this question, you should study each of the choices to find which is best. Consider choice "A" – Certainly an employee may discuss his complaint with fellow employees, but no change or improvement can result, and the complaint remains unresolved. Choice "B" is a poor choice since the head of the organization probably does not know what assignment you have been given, and taking your problem to him is known as "going over the head" of the supervisor. The supervisor, or person who made the assignment, is the person who can clarify it or correct any injustice. Choice "C" is, therefore, correct. To say nothing, as in choice "D," is unwise. Supervisors have and interest in knowing the problems employees are facing, and the employee is seeking a solution to his problem.

2) True/False Questions

The "true/false" or "right/wrong" form of question is sometimes used. Here a complete statement is given. Your job is to decide whether the statement is right or wrong.

SAMPLE: A roaming cell-phone call to a nearby city costs less than a non-roaming call to a distant city.

This statement is wrong, or false, since roaming calls are more expensive.

This is not a complete list of all possible question forms, although most of the others are variations of these common types. You will always get complete directions for answering questions. Be sure you understand *how* to mark your answers – ask questions until you do.

V. RECORDING YOUR ANSWERS

Computer terminals are used more and more today for many different kinds of exams.

For an examination with very few applicants, you may be told to record your answers in the test booklet itself. Separate answer sheets are much more common. If this separate answer sheet is to be scored by machine – and this is often the case – it is highly important that you mark your answers correctly in order to get credit.

An electronic scoring machine is often used in civil service offices because of the speed with which papers can be scored. Machine-scored answer sheets must be marked with a pencil, which will be given to you. This pencil has a high graphite content which responds to the electronic scoring machine. As a matter of fact, stray dots may register as answers, so do not let your pencil rest on the answer sheet while you are pondering the correct answer. Also, if your pencil lead breaks or is otherwise defective, ask for another.

Since the answer sheet will be dropped in a slot in the scoring machine, be careful not to bend the corners or get the paper crumpled.

The answer sheet normally has five vertical columns of numbers, with 30 numbers to a column. These numbers correspond to the question numbers in your test booklet. After each number, going across the page are four or five pairs of dotted lines. These short dotted lines have small letters or numbers above them. The first two pairs may also have a "T" or "F" above the letters. This indicates that the first two pairs only are to be used if the questions are of the true-false type. If the questions are multiple choice, disregard the "T" and "F" and pay attention only to the small letters or numbers.

Answer your questions in the manner of the sample that follows:

32. The largest city in the United States is
    A. Washington, D.C.
    B. New York City
    C. Chicago
    D. Detroit
    E. San Francisco

1) Choose the answer you think is best. (New York City is the largest, so "B" is correct.)
2) Find the row of dotted lines numbered the same as the question you are answering. (Find row number 32)
3) Find the pair of dotted lines corresponding to the answer. (Find the pair of lines under the mark "B.")
4) Make a solid black mark between the dotted lines.

VI. BEFORE THE TEST

Common sense will help you find procedures to follow to get ready for an examination. Too many of us, however, overlook these sensible measures. Indeed, nervousness and fatigue have been found to be the most serious reasons why applicants fail to do their best on civil service tests. Here is a list of reminders:

- Begin your preparation early – Don't wait until the last minute to go scurrying around for books and materials or to find out what the position is all about.
- Prepare continuously – An hour a night for a week is better than an all-night cram session. This has been definitely established. What is more, a night a week for a month will return better dividends than crowding your study into a shorter period of time.
- Locate the place of the exam – You have been sent a notice telling you when and where to report for the examination. If the location is in a different town or otherwise unfamiliar to you, it would be well to inquire the best route and learn something about the building.
- Relax the night before the test – Allow your mind to rest. Do not study at all that night. Plan some mild recreation or diversion; then go to bed early and get a good night's sleep.
- Get up early enough to make a leisurely trip to the place for the test – This way unforeseen events, traffic snarls, unfamiliar buildings, etc. will not upset you.
- Dress comfortably – A written test is not a fashion show. You will be known by number and not by name, so wear something comfortable.

- Leave excess paraphernalia at home – Shopping bags and odd bundles will get in your way. You need bring only the items mentioned in the official notice you received; usually everything you need is provided. Do not bring reference books to the exam. They will only confuse those last minutes and be taken away from you when in the test room.
- Arrive somewhat ahead of time – If because of transportation schedules you must get there very early, bring a newspaper or magazine to take your mind off yourself while waiting.
- Locate the examination room – When you have found the proper room, you will be directed to the seat or part of the room where you will sit. Sometimes you are given a sheet of instructions to read while you are waiting. Do not fill out any forms until you are told to do so; just read them and be prepared.
- Relax and prepare to listen to the instructions
- If you have any physical problem that may keep you from doing your best, be sure to tell the test administrator. If you are sick or in poor health, you really cannot do your best on the exam. You can come back and take the test some other time.

VII. AT THE TEST

The day of the test is here and you have the test booklet in your hand. The temptation to get going is very strong. Caution! There is more to success than knowing the right answers. You must know how to identify your papers and understand variations in the type of short-answer question used in this particular examination. Follow these suggestions for maximum results from your efforts:

1) Cooperate with the monitor

The test administrator has a duty to create a situation in which you can be as much at ease as possible. He will give instructions, tell you when to begin, check to see that you are marking your answer sheet correctly, and so on. He is not there to guard you, although he will see that your competitors do not take unfair advantage. He wants to help you do your best.

2) Listen to all instructions

Don't jump the gun! Wait until you understand all directions. In most civil service tests you get more time than you need to answer the questions. So don't be in a hurry. Read each word of instructions until you clearly understand the meaning. Study the examples, listen to all announcements and follow directions. Ask questions if you do not understand what to do.

3) Identify your papers

Civil service exams are usually identified by number only. You will be assigned a number; you must not put your name on your test papers. Be sure to copy your number correctly. Since more than one exam may be given, copy your exact examination title.

4) Plan your time

Unless you are told that a test is a "speed" or "rate of work" test, speed itself is usually not important. Time enough to answer all the questions will be provided, but this does not mean that you have all day. An overall time limit has been set. Divide the total time (in minutes) by the number of questions to determine the approximate time you have for each question.

5) Do not linger over difficult questions

If you come across a difficult question, mark it with a paper clip (useful to have along) and come back to it when you have been through the booklet. One caution if you do this – be sure to skip a number on your answer sheet as well. Check often to be sure that you have not lost your place and that you are marking in the row numbered the same as the question you are answering.

6) Read the questions

Be sure you know what the question asks! Many capable people are unsuccessful because they failed to *read* the questions correctly.

7) Answer all questions

Unless you have been instructed that a penalty will be deducted for incorrect answers, it is better to guess than to omit a question.

8) Speed tests

It is often better NOT to guess on speed tests. It has been found that on timed tests people are tempted to spend the last few seconds before time is called in marking answers at random – without even reading them – in the hope of picking up a few extra points. To discourage this practice, the instructions may warn you that your score will be "corrected" for guessing. That is, a penalty will be applied. The incorrect answers will be deducted from the correct ones, or some other penalty formula will be used.

9) Review your answers

If you finish before time is called, go back to the questions you guessed or omitted to give them further thought. Review other answers if you have time.

10) Return your test materials

If you are ready to leave before others have finished or time is called, take ALL your materials to the monitor and leave quietly. Never take any test material with you. The monitor can discover whose papers are not complete, and taking a test booklet may be grounds for disqualification.

VIII. EXAMINATION TECHNIQUES

1) Read the general instructions carefully. These are usually printed on the first page of the exam booklet. As a rule, these instructions refer to the timing of the examination; the fact that you should not start work until the signal and must stop work at a signal, etc. If there are any *special* instructions, such as a choice of questions to be answered, make sure that you note this instruction carefully.

2) When you are ready to start work on the examination, that is as soon as the signal has been given, read the instructions to each question booklet, underline any key words or phrases, such as *least, best, outline, describe* and the like. In this way you will tend to answer as requested rather than discover on reviewing your paper that you *listed without describing*, that you selected the *worst* choice rather than the *best* choice, etc.

3) If the examination is of the objective or multiple-choice type – that is, each question will also give a series of possible answers: A, B, C or D, and you are called upon to select the best answer and write the letter next to that answer on your answer paper – it is advisable to start answering each question in turn. There may be anywhere from 50 to 100 such questions in the three or four hours allotted and you can see how much time would be taken if you read through all the questions before beginning to answer any. Furthermore, if you come across a question or group of questions which you know would be difficult to answer, it would undoubtedly affect your handling of all the other questions.

4) If the examination is of the essay type and contains but a few questions, it is a moot point as to whether you should read all the questions before starting to answer any one. Of course, if you are given a choice – say five out of seven and the like – then it is essential to read all the questions so you can eliminate the two that are most difficult. If, however, you are asked to answer all the questions, there may be danger in trying to answer the easiest one first because you may find that you will spend too much time on it. The best technique is to answer the first question, then proceed to the second, etc.

5) Time your answers. Before the exam begins, write down the time it started, then add the time allowed for the examination and write down the time it must be completed, then divide the time available somewhat as follows:
   - If 3-1/2 hours are allowed, that would be 210 minutes. If you have 80 objective-type questions, that would be an average of 2-1/2 minutes per question. Allow yourself no more than 2 minutes per question, or a total of 160 minutes, which will permit about 50 minutes to review.
   - If for the time allotment of 210 minutes there are 7 essay questions to answer, that would average about 30 minutes a question. Give yourself only 25 minutes per question so that you have about 35 minutes to review.

6) The most important instruction is to *read each question* and make sure you know what is wanted. The second most important instruction is to *time yourself properly* so that you answer every question. The third most important instruction is to *answer every question*. Guess if you have to but include something for each question. Remember that you will receive no credit for a blank and will probably receive some credit if you write something in answer to an essay question. If you guess a letter – say "B" for a multiple-choice question – you may have guessed right. If you leave a blank as an answer to a multiple-choice question, the examiners may respect your feelings but it will not add a point to your score. Some exams may penalize you for wrong answers, so in such cases *only*, you may not want to guess unless you have some basis for your answer.

7) Suggestions
   a. Objective-type questions
      1. Examine the question booklet for proper sequence of pages and questions
      2. Read all instructions carefully
      3. Skip any question which seems too difficult; return to it after all other questions have been answered
      4. Apportion your time properly; do not spend too much time on any single question or group of questions

5. Note and underline key words – *all, most, fewest, least, best, worst, same, opposite*, etc.
6. Pay particular attention to negatives
7. Note unusual option, e.g., unduly long, short, complex, different or similar in content to the body of the question
8. Observe the use of "hedging" words – *probably, may, most likely*, etc.
9. Make sure that your answer is put next to the same number as the question
10. Do not second-guess unless you have good reason to believe the second answer is definitely more correct
11. Cross out original answer if you decide another answer is more accurate; do not erase until you are ready to hand your paper in
12. Answer all questions; guess unless instructed otherwise
13. Leave time for review

   b. Essay questions
1. Read each question carefully
2. Determine exactly what is wanted. Underline key words or phrases.
3. Decide on outline or paragraph answer
4. Include many different points and elements unless asked to develop any one or two points or elements
5. Show impartiality by giving pros and cons unless directed to select one side only
6. Make and write down any assumptions you find necessary to answer the questions
7. Watch your English, grammar, punctuation and choice of words
8. Time your answers; don't crowd material

8) Answering the essay question

Most essay questions can be answered by framing the specific response around several key words or ideas. Here are a few such key words or ideas:

M's: manpower, materials, methods, money, management
P's: purpose, program, policy, plan, procedure, practice, problems, pitfalls, personnel, public relations

   a. Six basic steps in handling problems:
1. Preliminary plan and background development
2. Collect information, data and facts
3. Analyze and interpret information, data and facts
4. Analyze and develop solutions as well as make recommendations
5. Prepare report and sell recommendations
6. Install recommendations and follow up effectiveness

   b. Pitfalls to avoid
1. *Taking things for granted* – A statement of the situation does not necessarily imply that each of the elements is necessarily true; for example, a complaint may be invalid and biased so that all that can be taken for granted is that a complaint has been registered

2. *Considering only one side of a situation* – Wherever possible, indicate several alternatives and then point out the reasons you selected the best one
3. *Failing to indicate follow up* – Whenever your answer indicates action on your part, make certain that you will take proper follow-up action to see how successful your recommendations, procedures or actions turn out to be
4. *Taking too long in answering any single question* – Remember to time your answers properly

IX. AFTER THE TEST

Scoring procedures differ in detail among civil service jurisdictions although the general principles are the same. Whether the papers are hand-scored or graded by machine we have described, they are nearly always graded by number. That is, the person who marks the paper knows only the number – never the name – of the applicant. Not until all the papers have been graded will they be matched with names. If other tests, such as training and experience or oral interview ratings have been given, scores will be combined. Different parts of the examination usually have different weights. For example, the written test might count 60 percent of the final grade, and a rating of training and experience 40 percent. In many jurisdictions, veterans will have a certain number of points added to their grades.

After the final grade has been determined, the names are placed in grade order and an eligible list is established. There are various methods for resolving ties between those who get the same final grade – probably the most common is to place first the name of the person whose application was received first. Job offers are made from the eligible list in the order the names appear on it. You will be notified of your grade and your rank as soon as all these computations have been made. This will be done as rapidly as possible.

People who are found to meet the requirements in the announcement are called "eligibles." Their names are put on a list of eligible candidates. An eligible's chances of getting a job depend on how high he stands on this list and how fast agencies are filling jobs from the list.

When a job is to be filled from a list of eligibles, the agency asks for the names of people on the list of eligibles for that job. When the civil service commission receives this request, it sends to the agency the names of the three people highest on this list. Or, if the job to be filled has specialized requirements, the office sends the agency the names of the top three persons who meet these requirements from the general list.

The appointing officer makes a choice from among the three people whose names were sent to him. If the selected person accepts the appointment, the names of the others are put back on the list to be considered for future openings.

That is the rule in hiring from all kinds of eligible lists, whether they are for typist, carpenter, chemist, or something else. For every vacancy, the appointing officer has his choice of any one of the top three eligibles on the list. This explains why the person whose name is on top of the list sometimes does not get an appointment when some of the persons lower on the list do. If the appointing officer chooses the second or third eligible, the No. 1 eligible does not get a job at once, but stays on the list until he is appointed or the list is terminated.

X. HOW TO PASS THE INTERVIEW TEST

The examination for which you applied requires an oral interview test. You have already taken the written test and you are now being called for the interview test – the final part of the formal examination.

You may think that it is not possible to prepare for an interview test and that there are no procedures to follow during an interview. Our purpose is to point out some things you can do in advance that will help you and some good rules to follow and pitfalls to avoid while you are being interviewed.

What is an interview supposed to test?

The written examination is designed to test the technical knowledge and competence of the candidate; the oral is designed to evaluate intangible qualities, not readily measured otherwise, and to establish a list showing the relative fitness of each candidate – as measured against his competitors – for the position sought. Scoring is not on the basis of "right" and "wrong," but on a sliding scale of values ranging from "not passable" to "outstanding." As a matter of fact, it is possible to achieve a relatively low score without a single "incorrect" answer because of evident weakness in the qualities being measured.

Occasionally, an examination may consist entirely of an oral test – either an individual or a group oral. In such cases, information is sought concerning the technical knowledges and abilities of the candidate, since there has been no written examination for this purpose. More commonly, however, an oral test is used to supplement a written examination.

Who conducts interviews?

The composition of oral boards varies among different jurisdictions. In nearly all, a representative of the personnel department serves as chairman. One of the members of the board may be a representative of the department in which the candidate would work. In some cases, "outside experts" are used, and, frequently, a businessman or some other representative of the general public is asked to serve. Labor and management or other special groups may be represented. The aim is to secure the services of experts in the appropriate field.

However the board is composed, it is a good idea (and not at all improper or unethical) to ascertain in advance of the interview who the members are and what groups they represent. When you are introduced to them, you will have some idea of their backgrounds and interests, and at least you will not stutter and stammer over their names.

What should be done before the interview?

While knowledge about the board members is useful and takes some of the surprise element out of the interview, there is other preparation which is more substantive. It *is* possible to prepare for an oral interview – in several ways:

1) Keep a copy of your application and review it carefully before the interview

This may be the only document before the oral board, and the starting point of the interview. Know what education and experience you have listed there, and the sequence and dates of all of it. Sometimes the board will ask you to review the highlights of your experience for them; you should not have to hem and haw doing it.

2) Study the class specification and the examination announcement

Usually, the oral board has one or both of these to guide them. The qualities, characteristics or knowledges required by the position sought are stated in these documents. They offer valuable clues as to the nature of the oral interview. For example, if the job involves supervisory responsibilities, the announcement will usually indicate that knowledge of modern supervisory methods and the qualifications of the candidate as a supervisor will be tested. If so, you can expect such questions, frequently in the form of a hypothetical situation which you are expected to solve. NEVER go into an oral without knowledge of the duties and responsibilities of the job you seek.

3) Think through each qualification required

Try to visualize the kind of questions you would ask if you were a board member. How well could you answer them? Try especially to appraise your own knowledge and background in each area, *measured against the job sought*, and identify any areas in which you are weak. Be critical and realistic – do not flatter yourself.

4) Do some general reading in areas in which you feel you may be weak

For example, if the job involves supervision and your past experience has NOT, some general reading in supervisory methods and practices, particularly in the field of human relations, might be useful. Do NOT study agency procedures or detailed manuals. The oral board will be testing your understanding and capacity, not your memory.

5) Get a good night's sleep and watch your general health and mental attitude

You will want a clear head at the interview. Take care of a cold or any other minor ailment, and of course, no hangovers.

What should be done on the day of the interview?

Now comes the day of the interview itself. Give yourself plenty of time to get there. Plan to arrive somewhat ahead of the scheduled time, particularly if your appointment is in the fore part of the day. If a previous candidate fails to appear, the board might be ready for you a bit early. By early afternoon an oral board is almost invariably behind schedule if there are many candidates, and you may have to wait. Take along a book or magazine to read, or your application to review, but leave any extraneous material in the waiting room when you go in for your interview. In any event, relax and compose yourself.

The matter of dress is important. The board is forming impressions about you – from your experience, your manners, your attitude, and your appearance. Give your personal appearance careful attention. Dress your best, but not your flashiest. Choose conservative, appropriate clothing, and be sure it is immaculate. This is a business interview, and your appearance should indicate that you regard it as such. Besides, being well groomed and properly dressed will help boost your confidence.

Sooner or later, someone will call your name and escort you into the interview room. *This is it.* From here on you are on your own. It is too late for any more preparation. But remember, you asked for this opportunity to prove your fitness, and you are here because your request was granted.

What happens when you go in?

The usual sequence of events will be as follows: The clerk (who is often the board stenographer) will introduce you to the chairman of the oral board, who will introduce you to the other members of the board. Acknowledge the introductions before you sit down. Do not be surprised if you find a microphone facing you or a stenotypist sitting by. Oral interviews are usually recorded in the event of an appeal or other review.

Usually the chairman of the board will open the interview by reviewing the highlights of your education and work experience from your application – primarily for the benefit of the other members of the board, as well as to get the material into the record. Do not interrupt or comment unless there is an error or significant misinterpretation; if that is the case, do not hesitate. But do not quibble about insignificant matters. Also, he will usually ask you some question about your education, experience or your present job – partly to get you to start talking and to establish the interviewing "rapport." He may start the actual questioning, or turn it over to one of the other members. Frequently, each member undertakes the questioning on a particular area, one in which he is perhaps most competent, so you can expect each member to participate in the examination. Because time is limited, you may also expect some rather abrupt switches in the direction the questioning takes, so do not be upset by it. Normally, a board member will not pursue a single line of questioning unless he discovers a particular strength or weakness.

After each member has participated, the chairman will usually ask whether any member has any further questions, then will ask you if you have anything you wish to add. Unless you are expecting this question, it may floor you. Worse, it may start you off on an extended, extemporaneous speech. The board is not usually seeking more information. The question is principally to offer you a last opportunity to present further qualifications or to indicate that you have nothing to add. So, if you feel that a significant qualification or characteristic has been overlooked, it is proper to point it out in a sentence or so. Do not compliment the board on the thoroughness of their examination – they have been sketchy, and you know it. If you wish, merely say, "No thank you, I have nothing further to add." This is a point where you can "talk yourself out" of a good impression or fail to present an important bit of information. Remember, *you close the interview yourself*.

The chairman will then say, "That is all, Mr. _____, thank you." Do not be startled; the interview is over, and quicker than you think. Thank him, gather your belongings and take your leave. Save your sigh of relief for the other side of the door.

How to put your best foot forward

Throughout this entire process, you may feel that the board individually and collectively is trying to pierce your defenses, seek out your hidden weaknesses and embarrass and confuse you. Actually, this is not true. They are obliged to make an appraisal of your qualifications for the job you are seeking, and they want to see you in your best light. Remember, they must interview all candidates and a non-cooperative candidate may become a failure in spite of their best efforts to bring out his qualifications. Here are 15 suggestions that will help you:

1) Be natural – Keep your attitude confident, not cocky

If you are not confident that you can do the job, do not expect the board to be. Do not apologize for your weaknesses, try to bring out your strong points. The board is interested in a positive, not negative, presentation. Cockiness will antagonize any board member and make him wonder if you are covering up a weakness by a false show of strength.

2) Get comfortable, but don't lounge or sprawl

Sit erectly but not stiffly. A careless posture may lead the board to conclude that you are careless in other things, or at least that you are not impressed by the importance of the occasion. Either conclusion is natural, even if incorrect. Do not fuss with your clothing, a pencil or an ashtray. Your hands may occasionally be useful to emphasize a point; do not let them become a point of distraction.

3) Do not wisecrack or make small talk

This is a serious situation, and your attitude should show that you consider it as such. Further, the time of the board is limited – they do not want to waste it, and neither should you.

4) Do not exaggerate your experience or abilities

In the first place, from information in the application or other interviews and sources, the board may know more about you than you think. Secondly, you probably will not get away with it. An experienced board is rather adept at spotting such a situation, so do not take the chance.

5) If you know a board member, do not make a point of it, yet do not hide it

Certainly you are not fooling him, and probably not the other members of the board. Do not try to take advantage of your acquaintanceship – it will probably do you little good.

6) Do not dominate the interview

Let the board do that. They will give you the clues – do not assume that you have to do all the talking. Realize that the board has a number of questions to ask you, and do not try to take up all the interview time by showing off your extensive knowledge of the answer to the first one.

7) Be attentive

You only have 20 minutes or so, and you should keep your attention at its sharpest throughout. When a member is addressing a problem or question to you, give him your undivided attention. Address your reply principally to him, but do not exclude the other board members.

8) Do not interrupt

A board member may be stating a problem for you to analyze. He will ask you a question when the time comes. Let him state the problem, and wait for the question.

9) Make sure you understand the question

Do not try to answer until you are sure what the question is. If it is not clear, restate it in your own words or ask the board member to clarify it for you. However, do not haggle about minor elements.

10) Reply promptly but not hastily

A common entry on oral board rating sheets is "candidate responded readily," or "candidate hesitated in replies." Respond as promptly and quickly as you can, but do not jump to a hasty, ill-considered answer.

11) Do not be peremptory in your answers

A brief answer is proper – but do not fire your answer back. That is a losing game from your point of view. The board member can probably ask questions much faster than you can answer them.

12) Do not try to create the answer you think the board member wants

He is interested in what kind of mind you have and how it works – not in playing games. Furthermore, he can usually spot this practice and will actually grade you down on it.

13) Do not switch sides in your reply merely to agree with a board member

Frequently, a member will take a contrary position merely to draw you out and to see if you are willing and able to defend your point of view. Do not start a debate, yet do not surrender a good position. If a position is worth taking, it is worth defending.

14) Do not be afraid to admit an error in judgment if you are shown to be wrong

The board knows that you are forced to reply without any opportunity for careful consideration. Your answer may be demonstrably wrong. If so, admit it and get on with the interview.

15) Do not dwell at length on your present job

The opening question may relate to your present assignment. Answer the question but do not go into an extended discussion. You are being examined for a *new* job, not your present one. As a matter of fact, try to phrase ALL your answers in terms of the job for which you are being examined.

Basis of Rating

Probably you will forget most of these "do's" and "don'ts" when you walk into the oral interview room. Even remembering them all will not ensure you a passing grade. Perhaps you did not have the qualifications in the first place. But remembering them will help you to put your best foot forward, without treading on the toes of the board members.

Rumor and popular opinion to the contrary notwithstanding, an oral board wants you to make the best appearance possible. They know you are under pressure – but they also want to see how you respond to it as a guide to what your reaction would be under the pressures of the job you seek. They will be influenced by the degree of poise you display, the personal traits you show and the manner in which you respond.

ABOUT THIS BOOK

This book contains tests divided into Examination Sections. Go through each test, answering every question in the margin. We have also attached a sample answer sheet at the back of the book that can be removed and used. At the end of each test look at the answer key and check your answers. On the ones you got wrong, look at the right answer choice and learn. Do not fill in the answers first. Do not memorize the questions and answers, but understand the answer and principles involved. On your test, the questions will likely be different from the samples. Questions are changed and new ones added. If you understand these past questions you should have success with any changes that arise. Tests may consist of several types of questions. We have additional books on each subject should more study be advisable or necessary for you. Finally, the more you study, the better prepared you will be. This book is intended to be the last thing you study before you walk into the examination room. Prior study of relevant texts is also recommended. NLC publishes some of these in our Fundamental Series. Knowledge and good sense are important factors in passing your exam. Good luck also helps. So now study this Passbook, absorb the material contained within and take that knowledge into the examination. Then do your best to pass that exam.

EXAMINATION SECTION

EXAMINATION SECTION
TEST 1

DIRECTIONS: Each question or incomplete statement is followed by several suggested answers or completions. Select the one that BEST answers the question or completes the statement. *PRINT THE LETTER OF THE CORRECT ANSWER IN THE SPACE AT THE RIGHT.*

1. A *flashed* or *flare* header is a

    A. dark-colored brick
    B. light-colored brick
    C. bat
    D. full-sized brick

1._____

2. A brick apron wall would MOST likely be used with

    A. wood frame construction
    B. steel frame construction
    C. masonry bearing walls
    D. none of the above

2._____

3. According to the building code, a hollow wall is built

    A. with hollow masonry units
    B. with solid masonry units
    C. without mortar
    D. to form interior walls only

3._____

4. The brick veneer of masonry wall is

    A. not joined to the wall in any way
    B. bonded to the wall
    C. tied to the wall
    D. separated from the wall by an appreciable air space

4._____

5. Increasing the amount of sand in a mortar for masonry will result in a mortar which is

    A. stronger
    B. more water resistant
    C. lower in shrinkage
    D. slower setting

5._____

6. Retempering of mortar is permissible

    A. with cement mortar
    B. with lime mortar
    C. with cement-lime mortar
    D. in no case

6._____

7. The frog in a brick

    A. is an imperfection
    B. is a trademark
    C. increases the weight of the brick
    D. provides a key for mortar

7._____

8. The MOST likely use of snap headers in an 8-inch brick wall is to

    A. improve the appearance of the wall
    B. increase the strength of the wall
    C. reduce the quantity of face brick in the wall
    D. simplify the laying of the brick

8._____

9. After a brick wall is completed, it is to be washed with a solution of muriatic acid. Washing is to be done from a swinging scaffold. The scaffold should be supported by

    A. manila rope
    B. hemp rope
    C. steel cables
    D. wrought iron chain

10. Before washing a brick wall with acid, mortar adhering to the face of the wall should be removed by using a

    A. stiff brush and a carborundum stone
    B. hammer
    C. hammer and chisel
    D. wooden mallet

11. In applying muriatic acid solution to a brick wall, the bricklayer should use a(n) _____ _____ pail and _____ brush.

    A. iron; wire
    B. wooden; fiber
    C. wooden; wire
    D. iron; fiber

12. A wood float is used to finish concrete surfaces when

    A. a smooth but gritty surface is desired
    B. a rough surface is desired
    C. a very smooth surface is desired
    D. the concrete mix is very stiff

13. Troweling of concrete should be done

    A. immediately after the concrete is struck off in the forms
    B. just before the concrete mix shows any stiffness
    C. after the concrete is stiff enough to walk on
    D. when the concrete is quite stiff but still workable

14. *Curing* of concrete is important

    A. if the mix is very wet
    B. if the mix is very dry
    C. regardless of the water-cement ratio of the mix
    D. in cold weather only

15. A mortar mix is called a 1:1:6 mix. The numbers refer to the following ingredients of the mortar:

    A. cement, water, and sand
    B. cement, lime, and sand
    C. cement, sand, and gravel
    D. lime, water, and sand

16. Mortar droppings inside a cavity wall are

    A. good because they strengthen the wall
    B. bad because they may block weep holes
    C. good because they make the wall more resistant to the passage of water
    D. bad because they prevent air circulation within the wall

Questions 17-21.

DIRECTIONS: Questions 17 through 21, inclusive, refer to the concrete masonry units shown in the sketches below.

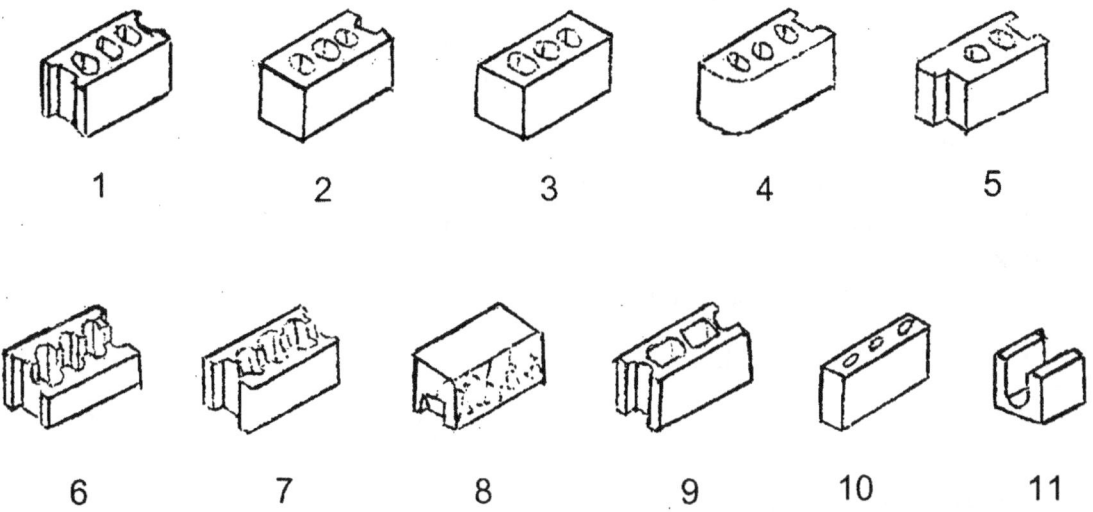

17. Of the above units, the one which would be used at the intersection of two walls is numbered

    A. 2   B. 5   C. 8   D. 11

18. Of the above units, the one which would be used as a header is numbered

    A. 1   B. 3   C. 4   D. 6

19. Of the above units, the one which would be used to form the sides of a door opening is numbered

    A. 1   B. 2   C. 4   D. 5

20. The unit which would be used in connection with steel reinforcement in a wall is numbered

    A. 1   B. 6   C. 9   D. 11

21. The unit which would be used in cavity wall construction is numbered

    A. 7   B. 8   C. 10   D. 11

22. A pail with a volume of one cubic foot holds exactly 7.48 gallons of water. A gallon of water occupies a space, in cubic inches, of

    A. 227   B. 229   C. 231   D. 233

23. A bullnose brick would MOST likely be used

    A. in arch work
    B. for window sills
    C. for backing
    D. for chimneys

24. Camber would MOST likely be found in

    A. solid brick walls B. cavity walls of brick
    C. wooden joists D. steel columns

25. Centering would MOST likely be used in the construction of brick

    A. arches B. sidewalks
    C. walls D. all of the above

26. A closer or closure brick is

    A. the last brick placed in a brick structure
    B. a brick adjoining a door or window opening in a wall
    C. a brick used to form the intersection of two walls
    D. the last brick placed in a course of brick work

27. Firebrick would be LEAST likely to be used in

    A. fire walls B. flues
    C. fireplaces D. furnace linings

28. A lewis is generally used to lift

    A. stone B. brick
    C. concrete block D. wood

29. The opposite of batter is

    A. camber B. miter C. chamfer D. overhang

30. The term *withe* or *wythe* is used in connection with

    A. floors B. spandrels C. walls D. openings

31. A lead in bricklaying corresponds in function MOST closely to

    A. a ground in plastering
    B. flashing in roofing
    C. a miter in carpentry
    D. a float in concrete work

32. Terra cotta tile which is usually scored so that it can be split easily on the job is USUALLY intended for

    A. backup work B. tile bearing walls
    C. tile partitions D. furring

33. A 12-inch brick wall built with standard (not modular) brick is actually 12 1/4 inches thick. The thickness of the mortar joint between a stretcher on one face of the wall and a header on the other is, in inches, MOST NEARLY

    A. 1/4 B. 3/8 C. 1/2 D. 5/8

34. Assume a 2 x 4 is 12'6" long. The number of board feet in this 2 x 4 is MOST NEARLY

    A. 7.9 B. 8.1 C. 8.3 D. 8.5

35. The sum of 5/12 and 1/4 is 35._____

    A. 7/12 B. 2/3 C. 3/4 D. 5/6

36. In brickwork, the terms *raked, struck,* and *weathered* refer to the 36._____

    A. bond
    B. type of mortar
    C. type of brick
    D. type of pointing

37. The furrow in the mortar of a bed joint should be 37._____

    A. deep
    B. shallow
    C. wide
    D. prohibited

38. Assume the masonry facing of a veneered wall is connected to the wall by dovetail anchors. The wall is MOST likely made of 38._____

    A. concrete
    B. wood
    C. stone masonry
    D. terra cotta tile

39. Upon opening a bag of cement, many lumps are found which cannot be crumbled by hand. The BEST thing to do in this case is 39._____

    A. sieve the cement to remove the lumps
    B. break up the lumps with a hammer
    C. use the cement as is but use more of it than would otherwise be used
    D. discard this bag and all others like it

40. In reinforced concrete work, wire chairs are GENERALLY used to 40._____

    A. reinforce sharp corners
    B. reinforce concrete in the interior of the member
    C. position reinforcing rods
    D. tie reinforcing rods together

KEY (CORRECT ANSWERS)

1. A	11. B	21. C	31. A
2. B	12. A	22. C	32. D
3. B	13. D	23. B	33. C
4. C	14. C	24. C	34. C
5. C	15. B	25. A	35. B
6. B	16. B	26. D	36. D
7. D	17. A	27. A	37. B
8. C	18. B	28. A	38. A
9. C	19. D	29. D	39. D
10. A	20. D	30. C	40. C

TEST 2

DIRECTIONS: Each question or incomplete statement is followed by several suggested answers or completions. Select the one that BEST answers the question or completes the statement. *PRINT THE LETTER OF THE CORRECT ANSWER IN THE SPACE AT THE RIGHT.*

1. The foundation for a brick wall should be at least four feet below ground surface. A shallower depth would be UNSATISFACTORY because   1.____

   A. the bearing value of the soil would be too small
   B. the foundation would be above the frost line
   C. the wall would not provide adequate insulation for the building
   D. burrowing animals could dig under the wall

2. In concrete work, wooden form spreaders   2.____

   A. are never removed
   B. should be removed before they are covered with concrete
   C. should be removed after they are well covered with concrete
   D. should be removed after the concrete has taken its initial set

3. Concrete for a 6-inch reinforced concrete wall has a slump of 2 inches. The defect that would MOST likely be found in the finished wall would be   3.____

   A. honeycombing   B. segregation
   C. excessive laitance   D. improper curing

4. Within practical limits, the MOST important factor governing the strength of a concrete mix is the ratio of cement to   4.____

   A. sand   B. gravel
   C. sand and gravel   D. water

5. A plan view of a building would be the BEST view to refer to in order to determine   5.____

   A. details of bond in a wall
   B. story height
   C. clear spacing between walls
   D. height of parapet

6. The interior surfaces of concrete form work are coated with oil PRIMARILY to   6.____

   A. provide concrete with smooth surfaces
   B. prevent honeycombing
   C. make form removal easier
   D. aid in curing the concrete

7. The volume of earth, in cubic yards, excavated from a trench 4' 0" wide by 5' 6" deep by 18' 6" long is MOST NEARLY   7.____

   A. 14.7   B. 15.1   C. 15.5   D. 15.9

8. A deformed bar used as reinforcement in reinforced concrete USUALLY

   A. is a twisted rod
   B. is bent at one or both ends
   C. has a different shape than the other bars in the pour
   D. has projecting lugs

9. The PRIMARY objection to continued troweling of a concrete floor when a smooth finish is desired is that such a practice

   A. makes a very slippery floor
   B. increases the cost
   C. produces a surface which will chalk or dust
   D. brings the coarse aggregate to the surface

10. When a chute is used to deposit concrete for a floor, the LEAST important consideration in placing the chute is

    A. the height of the discharge end above the floor
    B. the slope of the chute
    C. making provision to move the discharge end to any spot on the floor
    D. the sharpness of the angle where the chute changes direction horizontally

11. Beveled chamfer strips are used in the construction of formwork for concrete to

    A. eliminate right-angle corners in the forms
    B. make the forms watertight
    C. strengthen the forms
    D. position reinforcing bars

12. In reinforced concrete work, steel reinforcing bars USUALLY are

    A. bent at the steel mill
    B. heated to a red heat before bending on the job
    C. cut and welded on the job to form bends
    D. bent cold on a bar bending table

13. Of the following structural steel shapes, the one which would MOST likely be used for the lintel of a standard window in a brick wall is

    A. I   B. ⌐ C. ⊔   D. ⌐

14. In a pile of enameled brick, it would be very unusual to find a brick which was glazed on more than the following number of faces:

    A. 1   B. 2   C. 3   D. 4

15. To cut glazed brick,

    A. the identical method is used as in cutting common brick
    B. a power saw must be used
    C. a rotating abrasive disk should be used
    D. a hammer and chisel should be used

16. A bricklayer's level is placed on a flat surface which is apparently horizontal. The bubble is displaced one mark to the right. When the level is replaced on the surface with the ends of the level reversed, the bubble is again displaced one mark to the right. This indicates that

    A. the surface is horizontal
    B. the bubble tube is not set properly
    C. the bubble tube is set properly
    D. it is necessary to test the level on a known horizontal surface before any conclusion can be reached

17. The first course of a lead consists of three bricks. The height of this lead, in courses, would normally be

    A. 7   B. 6   C. 3   D. 4

18. Assume a wall consists of face brick and back-up tile. Before back-plastering the face brick (before the back-up units are laid), the joints in the back of the face brick should be

    A. cut flush   B. left as is
    C. carefully tooled   D. raked

19. Spalls would MOST probably be used by a

    A. carpenter   B. bricklayer
    C. stone mason   D. concrete worker

20. Tooling of face joints in brick work should be done

    A. after a course is completed
    B. immediately after laying four or five bricks
    C. after the mortar has acquired its initial set
    D. after the mortar has acquired its final set

21. A slump test would MOST likely be performed by a

    A. bricklayer   B. concrete worker
    C. carpenter   D. plumber

22. In brick work, a course consisting of brick set on end is known as _____ course.

    A. rowlock   B. belt   C. lacing   D. soldier

23. The same type of mortar would be used on all of the following units EXCEPT

    A. common brick   B. glazed brick
    C. fire brick   D. concrete block

24. Stone concrete block is inferior to cinder concrete block in

    A. strength   B. appearance
    C. durability   D. insulation

25. A coping is USUALLY held in place by

    A. mortar   B. nails   C. bolts   D. rivets

26. As used by bricklayers, *culling* is a terra used when

    A. cutting block to size
    B. selecting good brick from a pile
    C. making a furrow in the mortar bed
    D. laying the first brick in a wall

27. To obtain durability, exposed brickwork should be built of well-burned bricks. As used in the above sentence, durability means MOST NEARLY

    A. beauty
    B. water resistance
    C. strength
    D. long life

28. A common mistake is to assume that the strength of masonry is the most important factor. As used in the above sentence, assume means MOST NEARLY

    A. determine
    B. take for granted
    C. figure
    D. make sure

29. To produce a more plastic mortar, lime putty is added to cement mortar. As used in the above sentence, more plastic means MOST NEARLY

    A. whiter
    B. easier to work
    C. smoother
    D. denser

30. Copings should be made of impervious materials. As used in the above sentence, impervious means MOST NEARLY

    A. solid
    B. expensive
    C. water resistant
    D. strong

31. A steak weighed 2 pounds 4 ounces. How much did it cost at $4.60 per pound?

    A. $7.80   B. $8.75   C. $9.90   D. $10.35

32. During his summer vacation, a boy earned $45.00 per day and saved 60% of his earnings. If he worked 45 days, how much did he save during his vacation?

    A. $15.00   B. $18.00   C. $1215.00   D. $22.50

33. From his coin bank, a boy took 3 half dollars, 8 quarters, 7 dimes, 6 nickels, and 9 pennies to deposit in his school savings account. Express in dollars and cents the total amount of money he deposited.

    A. $2.82   B. $4.59   C. $6.42   D. $7.52

34. If a roast that requires 1 hour and 40 minutes of roasting time has been in the oven for 55 minutes, how many more minutes of roasting time are required?

    A. 30   B. 36   C. 45   D. 55

35. On the first day of its drive, a school raised $400, which was 33 1/3% of its Red Cross quota. How much was the quota?

    A. $1,200   B. $1,300   C. $1,400   D. $1,500

36. On a certain map, a distance of 10 miles is represented by 1/2 inch. If two towns are 3 1/2 inches apart on this map, express in miles the actual distance between the two towns.

   A. 70   B. 80   C. 90   D. 100

37. At an annual rate of $.40 per $100, what is the fire insurance premium for one year on a house that is insured for $80,000?

   A. $120   B. $160   C. $240   D. $320

38. A meter equals approximately 1.09 yards. How much longer, in yards, is a 100-meter dash than a 100-yard dash?

   A. 6   B. 8   C. 9   D. 12

39. A train leaves New York City at 8:10 A.M. and arrives in Buffalo at 4:45 P.M. on the same day. How long, in hours and minutes, does it take the train to make the trip?
   _____ hours, _____ minutes.

   A. 6; 22   B. 7; 16   C. 7; 28   D. 8; 35

40. A jacket that was marked at $125.00 was sold for $100. What was the rate of discount on the marked price?

   A. 10%   B. 15%   C. 18%   D. 20%

KEY (CORRECT ANSWERS)

1. B	11. A	21. B	31. D
2. B	12. D	22. D	32. C
3. A	13. C	23. C	33. B
4. D	14. B	24. D	34. C
5. C	15. C	25. A	35. A
6. C	16. C	26. B	36. A
7. B	17. B	27. D	37. D
8. D	18. A	28. B	38. C
9. C	19. C	29. B	39. D
10. D	20. C	30. C	40. D

EXAMINATION SECTION
TEST 1

DIRECTIONS: Each question or incomplete statement is followed by several suggested answers or completions. Select the one that BEST answers the question or completes the statement. *PRINT THE LETTER OF THE CORRECT ANSWER IN THE SPACE AT THE RIGHT.*

1. In a building, furring is USUALLY attached to the inside of a brick wall by galvanized

   A. pins
   B. screws
   C. ties
   D. anchor bolts

2. Brick is sometimes dipped in water before laying because

   A. the bricklayer prefers to handle wet brick
   B. the moisture absorbed makes the brick heavier
   C. a wet brick will not take moisture from the mortar
   D. a wet brick will not break as easily as a dry one

3. A piece of lumber measures 6 inches wide by 2 inches thick by 8 feet long. The number of board feet contained in the piece is

   A. 8 B. 10 C. 12 D. 48

4. The sum of 1/12 and 1/4 is

   A. 1/3 B. 5/12 C. 7/12 D. 3/8

5. The product of 12 and 2 1/3 is

   A. 27 B. 28 C. 29 D. 30

6. If 4 1/2 is subtracted from 7 1/5, the remainder is

   A. 3 7/10 B. 2 7/10 C. 3 3/10 D. 2 3/10

7. A slump test is performed on

   A. brick B. wood C. steel D. concrete

8. In brick work, a course consisting of bricks set upon their sides is known as a _____ course.

   A. soldier B. rowlock C. header D. stretcher

9. A small vertical recess or hollowed-out portion of a brick wall is called a

   A. chase B. gable C. corbel D. cope

10. Mortar for brick work MOST usually consists of

    A. lime, cement, and sand
    B. cement, sand, and water
    C. lime, cement, and water
    D. lime, cement, sand, and water

11. If mortar acquires an initial set (that is, becomes too stiff to work), it should be

    A. remixed without adding water
    B. remixed with added water
    C. used as it is
    D. discarded

12. A header brick differs from a stretcher brick in

    A. size
    B. shape
    C. surface finish
    D. position in the wall

13. The expression *two by four* refers to

    A. mortar   B. stone   C. wood   D. brick

14. Cut stone used in the construction of a brick wall would NOT be used for

    A. sills   B. coping   C. trip   D. backing

15. The length, thickness, and width of common brick are, in inches, respectively,

    A. 8 x 2 x 4
    B. 6 x 2 1/4 x 3 3/4
    C. 8 x 6 x 3 3/4
    D. 8 x 2 1/4 x 33

16. The terms *raked, struck, weather* are MOST likely to be used in the construction of

    A. walls   B. roofs   C. floors   D. foundations

17. The furrow in the mortar of a bed joint should be

    A. deep
    B. shallow
    C. wide
    D. parallel to the short side of the brick

18. Before starting to lay the bricks, mortar for bed joints should be spread out over a number of bricks. In general practice, this number is MOST NEARLY

    A. 32   B. 16   C. 8   D. 4

19. Of the following methods of making head joints in stretcher courses, the POOREST one is

    A. put plenty of mortar on the end of the brick and shove it into place
    B. spot a dab of mortar on the brick already in place, then throw plenty of mortar on it, and finally shove the brick being laid into this mortar
    C. shove the brick into a deep bed of mortar
    D. place the brick without mortar and then slush the joint

20. An inspector removes a brick which has just been laid. If the mortar does not adhere to the brick, it is an indication that

    A. the joint was not properly furrowed
    B. something is wrong with the mortar
    C. too much mortar was used
    D. not enough mortar was used

21. In masonry work, spalls are

    A. stones which have been rejected
    B. small stones used for closures
    C. chips of stone
    D. key-shaped bricks

22. Centering is used by a(n)

    A. electrician   B. bricklayer
    C. plumber   D. plasterer

23. A lintel is used in a

    A. roof   B. wall   C. floor   D. footing

24. Tooling of face joints in brick work should be done

    A. immediately after the brick is laid
    B. after the mortar has acquired initial set
    C. after the mortar has acquired final set
    D. on extensive jobs, after the wall is completed

25. A wall consists of stone facing and brick backing. Parging (or pargeting) should be done with

    A. stone-setting mortar
    B. brick mortar
    C. either type of mortar
    D. a mortar other than the two types specified

26. A worker's hourly rate is $8.52. If he works 11 1/2 hours, he should receive

    A. $97.38   B. $97.98   C. $ 98.61   D. $99.18

27. Water freezes at _____ °F.

    A. 0   B. 100   C. 50   D. 32

28. In brick work, pointing means

    A. laying brick at an angle
    B. filling exposed joints with mortar
    C. using the point of the trowel to furrow a bed
    D. laying the brick to a particular pattern

29. A dove-tail anchor would MOST likely be used to anchor

    A. individual bricks to one another
    B. individual stones to one another
    C. facing brick to terra cotta backing
    D. masonry facing to a concrete wall

30. A bonding or brushing mortar with a consistency of cream would MOST probably be used to lay   30.____

    A. common brick   B. face brick
    C. cinder concrete block   D. insulating fire brick

31. Upon opening a bag of cement, you find that there are many lumps in it which you cannot crumble in your hand. The BEST thing to do is to   31.____

    A. remove the lumps before using the cement
    B. discard the entire bag
    C. break up the lumps with a hammer
    D. use the cement as is

32. Twenty pints of water just fill a pail. The capacity of the pail, in gallons, is   32.____

    A. 2   B. 2 1/4   C. 2 1/2   D. 2 3/4

33. It is good practice to have the bottom of a footing for a wall at least four feet below the surface of the ground. This depth is specified to   33.____

    A. insure that the earth will provide a good support for the footing
    B. keep the bottom of the footing below the frost line
    C. allow for a shallow cellar
    D. keep the footing from showing

34. You are assisting a mason who is laying up concrete block for an exterior wall. He is careless and there are numerous smears of mortar on the outside surface of blocks which have just been placed. You should   34.____

    A. immediately wipe the mortar off with a wet rag
    B. allow the mortar to dry before removing it
    C. use a trowel to scrape it off immediately
    D. immediately wipe it off with an oily rag

35. A standard brick weighs, in pounds, about   35.____

    A. 1   B. 2   C. 4   D. 8

Questions 36-40.

DIRECTIONS: Questions 36 through 40, inclusive, refer to the concrete masonry units shown in the sketches below.

36. The unit which is called a stretcher is marked   36._____

    A. 1   B. 2   C. 3   D. 4

37. The unit which would be used to form the sides of door or window openings in a wall is marked   37._____

    A. 2   B. 4   C. 5   D. 6

38. A 12-inch wall is to be built with a brick facing and concrete block backing. The unit which would be required for this wall and would not ordinarily be used in a wall consisting of concrete block only is marked   38._____

    A. 5   B. 6   C. 9   D. 11

39. The unit which would MOST likely be used for an interior non-bearing partition is   39._____

    A. 7   B. 8   C. 10   D. 11

40. The unit which would BEST serve to support a floor joist is marked   40._____

    A. 3   B. 8   C. 9   D. 10

KEY (CORRECT ANSWERS)

1. C	11. D	21. C	31. B
2. C	12. D	22. B	32. C
3. A	13. C	23. B	33. B
4. A	14. D	24. B	34. B
5. B	15. D	25. A	35. C
6. B	16. A	26. B	36. A
7. D	17. B	27. D	37. C
8. B	18. D	28. B	38. B
9. A	19. D	29. D	39. C
10. D	20. B	30. D	40. B

TEST 2

DIRECTIONS: Each question or incomplete statement is followed by several suggested answers or completions. Select the one that BEST answers the question or completes the statement. *PRINT THE LETTER OF THE CORRECT ANSWER IN THE SPACE AT THE RIGHT.*

1. A bricklayer uses a lead in laying brickwork to   1.____

    A. tool joints
    B. place mortar beds
    C. cut brick
    D. maintain line and grade

2. A masonry unit 9" x 4 1/2" x 2 1/2" weighs two pounds. This unit is MOST probably a(n)   2.____

    A. insulating fire brick
    B. fireclay brick
    C. roman brick
    D. stone-faced concrete block

3. A 1:2:4 concrete contains for each bag of cement   3.____

    A. two wheelbarrows of sand and four of gravel
    B. sand weighing twice as much as a bag of cement and gravel weighing twice as much as the sand
    C. two cubic feet of sand and four of gravel
    D. one bag of lime, two of sand, and four of gravel

4. A short stairway is constructed of brick. The brick forming the nosing of the treads should be   4.____

    A. full headers
    B. half headers
    C. stretchers
    D. splits

5. On a given job, concrete for a floor is being chuted into place. The lower end of the chute is 8 feet above the floor. The end of the chute can be moved about horizontally. Which one of the following statements is MOST NEARLY correct?   5.____

    A. Moving the end of the chute is poor practice because concrete should be spread from one location.
    B. The 8-foot drop is good practice as it prevents clogging the end of the chute.
    C. The 8-foot drop is poor practice because it causes segregation.
    D. The height of drop is unimportant as long as the end of the chute can be moved about.

6. Terra cotta units would be used in a wall as   6.____

    A. backing
    B. facing
    C. either backing or facing, depending upon type
    D. fireproofing only

7. A carborundum stone would MOST likely be used to   7.____

    A. remove form marks from concrete
    B. form mortar joints in brickwork

C. smooth marble walls
D. dress fieldstone walls

8. If 1,233 bricks are required for 100 square feet of 8-inch wall, the number of bricks required for 150 square feet of 12-inch wall is MOST NEARLY

   A. 2,466   B. 2,569   C. 2,672   D. 2,775

Questions 9-12.

DIRECTIONS: Questions 9 through 12 refer to the brickwork units shown in the sketches below.

9. Common bond is marked

   A. 1   B. 2   C. 3   D. 4

10. English bond is marked

    A. 1   B. 2   C. 3   D. 5

11. The bond marked 6 would be used PRINCIPALLY for

    A. bearing walls
    B. veneered walls
    C. faced walls
    D. sidewalks

12. For a wall using face brick with common brick backing and all full headers, the bond which would require the LARGEST number of face brick per 100 square feet is marked

    A. 2   B. 3   C. 4   D. 5

13. It is CORRECT to say that

    A. bond affects the appearance of the wall only
    B. bond has no effect on the strength of a wall
    C. proper bond increases the strength of a wall
    D. the bond depends only upon the type of brick used to construct the wall

14. In brick work, *filling in* could not be done on a wall which had a thickness, in inches, of

    A. 8   B. 12   C. 16   D. 20

15. Projecting courses of masonry at the corners of buildings are known as 15._____

    A. quoins   B. coping   C. culls   D. batters

16. Steel columns in buildings are encased in concrete to 16._____

    A. strengthen the columns
    B. provide a surface for plastering
    C. give protection from fire
    D. comply with architectural plans

17. In concrete work, wooden form spreaders 17._____

    A. are never used
    B. should be removed as soon as the concrete is placed
    C. should be removed after the concrete has attained initial set
    D. should be removed after the concrete has attained final set

18. An advantage of cinder concrete block over stone concrete block is that the cinder concrete block is 18._____

    A. stronger   B. heavier
    C. a better insulator D. better in appearance

19. The use of bats in brickwork is 19._____

    A. good, because it cuts the amount of face brick required
    B. good, because it increases the strength of the wall
    C. sometimes required by the bond
    D. never justified

Questions 20-24.

DIRECTIONS: Questions 20 through 24 refer to the four mortars which are described below.

Mortar A - 1 part cement, 1/4 part lime putty, 3 parts sand
Mortar B - 1 part cement, 1 part lime putty, 6 parts sand
Mortar C - 1 part cement, 2 parts lime putty, 9 parts sand
Mortar D - 1/4 part cement, 2 parts lime putty, 7 parts sand

20. The mortar to use for reinforced brickwork is Mortar 20._____

    A. A   B. B   C. C   D. D

21. Mortar D would be MOST appropriate for 21._____

    A. masonry work below grade
    B. masonry work in severe (cold) climates
    C. non-bearing walls
    D. furnace linings

22. The mortar that would MOST likely be used for the bearing walls of a two-story building is either Mortar 22._____

    A. A or B   B. B or C   C. C or D   D. A or D

23. The mortar that would be used to lay insulating fire brick is Mortar

   A. A
   B. B or C
   C. D
   D. none of the above

24. Of the following, the kind of bar that would be MOST satisfactory for reinforcing concrete would be one that

   A. had a rusty surface
   B. was covered with grease
   C. was painted
   D. was oiled

25. Concrete for a thin, reinforced wall section should have a slump, in inches, of MOST NEARLY

   A. 1
   B. 2 1/2
   C. 6
   D. 10

26. Within reasonable limits and for a given amount of cement, the MOST important factor governing the strength of concrete is the amount of _____ added.

   A. water
   B. sand and gravel
   C. sand
   D. gravel

27. Terrazzo is made of

   A. clay
   B. marble chips and neat cement
   C. sand and neat cement
   D. asbestos and neat cement

28. The number of cubic feet in 3 cubic yards is

   A. 81
   B. 82
   C. 83
   D. 84

29. A cubic foot of loose, dry sand would weigh, in pounds, MOST NEARLY

   A. 25
   B. 50
   C. 75
   D. 100

30. The number of cubic yards in 47 cubic feet is MOST NEARLY

   A. 1.70
   B. 1.74
   C. 1.78
   D. 1.82

31. A wall 8'0" high by 12'6" long has a window opening 4'0" high by 3'6" wide. The net area of the wall (allowing for the window opening) is, in square feet,

   A. 86
   B. 87
   C. 88
   D. 89

32. Rafters would be used in the construction of

   A. roofs
   B. floors
   C. walls
   D. columns

33. A trimmer arch would be used in construction involving

   A. windows
   B. floor openings
   C. chimneys
   D. bulkheads

34. Coping would be placed by a

   A. carpenter
   B. mason
   C. plumber
   D. roofer

35. Before placing concrete in forms, the inside surfaces of the forms should be covered with   35.____

   A. oil   B. water   C. paint   D. wax

36. In laying up ashlar masonry walls, it is good practice to   36.____

   A. pin up the stones with spalls
   B. drop the stones into place
   C. settle each stone in place with a maul
   D. slide stones over stones which have already been laid

37. Of the following materials, the one which is MOST acceptable and commonly used in reinforced concrete construction to form chairs is   37.____

   A. brick   B. wood
   C. wire   D. cinder block

Questions 38-40.

DIRECTIONS: Questions 38 through 40 are to be answered SOLELY in accordance with the information in the paragraph given below.

Before placing the concrete, check that the forms are rigid and well braced, and place the concrete within 45 minutes after mixing it. Fill the forms to the top with the wearing-course concrete. Level off the surfaces with a strikeboard. When the concrete becomes stiff but still workable (in a few hours), finish the surface with a wood float. This fills the hollows and compacts the concrete, and produces a smooth but gritty finish. For a non-gritty and smoother surface (but one that is more slippery when wet), follow up with a steel trowel after the water sheen from the wood-troweling starts to disappear. If you wish, slant the tread forward a fraction of an inch so that it will shed rain water.

38. Slanting the tread a fraction of an inch gives a surface that will   38.____

   A. have added strength   B. not be slippery when wet
   C. shed rain water   D. not have hollows

39. In addition to giving a smooth but gritty finish, the use of a wood float will tend to   39.____

   A. give a finish that is slippery when wet
   B. compact the concrete
   C. give a better wearing course
   D. provide hollows to retain rain water

40. Which one of the following statements is MOST NEARLY correct?   40.____

   A. Having checked the forms, one may place the concrete immediately after mixing same.
   B. One must wait at least 15 minutes after mixing the concrete before it may be placed in the forms.
   C. A gritty compact finish and one which is more slippery when wet will result with the use of a wood float.
   D. A steel trowel used promptly after a wood float will tend to give a non-gritty smooth finish.

KEY (CORRECT ANSWERS)

1.	D	11.	C	21.	C	31.	A
2.	A	12.	A	22.	B	32.	A
3.	C	13.	C	23.	D	33.	C
4.	A	14.	A	24.	A	34.	B
5.	C	15.	A	25.	C	35.	A
6.	C	16.	C	26.	A	36.	C
7.	A	17.	B	27.	B	37.	C
8.	D	18.	C	28.	A	38.	C
9.	A	19.	C	29.	D	39.	B
10.	B	20.	A	30.	B	40.	A

EXAMINATION SECTION
TEST 1

DIRECTIONS: Each question or incomplete statement is followed by several suggested answers or completions. Select the one that BEST answers the question or completes the statement. *PRINT THE LETTER OF THE CORRECT ANSWER IN THE SPACE AT THE RIGHT.*

1. The sketch below shows a concrete building wall and footing with a dumbbell shaped sheet of rubber joining then.

   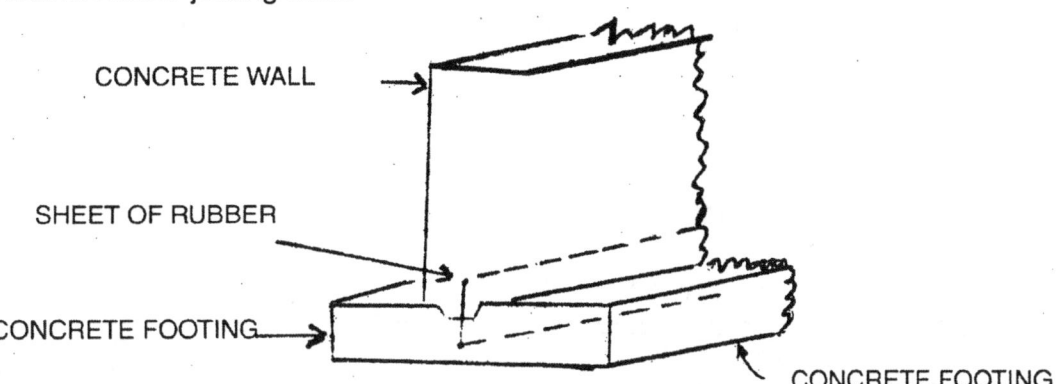

   The MAIN purpose of the sheet of rubber between the footing and the wall is to

   A. cut down the loss of heat from the building
   B. prevent termites from entering into the building through the joint
   C. prevent the flow of water through the joint
   D. provide a flexible joint between the wall and the footing

2. A chase is USUALLY put on the inside face of a brick wall to

   A. allow for expansion of the wall
   B. provide space for a pipe
   C. act as a mortar drop during construction
   D. moisture-proof the back side of the wall

3. The sketch below shows a cap stone set on a brick wall.

   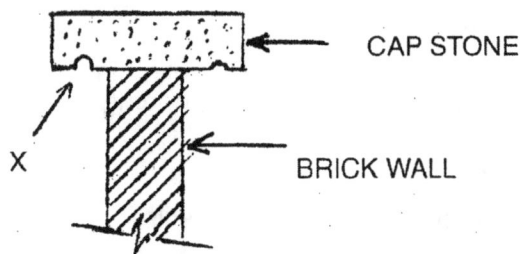

   The MAIN purpose of the groove marked X in the cap stone is to

   A. save on material
   B. make the projection appear smaller
   C. prevent rainwater on the cap stone from reaching the wall
   D. provide a finger grip when setting the cap stone

4. The sketch shown below represents a part of a brick wall.

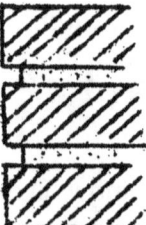

The type of mortar joint shown in the diagram is known as a _____ joint.

   A. weathered   B. raked   C. cut   D. struck

Questions 5-8.

DIRECTIONS: Questions 5 through 8 refer to the FRONT ELEVATION OF A BRICK BUILDING shown below.

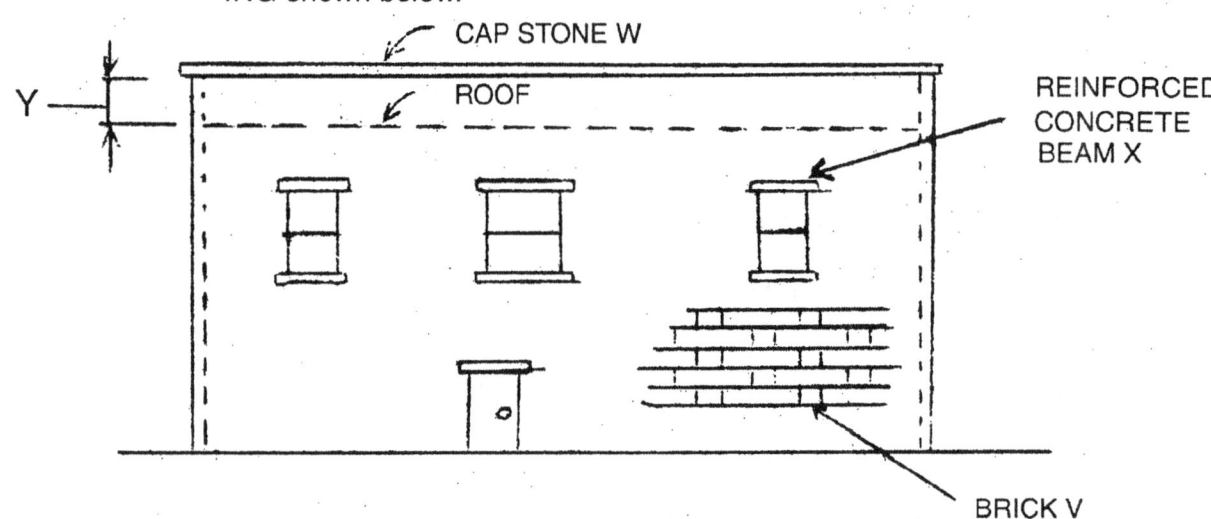

5. The brick indicated by letter V is called a

   A. header   B. rowlock   C. corbel   D. stretcher

6. The cap stone W is known as a

   A. baffling   B. plinthing
   C. creneling   D. coping

7. The reinforced concrete beam X is a

   A. lintel   B. batten   C. stile   D. rafter

8. The part of the wall Y that extends above the roof is the

   A. parapet   B. wainscot   C. apron   D. skirt

9. The term *corbelling* generally refers to

   A. the cutting of flagstones with a circular saw to form circular pieces
   B. the erection of a scaffold to lay a circular brick wall

C. a method of constructing concrete walls by pouring the concrete in flat panels and then tilting them into a vertical position
D. the stepping out of several courses of brick to form a ledge

10. In masonry cavity or veneer walls, the PURPOSE of providing an opening through the mortar joints at regular intervals is to allow for

    A. lateral expansion
    B. drainage of moisture
    C. inspection of the brick work
    D. the insertion of expansion bolts

10._____

11. The sketch below shows a reinforced concrete wall and footing.

11._____

The concrete section marked E is USUALLY called a

    A. balustrade   B. buttress
    C. breach   D. branch

12. The sketch shown at the right is the plan of a concrete column. The bevel X on each corner is known as a(n)
    A. kerf
    B. incline
    C. chamfer
    D. bend

12._____

13. The process of keeping freshly poured concrete damp for a period of days after it is poured is known as

    A. curing   B. hibernating
    C. dousing   D. bathing

13._____

14. Concrete, mixed at a central plant and ready to be poured at time of delivery at a job site, is known as _____ concrete.

    A. haul-mix   B. ready-mix
    C. house-mix   D. precast

14._____

15. The test on fresh concrete to show its stiffness is known as the _____ test.

    A. slump   B. slop   C. slack   D. slip

15._____

16. A brick masonry wall is leaking because the mortar joints have cracked. The process of cutting away the defective mortar to a depth of at least 1/2 inch and then replacing it with the proper mortar is called _____ pointing.

   A. score B. jack C. channel D. tuck

17. The grooved wheels in a block used in raising loads are known as

   A. pins B. shackles C. beckets D. sheaves

18. Of the following devices, the one that should be used for raising and lowering heavy stones is a(n)

   A. windlass B. adze C. cant D. jitney

19. A spall is a _____ brick.

   A. blistered
   B. chip of a
   C. pockmarked
   D. scored

20. A snap tie would be used MOST often in the construction of a _____ wall.

   A. brick
   B. concrete block
   C. concrete
   D. rubble

KEY (CORRECT ANSWERS)

1.	C	11.	B
2.	B	12.	C
3.	C	13.	A
4.	B	14.	B
5.	A	15.	A
6.	D	16.	D
7.	A	17.	D
8.	A	18.	A
9.	D	19.	B
10.	B	20.	C

TEST 2

DIRECTIONS: Each question or incomplete statement is followed by several suggested answers or completions. Select the one that BEST answers the question or completes the statement. *PRINT THE LETTER OF THE CORRECT ANSWER IN THE SPACE AT THE RIGHT.*

1. The MAIN reason for oiling the inside faces of wood forms against which concrete will be placed is to

    A. prevent the formation of hairline cracks in the concrete
    B. give the concrete surface a darker color tone
    C. prevent the forms from sticking to the concrete
    D. accelerate the setting of the concrete

    1.____

2. After placing fresh concrete in the wood forms of a floor slab, water containing fine particles may rise to the surface.
   This will occur MOST frequently if the

    A. concrete is vibrated excessively
    B. concrete is dropped into the form from a wheelbarrow
    C. aggregate is very dry
    D. temperature of the fresh concrete rises to 90°F

    2.____

3. Thin, dressed, squared stone used for facing a wall is known as

    A. ashlar   B. strap   C. fillet   D. mill

    3.____

4. A special type of portland cement which causes the concrete to harden more quickly than ordinary portland cement is USUALLY known as _____ cement.

    A. fast-hardening   B. high-early-strength
    C. air-entrained   D. extra-ordinary

    4.____

5. In cavity wall construction, the metal wires placed between the two separate parts of the wall are known as

    A. stirrups   B. escutcheons
    C. ties   D. girts

    5.____

6. The type of scaffold that is MOST frequently used when repointing leaky brick joints near the top of a high-rise brick apartment building that has no fire escapes is the _____ scaffold.

    A. trestle   B. swing
    C. wood pole   D. rolling

    6.____

7. Of the following items, the ones that should be used to fasten wood strips to a masonry wall are masonry

    A. wedges   B. splints   C. nails   D. spiders

    7.____

8. Of the following types of brick, the one that should be used to line the inside surface of a boiler furnace is the _____ brick.

    A. face   B. glazed   C. fire   D. enameled

    8.____

9. A strong water-proof material that is used to cover equipment to protect it from rain or snow is a

   A. template
   B. trammel
   C. trabeate
   D. tarpaulin

10. The bottom of a reinforced concrete column USUALLY rests on a

    A. bed
    B. footing
    C. grillage
    D. plate

11. A hand cutting tool that resembles a small pick and is used by bricklayers for fire brick work is known as a(n)

    A. adze
    B. gaff
    C. scutch
    D. chip

12. Of the following, the building member that is LEAST related to the others in function is the

    A. pier
    B. column
    C. pilaster
    D. sill

13. A course of 4" x 2 3/8" x 8" bricks is set in a wall so that the 2 3/8" x 8" side is in the front face of the wall with the 8" length vertical.
    This course is called a _____ course.

    A. rowlock
    B. soldier
    C. king
    D. belt

14. A kiln should LEAST likely be used to

    A. dry lumber
    B. burn lime
    C. bake brick
    D. dry concrete

15. In the construction of a brick wall, the LAST brick which finishes a horizontal course is known as the _____ brick.

    A. clincher
    B. closer
    C. liner
    D. keyer

16. Of the following locations, a concrete culvert would MOST likely be found

    A. on a roof of a building
    B. under a roadway
    C. under a tunnel
    D. on a wharf

17. Of the following, the MOST practical device to use to deposit fresh concrete in places that are difficult to reach is a

    A. scupper
    B. scuttle
    C. catamaran
    D. chute

18. Of the following types of rope, the one that is MOST susceptible to dry rot when not stored properly is

    A. nylon
    B. manila
    C. polyester
    D. polypropylene

19. Of the following locations, an outrigger should MOST often be built

    A. on a roof
    B. in a basement
    C. in a dumbwaiter
    D. in a boiler furnace

20. A mixture of hydrochloric acid (1 part by volume) and water (4 parts by volume) used to remove mortar stains from brick is known as _____ acid.   20._____

    A. builder's   B. mason's   C. Dutch   D. French

KEY (CORRECT ANSWERS)

1.	C	11.	C
2.	A	12.	D
3.	A	13.	B
4.	B	14.	D
5.	C	15.	B
6.	B	16.	B
7.	C	17.	D
8.	C	18.	B
9.	D	19.	A
10.	B	20.	A

TEST 3

DIRECTIONS: Each question or incomplete statement is followed by several suggested answers or completions. Select the one that BEST answers the question or completes the statement. *PRINT THE LETTER OF THE CORRECT ANSWER IN THE SPACE AT THE RIGHT.*

1. A pure cement uncut by a sand mixture is known as _____ cement.   1.____
   A. unspiked   B. mason's   C. white   D. neat

2. In reinforced concrete work, the diameter of a #6 reinforcing bar is MOST NEARLY _____ inch.   2.____
   A. 1/4   B. 1/2   C. 5/8   D. 3/4

3. In a 1:2: 3 1/4 concrete sidewalk mix, the 3 1/4 refers to the   3.____
   A. cement   B. admixture   C. stone   D. sand

4. Cinder concrete block is SUPERIOR to stone concrete block in   4.____
   A. strength
   C. durability
   B. the ability to insulate
   D. appearance

5. The sketch shown at the right shows the top of a concrete block.   5.____
   The block is called a
   A. broach
   B. bull nose
   C. buffer
   D. bollard

6. Lampblack is used in concrete for sidewalks PRIMARILY to   6.____
   A. make the concrete surface slip-proof
   B. give the concrete a darker shade
   C. accelerate the setting of the concrete
   D. increase the strength of the concrete

7. *Honeycomb* is a defect that occurs in   7.____
   A. concrete
   C. common brick
   B. plaster
   D. glass brick

8. Common red brick is composed PRIMARILY of   8.____
   A. clay
   C. asbestos
   B. sand
   D. hydrated lime

9. The substance, which when added to a concrete mix gives it color, is known as a   9.____
   A. vehicle   B. solvent   C. charger   D. pigment

10. Of the following materials, the one that is used as an aggregate in lightweight concrete is   10.____
    A. transite   B. hematite   C. bauxite   D. perlite

30

11. The weight of a cubic foot of concrete, made of regular cement, sand, and stone, is MOST NEARLY _____ lbs. 11.____

 A. 100 B. 125 C. 150 D. 175

12. Of the following materials, the one that is USUALLY used to fill the expansion joint of a reinforced concrete roadway slab poured on earth is a premolded _____ filler. 12.____

 A. gypsum B. mastic C. plaster D. lead

13. In first class reinforced concrete work, the horizontal reinforcement in a floor slab is USUALLY supported on 13.____

 A. bollards B. bolsters C. battens D. bats

14. A masonry block provided with a groove to receive metal flashing is known as a _____ block. 14.____

 A. raggle or reglet B. random or irregular
 C. ranger or soldier D. ratchet or slope

15. The 3/4" space between the bottom of a pump bed plate and the top of the concrete foundation supporting it should USUALLY be filled with 15.____

 A. plaster of paris B. a caulking compound
 C. a grout mixture D. bitumastic asphalt

16. In a concrete mix of 1:2:2 3/4, the 1 refers to the amount of 16.____

 A. admixture B. coarse aggregate
 C. sand D. cement

17. In a 1:1:6 mortar mix, the 6 refers to the amount of 17.____

 A. sand B. lime
 C. coarse aggregate D. cement

18. The number of bags of cement in 3/4 of a barrel of cement is MOST NEARLY 18.____

 A. 2 B. 2 1/2 C. 3 D. 3 3/4

19. In building construction, pieces of material which have been rejected as not suitable to be used are known as 19.____

 A. curds B. culls C. cairns D. cusps

20. The sketch shown at the right shows the top of a concrete block.
Of the following locations, this block should MOST often be used 20.____

KEY (CORRECT ANSWERS)

1.	D	11.	C
2.	D	12.	B
3.	C	13.	B
4.	B	14.	A
5.	B	15.	C
6.	B	16.	D
7.	A	17.	A
8.	A	18.	C
9.	D	19.	B
10.	D	20.	A

TEST 4

DIRECTIONS: Each question or incomplete statement is followed by several suggested answers or completions. Select the one that BEST answers the question or completes the statement. *PRINT THE LETTER OF THE CORRECT ANSWER IN THE SPACE AT THE RIGHT.*

1. Of the following, the tool MOST frequently used by a bricklayer is a   1.____

    A. trowel B. jointer C. hoe D. shovel

2. Fresh concrete is usually poured under water by using vertical steel pipe and a hopper for receiving the concrete.   2.____
    This method is known as the _____ method.

    A. Frasch B. Proctor C. Tremie D. Atterberg

3. The shape of the face of the head of a bricklayer's hammer is   3.____

    A. round B. square
    C. elliptical D. hexagonal

4. The metal or wood tool used to strike off and level freshly poured concrete is a   4.____

    A. screed B. squeegee C. slicker D. scupper

5.   5.____

    [Diagram: 22" long steel blade, 4½" tall, with 54" wood handle (not shown), with triangular teeth on bottom edge]

    The tool shown in the above sketch is a concrete

    A. placer B. kumalong C. flute D. rake

6. The tool shown in the sketch at the right is a   6.____

    A. bricklayer's set
    B. wire lather's cutter
    C. stone mason's chisel
    D. concrete mason's caulker 8"

    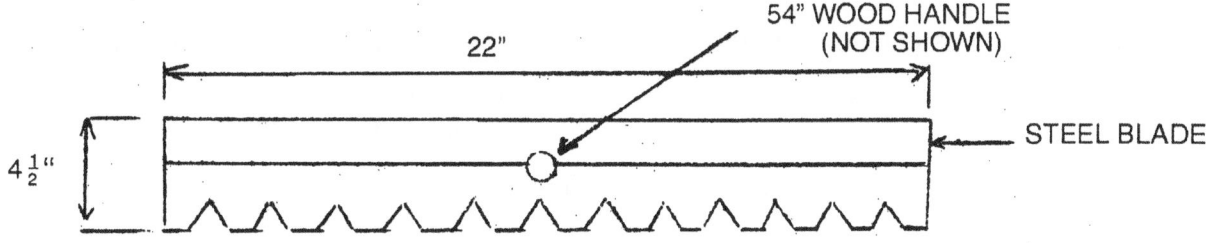

7. Of the following, the heater that is MOST frequently used in the winter time to heat the air around freshly poured concrete to prevent the concrete from freezing is a   7.____

    A. Davy lamp B. Bunsen burner
    C. salamander D. skewer

33

8. The tool shown in the sketch at the right is a _____ trowel.
   A. buttering
   B. cross joint
   C. gauging
   D. duck bill

9. Shown at the right is a sketch of a knot used in rigging. The knot is a _____ hitch.
   A. timber
   B. timber hitch and a half
   C. half
   D. clove

10. For maximum safety when using an 18-foot ladder set against a wall, the helper should place the base of the ladder so that it extends from the face of the wall a distance of MOST NEARLY

   A. 2'6"   B. 4'6"   C. 6'0"   D. 9'0"

11. Of the following types of fire extinguisher, the BEST one to use on a gasoline fire is
   A. soda acid
   B. pump tank
   C. foam
   D. cartridge actuated

12. The handles of a loaded wheelbarrow should be raised to the traveling position by lifting with the
   A. back muscles, keeping the back stooped backwards from the vertical position
   B. back muscles, keeping the back stooped forward from the vertical position
   C. leg muscles, keeping the back in a vertical position
   D. leg muscles, keeping the back in a horizontal position

13. The number of cubic feet in a concrete sidewalk consisting of fifteen squares 5 feet by 5 feet by 4 inches deep is MOST NEARLY

   A. 100   B. 125   C. 250   D. 600

14. The sketch at the right shows a section of a concrete wall.
   The dimension X has a value of MOST NEARLY

   A. 2' 7 3/4"
   B. 2' 8 1/4"
   C. 2' 9 1/2"
   D. 2' 10 3/4"

15. The total number of cubic feet of concrete in twenty-three round concrete fence post footings, the dimension of which are 3 feet by 8 inches in diameter (neglect the volume of the pipe), is MOST NEARLY   15.____

    A. 19   B. 21   C. 23   D. 25

16. The run of a reinforced concrete staircase which has 11 steps, each 9 1/2 inches wide (exclusive of the nosing), is   16.____

    A. 7'11"   B. 8'9"   C. 9'6"   D. 10'2"

Questions 17-19.

DIRECTIONS: Questions 17 through 19 are to be answered SOLELY on the basis of the following passage.

It is best to avoid surface water on freshly poured concrete in the first place. However, when there is a very small amount present, the recommended procedure is to allow it to evaporate before finishing. If there is considerable water, it is removed with a broom, belt, float, or by other convenient means. It is never good practice to sprinkle dry cement, or a mixture of cement and fine aggregate, on concrete to take up surface water. Such fine materials form a layer on the surface that is likely to dust or hair check when the concrete hardens.

17. The MAIN subject of the above passage is: 17.____

    A. Surface cracking of concrete
    B. Evaporation of water from freshly poured concrete
    C. Removing surface water from concrete
    D. Final adjustments of ingredients in the concrete mix

18. According to the passage, the sprinkling of dry cement on the surface of a concrete mix would MOST likely   18.____

    A. prevent the mix from setting
    B. cause discoloration on the surface of the concrete
    C. cause the coarse aggregate to settle out too quickly
    D. cause powdering and small cracks on the surface of the concrete

19. According to the passage, the thing to do when considerable surface water is present on the freshly poured concrete is to   19.____

    A. dump the concrete back into the mixer and drain the water
    B. allow the water to evaporate before finishing
    C. remove the water with a broom, belt, or float
    D. add more fine aggregate but not cement

20. Scaffolds shall be level and set on *firm* ground.   20.____
    As used in the above sentence, the word *firm* means MOST NEARLY

    A. stable   B. loose   C. weak   D. flimsy

KEY (CORRECT ANSWERS)

1. A
2. C
3. B
4. A
5. D

6. C
7. C
8. B
9. C
10. B

11. C
12. C
13. B
14. D
15. C

16. B
17. C
18. D
19. C
20. A

EXAMINATION SECTION
TEST 1

DIRECTIONS: Each question or incomplete statement is followed by several suggested answers or completions. Select the one that BEST answers the question or completes the statement. *PRINT THE LETTER OF THE CORRECT ANSWER IN THE SPACE AT THE RIGHT.*

Questions 1-16.

DIRECTIONS: Questions 1 through 16 are to be answered on the basis of the following tools. These tools are NOT shown to scale.

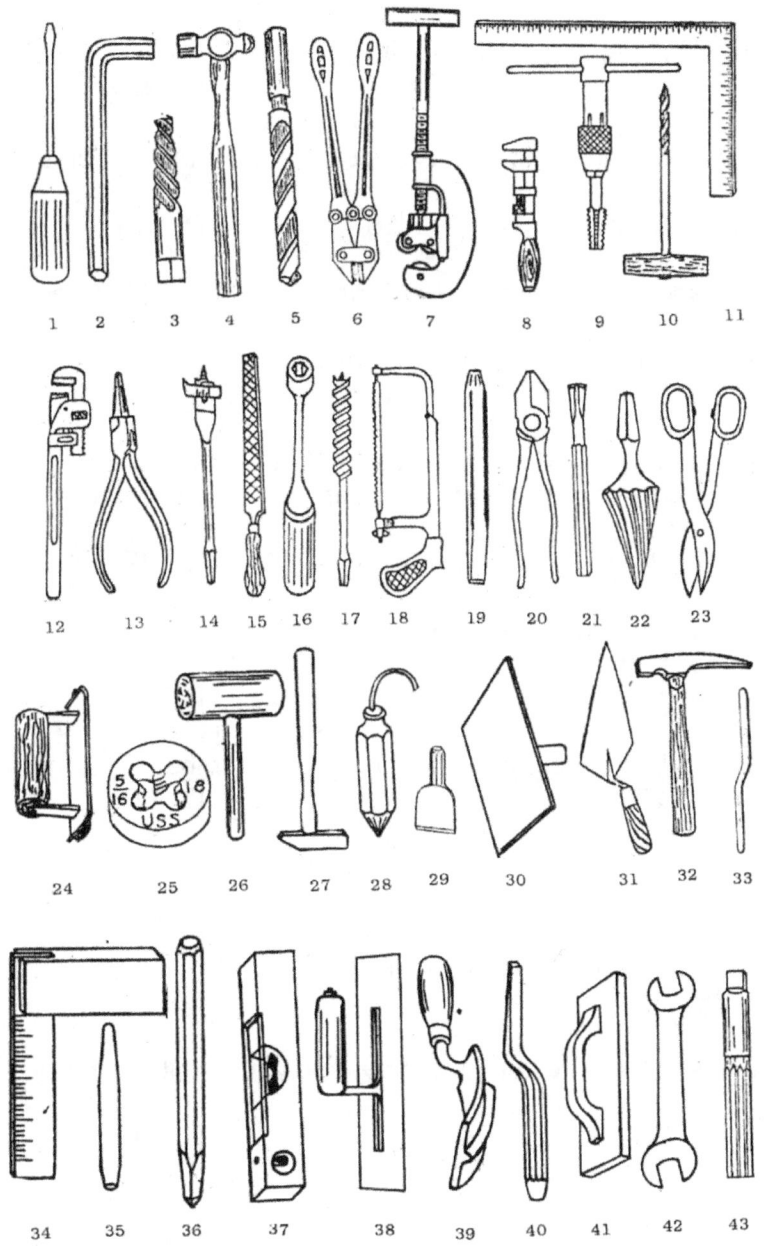

2 (#1)

1. In order to cut a piece of 5/16" diameter steel scaffold hoisting cable, you should use tool number
   A. 6   B. 7   C. 19   D. 23

   1._____

2. Scaffold planks are secured to joisting irons by means of lag screws. To properly tighten these lag screws, you should use tool number
   A. 12   B. 13   C. 20   D. 42

   2._____

3. While installing a steel angle iron lintel, you find that the threads on the embedded holding bolts are damaged. You should repair the threads by using tool number
   A. 7   B. 9   C. 25   D. 43

   3._____

4. It is necessary to cut a hole in a concrete foundation wall in order to place a small bolt. To cut this small hole, you should use tool number
   A. 14   B. 19   C. 21   D. 40

   4._____

5. If tool number 17 bears the mark "7," this tool should be used to drill holes having a diameter of
   A. 7/64"   B. 7/32"   C. 7/16"   D. 7/8"

   5._____

6. If the marking on the blade of tool number 18 reads "10-18," the "18" refers to the
   A. number of teeth per inch   B. weight
   C. thickness   D. length

   6._____

7. If two points are separated by a vertical distance of 12 feet, the tool that should be used to make certain that the points are in *perfect* vertical alignment is number
   A. 11   B. 28   C. 34   D. 37

   7._____

8. A ¾" diameter hole must be made in a steel floor beam. The tool you should use is number
   A. 3   B. 5   C. 9   D. 22

   8._____

9. To cut the corner off a building brick, you should use tool number
   A. 4   B. 27   C. 29   D. 36

   9._____

10. A 2" x 2" x $^3/_{16}$" steel angle should be cut using tool number
    A. 6   B. 7   C. 18   D. 19

    10._____

11. The term "snips" should be applied to tool number
    A. 6   B. 13   C. 20   D. 23

    11._____

12. To line-up the bolt holes in two structural steel beams, you should use tool number
    A. 1   B. 33   C. 35   D. 36

    12._____

13. A "hawk" is tool number 13._____
    A. 29   B. 30   C. 38   D. 41

14. After an 8" thick brick wall has been erected, it is discovered that a hole 14._____
    should have been left for a 4" sewer pipe.
    To cut that hole, you should use tool number
    A. 5   B. 19   C. 32   D. 36

15. A "float" is tool number 15._____
    A. 30   B. 31   C. 33   D. 41

16. A "Stillson" is tool number 16._____
    A. 2   B. 8   C. 12   D. 22

Questions 17-33.

DIRECTIONS: Questions 17 through 33 are concerned with terms commonly used in the bricklayer trade. Answer these questions by selecting the meaning as used in the trade.

17. A "skewback" is part of a(n) 17._____
    A. column   B. beam   C. arch   D. parapet

18. A "snap header" is a 18._____
    A. bond stone   B. false header
    C. glazed brick   D. rounded bond brick

19. A "putlog" is a part of a 19._____
    A. roof   B. scaffold   C. foundation   D. ladder

20. A "corbel" is a 20._____
    A. hole   B. recess   C. projection   D. chase

21. A "reglet" is usually found in a 21._____
    A. glazed block   B. fire brick
    C. common brick   D. flashing block

22. "Efflorescence" is caused by 22._____
    A. erosion   B. expansion   C. salts   D. freezing

23. "Parging" is usually applied only to _____ walls. 23._____
    A. veneered   B. faced   C. foundation   D. hollow

24. A "salmon" brick is one that is 24._____
    A. oversized   B. glazed   C. underburned   D. overburned

25. "Centering" is used in connection with 25._____
    A. archways   B. parapets
    C. window sills   D. roof penthouses

26. A "reveal" usually occurs at
    A. windows   B. chimneys   C. parapets   D. doorways

27. A "chase" is like a
    A. projection   B. belt course   C. recess   D. parapet

28. "Bulking" occurs when sand is
    A. shifted   B. rammed   C. moistened   D. dried

29. "Weep holes" are usually placed in _____ walls.
    A. solid brick B. veneered   C. cavity   D. combination

30. A "compass brick" is
    A. rounded on one end   B. circular
    C. square   D. wedge-shaped

31. A "storey pole" is used with
    A. scaffolds   B. vertical distances
    C. flags   D. platforms

32. A "dove-tail" anchor would MOST likely bond brick veneer to a _____ wall.
    A. concrete   B. cinder block
    C. wood frame   D. brick

33. A "fore cut" is made in a
    A. column   B. joist   C. stud   D. rafter

34. In high-rise concrete buildings, the underside of the floor slabs are frequently painted.
    Before painting, the underside surfaces should be
    A. troweled   B. floated   C. screeded   D. rubbed

35. In laying a cavity wall, a bricklayer will sometimes place a wood board on top of the ties.
    The MAIN purpose for using this board is to
    A. maintain proper width of cavity   B. catch any mortar droppings
    C. aid in keeping courses level   D. properly space the ties

36. Sometimes two different grades of brick are used in the exterior wall of a building. Face brick is used on the outside face and a backing brick is used for the inside.
    The MAIN reason for this practice is
    A. speed in erection
    B. lower cost
    C. increased strength of the wall
    D. greater resistance to water penetration

37. When cement mortar stiffens before it can be used, it is possible to make it workable once again by retempering.
Such retempering is considered
   A. *good*, because it prevents waste of the expensive mortar
   B. *good*, because it prevents delay in the work
   C. *bad*, because it weakens the mortar
   D. *bad*, because it requires additional labor cost

38. The MAIN reason for removing nails from used lumber is that
   A. nails which are not bent can be used again
   B. workers may be injured by projecting nails
   C. the nails might rust and not be re-usable
   D. it will be easier to pile up the lumber

39. It is considered *good* practice to cut glazed brick using a(n)
   A. mason's hammer   B. abrasive wheel
   C. wide chisel   D. hacksaw

40. The MAIN purpose of adding calcium chloride to a mortar mix is to
   A. color the mortar   B. increase its workability
   C. reduce its freezing temperature   D. speed up its setting rate

KEY (CORRECT ANSWERS)

1.	A	11.	D	21.	D	31.	B
2.	D	12.	C	22.	C	32.	A
3.	C	13.	B	23.	B	33.	B
4.	C	14.	D	24.	C	34.	D
5.	C	15.	D	25.	A	35.	B
6.	A	16.	C	26.	A	36.	B
7.	B	17.	C	27.	C	37.	C
8.	B	18.	B	28.	C	38.	B
9.	C	19.	B	29.	C	39.	B
10.	C	20.	C	30.	D	40.	D

TEST 2

DIRECTIONS: Each question or incomplete statement is followed by several suggested answers or completions. Select the one that BEST answers the question or completes the statement. *PRINT THE LETTER OF THE CORRECT ANSWER IN THE SPACE AT THE RIGHT.*

Questions 1-8.

DIRECTIONS: Questions 1 through 16 are to be answered on the basis of the following concrete masonry units.

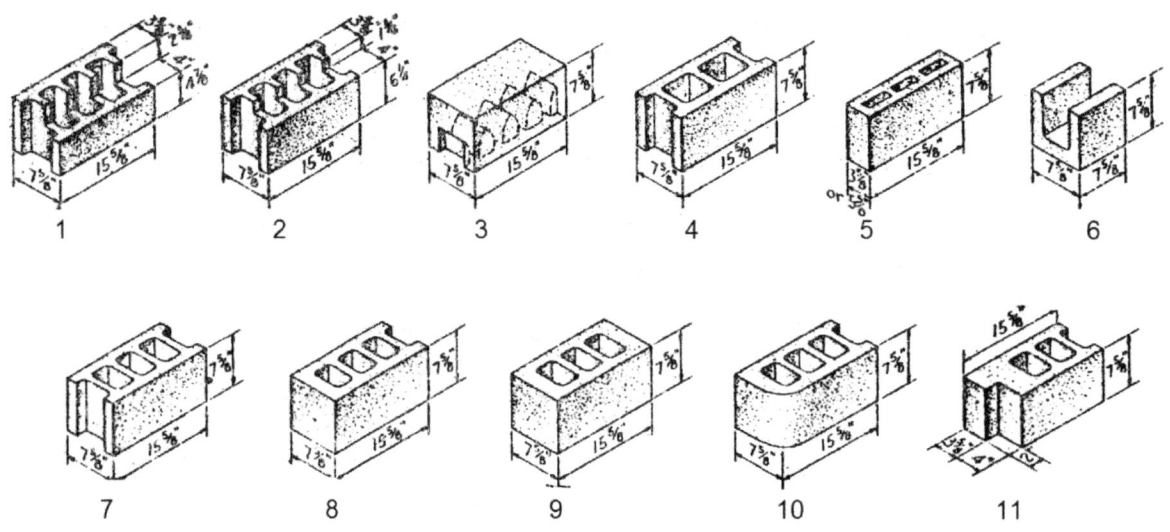

CONCRETE MASONRY UNITS

1. The unit that should be used for bonding with brick facing is number
 A. 2   B. 3   C. 6   D. 10

2. The unit that should be used at the side of a door opening is number
 A. 1   B. 3   C. 6   D. 11

3. The unit known as a "bull nose" is number
 A. 1   B. 8   C. 10   D. 11

4. The unit that should be used to make a lintel is number
 A. 6   B. 7   C. 9   D. 10

5. The unit that should be used at the outside corner of a wall is number
 A. 3   B. 6   C. 7   D. 8

6. The unit that should be used in a 16" square free-standing pier is number
 A. 4   B. 7   C. 8   D. 9

7. The unit known as a "stretcher" is number
 A. 4   B. 6   C. 10   D. 11

1.____
2.____
3.____
4.____
5.____
6.____
7.____

42

8. The unit that should be used to support a floor joist is number 8.____
   A. 2   B. 3   C. 6   D. 9

9. Cinder concrete blocks, as compared with stone concrete blocks, are 9.____
   A. heavier   B. more waterproof
   C. stronger   D. better insulators

10. The MAIN reason why a job site should be kept as neat as possible is that this practice 10.____
    A. makes it easier to locate materials
    B. increases the availability of storage space
    C. improves morale by providing better working conditions
    D. reduces the likelihood of workers being involved in accidents

Questions 11-13.

DIRECTIONS: Questions 11 through 13 are to be answered on the basis of the sketches shown at the right of each question.

11. The wall shown is a _____ wall. 11.____
    A. cavity
    B. block
    C. rowlock
    D. veneer

12. The groove which is cut in the coping shown is a(n) 12.____
    A. caulking groove
    B. expansion joint
    C. drip
    D. expansion slot

13. The wall shown is a _____ wall. 13.____
    A. cavity
    B. block
    C. rowlock
    D. veneer

14. The MOST important factor governing the strength of a concrete mix is the ratio 14._____
    of cement to
    A. water   B. gravel
    C. sand   D. sand and gravel combined

15. The MOST important safety precaution that one should take when using a 15._____
    pneumatic hammer to chip concrete is to wear
    A. safety shoes   B. goggles
    C. a long-sleeve shirt   D. a hard hat

16. The rate at which fresh concrete hardens 16._____
    A. will increase with a rise in temperature
    B. will increase with a fall in temperature
    C. will increase with any large change in temperature
    D. is independent of the temperature

17. The MAIN reason why re-bars should NOT be painted is that the paint will 17._____
    A. be removed when the concrete is poured
    B. reduce the bond between the concrete and the steel
    C. not be seen since the re-bars are buried in the concrete
    D. greatly increase the cost

Questions 18-23.

DIRECTIONS: Questions 18 through 23 are to be answered on the basis of the following mortar joints.

MORTAR JOINTS

18. A raked joint is number 18._____
    A. 1   B. 2   C. 3   D. 4

19. A V joint is number 19._____
    A. 3   B. 4   C. 5   D. 6

20. A flush joint is number 20._____
    A. 1   B. 2   C. 3   D. 4

21. A weather joint is number
    A. 3   B. 4   C. 5   D. 6

22. A struck joint is number
    A. 1   B. 2   C. 3   D. 4

23. A concave joint is number
    A. 1   B. 3   C. 4   D. 6

Questions 24-28.

DIRECTIONS: Questions 24 through 28 are to be answered on the basis of the following pattern bonds.

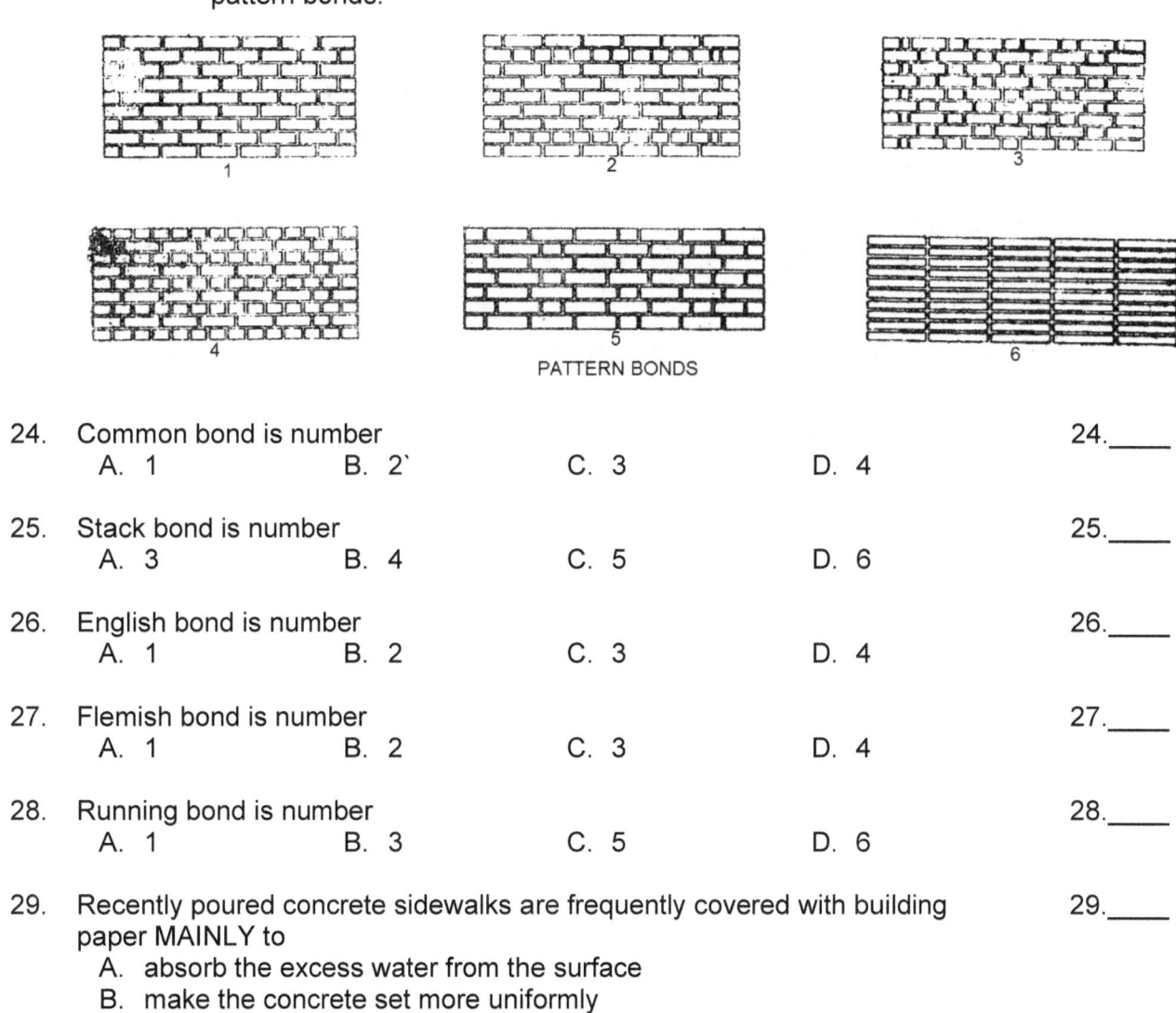

PATTERN BONDS

24. Common bond is number
    A. 1   B. 2   C. 3   D. 4

25. Stack bond is number
    A. 3   B. 4   C. 5   D. 6

26. English bond is number
    A. 1   B. 2   C. 3   D. 4

27. Flemish bond is number
    A. 1   B. 2   C. 3   D. 4

28. Running bond is number
    A. 1   B. 3   C. 5   D. 6

29. Recently poured concrete sidewalks are frequently covered with building paper MAINLY to
    A. absorb the excess water from the surface
    B. make the concrete set more uniformly
    C. prevent pedestrians from walking on it
    D. protect the concrete from wind-blown dust and dirt

30. The practice of oiling forms prior to placing concrete is considered 30.____
    A. *poor*, since oil may get on the rods
    B. *poor*, since this discolors the concrete surface
    C. *good*, since this makes the concrete flow better
    D. *good*, since this makes stripping easier

KEY (CORRECT ANSWERS)

1.	A	11.	A	21.	D
2.	D	12.	C	22.	B
3.	C	13.	D	23.	C
4.	A	14.	A	24.	B
5.	D	15.	B	25.	D
6.	D	16.	A	26.	D
7.	A	17.	B	27.	C
8.	B	18.	C	28.	A
9.	D	19.	C	29.	B
10.	D	20.	A	30.	D

EXAMINATION SECTION
TEST 1

DIRECTIONS: Each question or incomplete statement is followed by several suggested answers or completions. Select the one that BEST answers the question or completes the statement. *PRINT THE LETTER OF THE CORRECT ANSWER IN THE SPACE AT THE RIGHT.*

1. Coating reinforcing rods with oil before placing them in the forms is

   A. *good* practice, because it prevents rusting
   B. *poor* practice, because it makes the rods difficult to handle
   C. *good* practice if the forms are oiled
   D. *poor* practice because it destroys the bond between the concrete and the rods

2. If the mixing plant should break down after one-half the concrete has been mixed for a floor, the BEST thing to do would be to

   A. take the concrete out of the forms and throw it away
   B. spread the available concrete evenly over the floor area
   C. block off one-half of the floor area and place the available concrete in the blocked-off area
   D. keep mixing the concrete in the forms with shovels until the plant is repaired

3. Splicing of reinforcing bars is accomplished by

   A. using wire ties
   B. underlapping the bars
   C. hooking the bars
   D. using metal clips

Questions 4-6.

DIRECTIONS: Questions 4 through 6 are to be answered on the basis of the following specification.

The minimum time of mixing shall be one minute per cubic yard after all the material, including the water, has been placed in the drum, and the drum shall be reversed for an additional two minutes. Mixing water shall be added only in the presence of the inspector.

4. From the above specifications, it is REASONABLE to conclude that

   A. the total mixing time of all the material, including the water, shall be at least 3 minutes for a one-yard batch
   B. the total mixing time of all the material, including the water, shall not be more than 3 minutes
   C. after the material has been mixed for 1 minute, the drum should be discharged and reversed for 2 minutes
   D. the material is mixed for one minute, the water is then added, and mixing continues for 2 more minutes

5. The above specification requires the presence of the inspector at the time the mixing water is added. The PRIMARY reason for this is that he should

   A. see the permit from the water department
   B. obtain the truck number
   C. check the amount of water added
   D. check the quality of water added

6. The above specification MOST likely refers to

    A. transit mix concrete
    B. mortar for brick masonry
    C. plaster for scratch coat
    D. plaster for finish coat

7. In lightweight concrete, the lightweight material is substituted PRIMARILY for

    A. water   B. sand   C. cement   D. gravel

8. One method of dewatering an excavation for a foundation is by the use of

    A. inverted siphons   B. well points
    C. line holes   D. suction heads

9. An excavation for a concrete footing to support a structural steel column was dug 4" too deep.
   Of the following, the BEST construction practice would be to

    A. backfill the 4" with stone
    B. backfill the 4" with sand
    C. lower the entire footing 4"
    D. make the footing 4" thicker

10. Spudding, in a pile driving operation, is used PRIMARILY to

    A. remove a broken pile
    B. pass an obstruction
    C. compact the soil in the area
    D. splice piles

11. Where walers and form ties are used in wood formwork for tall vertical concrete walls, the walers are

    A. more closely spaced at the top of the wall than at the bottom
    B. evenly spaced at the top to the bottom of the wall
    C. more closely spaced at the bottom of the wall than at the top
    D. more closely spaced at the middle of the wall than at either the top or the bottom

12. If a station wall tile panel is to be completed using the pattern shown, which is made up of three different sized tiles, then the additional number of tiles required for completion is

    A. 8
    B. 10
    C. 12
    D. 14

    SUBWAY WALL TILE PANEL

13. Specifications state that the column dowels are embedded 24 diameters in the footing. The length of embedment for a number 6 bar is _____ inches.

    A. 6   B. 12   C. 18   D. 24

14. The specifications for a construction job state: Cement content shall not exceed 7 1/2 sacks nor be less than 6 sacks per cubic yard of concrete.
    The ratio of the number of sacks of cement per cubic yard of concrete is known as the

    A. water-cement ratio   B. yield
    C. ultimate strength   D. cement factor

15. Specifications for a building state that reinforcing bars must lap 40 diameters in the concrete.
    The length of lap for a number 5 bar should be _____ inches.

    A. 15   B. 25   C. 30   D. 35

16. In concrete work, a dummy joint is MOST similar in purpose to a(n) _____ joint.

    A. construction   B. expansion
    C. contraction   D. shear

17. After mixing, the time of initial set of concrete should NOT be less than approximately

    A. one hour   B. three hours
    C. twenty-four hours D. seven days

18. The term *key* in concrete work indicates the method of

    A. tieing forms together
    B. uniting two succeeding days pours
    C. wiring of reinforcing rods
    D. splicing of reinforcing rods

19. Holes left in the bottoms of forms for concrete walls are PRIMARILY for the purpose of

    A. inspection of reinforcement
    B. placement of steel
    C. cleaning out of forms
    D. easy removal of forms

20. Of the following materials, the one that is MOST frequently used as a water stop at a joint in a concrete wall is

    A. stainless steel   B. copper
    C. galvanized iron   D. tin

21. A concrete mix is specified as $1:1\frac{1}{2}:3$.
    The order in which the materials are specified is

    A. sand, gravel, cement   B. cement, gravel, sand
    C. gravel, sand, cement   D. cement, sand, gravel

22. *Corbeling* results in
    A. strengthening a concrete column
    B. waterproofing a foundation wall
    C. anchoring a steel girder to a bearing wall
    D. increasing the thickness of a brick wall

23. One of the unit price items in the contract for extra or omitted work in a building is reinforcing steel in place.
    This price is MOST likely _____/pound.
    A. 12¢   B. $1.20   C. $12.00   D. $120.00

24. The specifications require that porous fill be placed under a concrete slab.
    The material LEAST likely to be permitted as porous fill is
    A. crushed stone   B. sand
    C. gravel   D. loam

25. If concrete weighs 4000 pounds per cubic yard, the weight of a slab of concrete 2'6" by 6'9" by 3'2" is, in pounds, MOST NEARLY
    A. 7920   B. 7830   C. 7740   D. 7650

KEY (CORRECT ANSWERS)

1. D		11. C	
2. C		12. C	
3. A		13. C	
4. A		14. D	
5. C		15. B	
6. A		16. C	
7. D		17. A	
8. B		18. B	
9. D		19. C	
10. B		20. B	

21. D
22. D
23. B
24. D
25. A

TEST 2

DIRECTIONS: Each question or incomplete statement is followed by several suggested answers or completions. Select the one that BEST answers the question or completes the statement. *PRINT THE LETTER OF THE CORRECT ANSWER IN THE SPACE AT THE RIGHT.*

1. The specifications for a construction job state that the bench top of a table shall be made of 1/2 inch transite. Transite is a(n)

    A. thermo-setting plastic
    B. titanium steel alloy
    C. gypsum-cement product
    D. asbestos-cement product

2. High early strength cement is designated as Type

    A. I   B. II   C. III   D. IV

3. The average weight of stone concrete is MOST NEARLY _____ pounds/cubic foot.

    A. 100   B. 150   C. 200   D. 250

4. A mortar joint in a brick wall in which the joint is made flush with the brick is called a _____ joint.

    A. cut   B. weather   C. painted   D. stripped

5. Quarry tile is made of

    A. marble
    B. cement and sand
    C. clay
    D. limestone

6. When constructing cellar concrete floors resting on earth, the item that should be checked MOST carefully is that

    A. the earth is dry before pouring
    B. the earth is wet before pouring
    C. all backfill is properly compacted
    D. all backfill is granular soil

7. When building the formwork for a 12" doubly reinforced concrete wall, the USUAL order of construction is: Place the

    A. formwork for both faces of the wall and then place the reinforcing steel
    B. reinforcing steel and then place the formwork for both faces of the wall
    C. formwork for one face of the wall, place the reinforcing steel, and then place the formwork for the other face of the wall
    D. formwork for one face of the wall, place the reinforcing steel for one face, place the formwork for the other face of the wall, and then place the reinforcement for the second face

8. Of the following, the BEST time to apply the final coat in a three-coat plastering job is when the second coat is

    A. completely set and nearly dry
    B. completely set and completely dry
    C. nearly set and nearly dry
    D. nearly set and completely dry

9. The side forms for a 4-inch thick sidewalk 5 feet wide are in place.
   Of the following, the BEST way to see that the concrete is of proper thickness is to

   A. test the compactness of the subgrade to be certain there will be no settlement
   B. measure the depth of the side forms to the subgrade
   C. have a surveying party check the elevation of the subgrade
   D. measure the distance between the forms

10. By trial, it is found that by using 2 cubic feet of sand, a 5 cubic foot batch of concrete is produced.
    Using the same proportions, the amount of sand, in cubic feet, required to produce 2 cubic yards of concrete is MOST NEARLY

    A. 7   B. 22   C. 27   D. 45

11. Tooling of the face joints of a brick wall under construction should be done

    A. after the mortar has acquired its initial set
    B. after the entire wall is laid
    C. after the mortar has acquired its final set
    D. as each brick is laid

12. A 10-inch foundation wall is 11 feet long and 15 feet high.
    If the compressive strength of the wall is 300 pounds per square inch, the MAXIMUM permissible load on this wall is _____ lbs.

    A. 540,000   B. 495,000   C. 396,000   D. 33,000

13. It is INCORRECT to state that

    A. neat cement contains cement and water
    B. salt is used to hasten the setting of concrete
    C. the strength of concrete is affected by the water ratio
    D. a sidewalk should slope toward the street

14. On a plan, the symbol shown at the right represents

    A. brick
    B. cinder concrete block
    C. hollow clay tile
    D. gypsum block

15. Where a continuous concrete floor slab is supported on concrete beams and girders, poured integrally, the BEST place to make a construction joint is at a point

    A. midway between the beams
    B. directly over the center of a beam
    C. a distance from the face of the beam equal to the depth of the beam
    D. one-third of the distance from the face of the beam to the center of the beam

16. A neat line

    A. is the result of good workmanship
    B. is used in concrete construction only
    C. defines an outer limit of a structure
    D. defines an outer limit of excavation for a structure

17. Continued trowelling of a cement-finish floor for a building is

    A. *good* practice because it provides a smooth floor
    B. *poor* practice because it produces a slippery floor
    C. *poor* practice because it brings the fines to the surface
    D. *good* practice because it insures proper mixing of the cement finish

18. In reinforced concrete formwork, a beveled chamfer strip is used to

    A. reinforce the outside of the forms
    B. reinforce the inside of the forms
    C. seal leaks in the forms
    D. do none of the above

19. The following statement appears in a set of specifications for a reinforced concrete housing construction job: At the contractor's option, the column sizes shown between the first and second floor on the column schedule may be carried up through all the upper stories. The same steel required by the drawings for each floor height shall be used but shall be re-spaced and the ties made larger to meet the changed column sizes.
    You may conclude from the above that

    A. a contractor who accepts the option will be wasting money
    B. a contractor may build stronger columns than those called for in the schedule
    C. it is possible to save on reinforcing steel by making use of this clause
    D. the smaller the column the larger the required ties

20. In preparing a concrete surface for painting, a *sparkle* (sometimes called spackle) mixture is specified.
    This would be used

    A. for patching holes
    B. for cleaning the wall
    C. as a primer coat
    D. to provide a glossy surface

21. Before laying concrete on an earth surface, it is good practice to

    A. wet down and ram the earth
    B. thoroughly dry the earth
    C. loosen the earth thoroughly
    D. place a canvas between the earth and the poured concrete

22. Troweling the top surface of poured concrete

    A. weakens the concrete
    B. introduces dirt into the concrete

C. helps to make it waterproof
D. makes the concrete more flexible

23. The strength of brick walls is based upon the type of mortar used. The relative strength of the various types of mortar, in descending order, is

    A. cement, lime, cement-lime
    B. lime, cement-lime, cement
    C. cement-lime, cement, lime
    D. cement, cement-lime, lime

24. Spreaders are used in connection with forms for concrete to

    A. hold the walls of a form the correct distance apart
    B. anchor a form to the ground
    C. make a form watertight
    D. make the cement spread evenly through the form

25. Curing of concrete means

    A. finishing the surface of the concrete
    B. softening stiff concrete by adding water
    C. keeping the concrete wet while setting
    D. the salvaging of frozen concrete

KEY (CORRECT ANSWERS)

1.	D	11.	A
2.	C	12.	C
3.	B	13.	B
4.	A	14.	B
5.	C	15.	A
6.	C	16.	C
7.	C	17.	C
8.	A	18.	D
9.	B	19.	B
10.	B	20.	A

21. A
22. C
23. D
24. A
25. C

TEST 3

DIRECTIONS: Each question or incomplete statement is followed by several suggested answers or completions. Select the one that BEST answers the question or completes the statement. *PRINT THE LETTER OF THE CORRECT ANSWER IN THE SPACE AT THE RIGHT.*

1. For a building, the number of reinforcing bars in a slab would be indicated on the   1.____

    A. architectural plans
    B. structural engineer's plans
    C. reinforcing steel shop drawings
    D. standard detail drawings

2. Of the following, the designation that would apply to brick is   2.____

    A. Grade A
    B. Grade SW
    C. Select Quality
    D. No. 1 Common

3. It is NOT necessary to wear protective goggles when   3.____

    A. drilling rivet holes in a steel beam
    B. sharpening tools on a power grinder
    C. welding a steel plate to a pipe column
    D. laying up a cinder block partition

Questions 4-5.

DIRECTIONS: Questions 4 and 5 refer to the following statement and sketch.

A specification reads: Net cross-sectional area of a masonry unit shall be taken as the gross cross-sectional area minus the area of cores or cellular space.

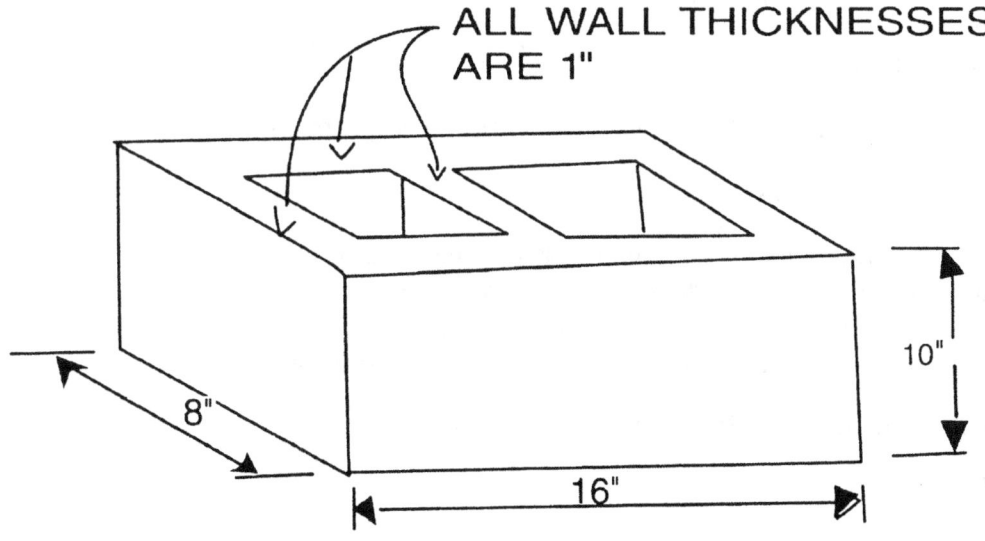

4. The gross cross-sectional area is _____ square inches.   4.____

    A. 64   B. 84   C. 128   D. 144

55

5. The net cross-sectional area is _____ square inches.

   A. 128 B. 112 C. 77 D. 50

6. The concrete surface of a reinforced concrete building is inch below the finished floor. Of the following, the floor finish MOST likely to be installed is

   A. wood flooring
   B. ceramic tile
   C. asphalt tile
   D. terrazzo

7. Concrete with a slump of 2 inches would MOST likely be used for

   A. floors
   B. thin wall sections
   C. columns
   D. deep beams

8. In a 1:1:6 mortar for brickwork, the middle figure USUALLY represents the proportion of

   A. cement B. lime C. sand D. gypsum

9. A reveal in a brickwork USUALLY occurs at

   A. the corners of the building
   B. windows
   C. the intersection of the brick wall and the foundation wall
   D. the intersection of the roof and parapet

10. Salmon brick are USUALLY brick that are

    A. oversized
    B. overburned
    C. underburned
    D. glazed

11. It is permissible to use bats in the face of a brick wall in order to

    A. reinforce the bond
    B. substitute for the use of ties
    C. provide imitation bond
    D. provide closure

12. At the ready mix concrete plant, the sand for the concrete mix has a greater than usual percent of moisture.
    The BEST procedure is to

    A. ignore the fact since it will have no effect on the concrete mix
    B. notify the concrete truckdrivers to reduce the amount of water to be added
    C. hold up the delivery of concrete until the excess moisture evaporates
    D. reject the sand as unfit for use as a concrete aggregate

13. The hammer shown at the right would be used by a

    A. carpenter
    B. bricklayer
    C. tinsmith
    D. plumber

14. Brickwork is said to be laid up in common bond when it

    A. has a header course after every five stretcher courses
    B. is made up entirely of header courses
    C. is made up entirely of stretcher courses
    D. has a stretcher course after every five header courses

15. If concrete which is being put into a sloping metal chute for deposit into place has difficulty flowing down the chute, the BEST remedy would be to

    A. pound the chute with a sledge hammer
    B. add more water to the concrete mix
    C. increase the slope of the chute if possible
    D. oil the chute to reduce friction

16. Reinforced concrete is concrete which has been strengthened by the addition of

    A. long steel reinforcing rods
    B. chemical strengtheners
    C. additional cement
    D. additional coarse aggregate

17. In a building, precast concrete plank would MOST likely be used in

    A. a roof
    B. demountable partitions
    C. the foundation footings
    D. the foundation walls

18. Good construction practice requires that ordinary concrete be kept moist after placing for a MINIMUM of

    A. 24 hours   B. 48 hours   C. 7 days   D. 28 days

19. *Retempering* of concrete is prohibited during a concrete pour. Retempering means

    A. adding extra cement to the mix before it leaves the mixer
    B. adding extra aggregate to the mix before it leaves the mixer
    C. increasing mixing time
    D. mixing concrete in the mixer after it has partially set

20. Of the following, the MOST important item to consider when a concrete slab is to be supported by the earth is whether the earth is

    A. properly compacted
    B. sufficiently porous
    C. wet before pouring the concrete
    D. thoroughly dry before pouring the concrete

21. When placing concrete, a vibrator should be used to

    A. prevent segregation in the concrete
    B. consolidate the concrete
    C. increase the air content in the concrete
    D. help move the concrete in the forms

22. The specification of grouting states: The contractor shall furnish all material and labor for properly bedding on Portland cement grout, the equipment or its supporting base. Grout of this type would USUALLY consist of

    A. Portland cement *only*
    B. 1 part Portland cement and 1 part sand
    C. 1 part Portland cement and 4 parts sand
    D. 1 part Portland cement and 8 parts sand

23. Referring to the above question, the thickness of grout for the bases of machinery and equipment normally found in buildings would be, in inches, MOST NEARLY _____ inch(es).

    A. 1/4   B. 1/2   C. 1   D. 3

24. A new 9" thick concrete floor is to be poured in a 90' x 100' cellar. This will require a quantity of concrete of about _____ cubic yards.

    A. 47   B. 562   C. 250   D. 6750

25. A concrete test specimen, 6" diameter x 12" high, fails when stressed at 3000 lbs/sq.in. The total load causing failure is MOST NEARLY

    A. 1500#   B. 3000#   C. 42500#   D. 85000#

KEY (CORRECT ANSWERS)

1. C		11. D	
2. B		12. B	
3. D		13. B	
4. C		14. A	
5. D		15. C	
6. C		16. A	
7. A		17. A	
8. B		18. C	
9. B		19. D	
10. C		20. A	

21. B
22. B
23. C
24. C
25. D

ARITHMETICAL REASONING

EXAMINATION SECTION
TEST 1

DIRECTIONS: Each question or incomplete statement is followed by several suggested answers or completions. Select the one that BEST answers the question or completes the statement. *PRINT THE LETTER OF THE CORRECT ANSWER IN THE SPACE AT THE RIGHT.*

1. If it takes 2 men 9 days to do a job, how many men are needed to do the same job in 3 days?

    A. 4　　B. 5　　C. 6　　D. 7

2. Suppose that a department operates 1,644 buildings. If one employee is needed for every 2 buildings, and one foreman is needed for every 18 employees, the number of foremen needed is CLOSEST to

    A. 45　　B. 50　　C. 55　　D. 60

3. If 60 bars of soap cost the same as 2 gallons of wax, how many bars of soap can be bought for the price of 5 gallons of wax?

    A. 120　　B. 150　　C. 180　　D. 300

4. An employee waxes 275 sq.ft. of floor on Monday, 352 sq.ft. on Tuesday, 179 sq.ft. on Wednesday, and 302 sq.ft. on Thursday.
In order to average 280 sq.ft. of floor waxed a day, how many square feet of floor must he wax on Friday?

    A. 264　　B. 278　　C. 292　　D. 358

5. A project covers 35 acres altogether. Lawns, playgrounds, and walks take up 28 acres and the rest is given over to buildings.
What percentage of the total area is given over to buildings?

    A. 7%　　B. 20%　　C. 25%　　D. 28%

6. When preparing for a mopping operation, fill the standard 16 quart bucket to the 3/4 full mark with warm water. Then add detergent at the rate of 2 oz. per gallon of water and disinfectant at the rate of 1 oz. to 3 gallons of water. According to these directions, the amount of detergent and disinfectant to add to 3/4 of a bucket of warm water is _____ oz. detergent and _____ oz. disinfectant.

    A. 4; 1/2　　B. 5; 3/4　　C. 6; 1　　D. 8; 1 1/4

7. If corn brooms weigh 32 lbs. a dozen, the average weight of one corn broom is CLOSEST to _____ lbs. _____ oz.

    A. 2; 14　　B. 2; 11　　C. 2; 9　　D. 2; 6

8. At the beginning of the year, a foreman has 7 dozen electric bulbs in stock. During the year, he receives a shipment of 14 dozen bulbs, and also replaces 5 burned out bulbs a month in each of 3 buildings in his area. How many electric bulbs does he have on hand at the end of the year? _____ dozen.

   A. 3   B. 6   C. 8   D. 12

9. A project has 4 buildings, each 14 floors high. Each floor has 10 apartments.
   If 35% of the apartments in the project have 3 rooms or less, how many apartments have 4 or more rooms?

   A. 196   B. 210   C. 364   D. 406

10. An employee takes 1 hour and 30 minutes a day to sweep 30 flights of stairs. How many flights of stairs does he sweep in a month if he spends a total of 30 hours doing this job and works at the same rate?

    A. 200   B. 300   C. 600   D. 900

11. During a month, Employee A washed 30 windows, Employee B washed 4 times as many windows as Employee A, and Employee C washed half as many windows as Employee B. The TOTAL number of windows washed by all three men together during this month is

    A. 180   B. 210   C. 240   D. 330

12. How much would it cost to completely fence in the playground area shown at the right with fencing costing $7.50 a foot?
    A. $615.00
    B. $820.00
    C. $885.00
    D. $960.00

13. A drill bit measures .625 inches. The fractional equivalent, in inches, is

    A. 9/16   B. 5/8   C. 11/16   D. 3/4

14. The number of cubic yards of sand required to fill a bin measuring 12 feet by 6 feet by 4 feet is MOST NEARLY

    A. 8   B. 11   C. 48   D. 96

15. Assume that you are assigned to put down floor tiles in a room measuring 8 feet by 10 feet. Individual tiles measure 9 inches by 9 inches.
    The total number of floor tiles required to cover the entire floor is MOST NEARLY

    A. 107   B. 121   C. 142   D. 160

16. Lumber is usually sold by the board foot, and a board foot is defined as a board one foot square and one inch thick.
    If the price of one board foot of lumber is 90 cents and you need 20 feet of lumber 6 inches wide and 1 inch thick, the cost of the 20 feet of lumber is

    A. $9.00   B. $12.00   C. $18.00   D. $24.00

17. For a certain plumbing repair job, you need three lengths of pipe, 12 1/4 inches, 6 1/2 inches, and 8 5/8 inches.
    If you cut these three lengths from the same piece of pipe, which is 36 inches long, and each cut consumes 1/8 inch of pipe, the length of pipe REMAINING after you have cut out your three pieces should be _____ inches.

    A. 7 1/4   B. 7 7/8   C. 8 1/4   D. 8 7/8

18. A maintenance bond for a roadway pavement is in an amount of 10% of the estimated cost.
    If the estimated cost is $8,000,000, the maintenance bond is

    A. $8,000   B. $80,000   C. $800,000   D. $8,000,000

19. Specifications require that a core be taken every 700 square yards of paved roadway or fraction thereof. A 100 foot by 200 foot rectangular area would require _____ core(s).

    A. 1   B. 2   C. 3   D. 4

20. An applicant must file a map at a scale of 1" = 40'. Six inches on the map represents _____ feet on the ground.

    A. 600   B. 240   C. 120   D. 60

21. A 100' x 110' lot has an area of MOST NEARLY _____ acre.

    A. 1/8   B. 1/4   C. 3/8   D. 1/2

22. 1 inch is MOST NEARLY equal to _____ feet.

    A. .02   B. .04   C. .06   D. .08

23. The area of the triangle EFG shown at the right is MOST NEARLY _____ sq. ft.

    A. 36   B. 42   C. 48   D. 54

24. Specifications state: As further security for the faithful performance of this contract, the Comptroller shall deduct, and retain until the final payment, 10% of the value of the work certified for payment in each partial payment voucher, until the amount so deducted and retained shall equal 5% of the contract price or in the case of a unit price contract, 5% of the estimated amount to be paid to the Contractor under the contract.
    For a $300,000 contract, the amount to be retained at the end of the contract is

    A. $5,000   B. $10,000   C. $15,000   D. $20,000

25. Asphalt was laid for a length of 210 feet on the entire width of a street whose curb-to-curb distance is 30 feet. The number of square yards covered with asphalt is MOST NEARLY

    A. 210   B. 700   C. 2,100   D. 6,300

KEY (CORRECT ANSWERS)

1. C
2. A
3. B
4. C
5. B

6. C
7. B
8. B
9. C
10. C

11. B
12. C
13. B
14. B
15. C

16. A
17. C
18. C
19. D
20. B

21. B
22. D
23. A
24. C
25. B

SOLUTIONS TO PROBLEMS

1. (2)(9) = 18 man-days. Then, 18 ÷ 3 = 6 men

2. The number of employees = 1644 ÷ 2 = 822. The number of foremen needed = 822 ÷ 18 ≈ 45

3. 1 gallon of wax costs the same as 60 ÷ 2 = 30 bars of soap. Thus, 5 gallons of wax costs the same as (5)(30) = 150 bars of soap.

4. To average 280 sq.ft. for five days means a total of (5)(280) = 1400 sq.ft. for all five days. The number of square feet to be waxed on Friday = 1400 - (275+352+179+302) = 292

5. The acreage for buildings is 35 - 28 = 7. Then, 7/35 = 20%

6. (16)(3/4) = 12 quarts = 3 gallons. The amount of detergent, in ounces, is (2)(3) = 6. The amount of disinfectant is 1 oz.

7. One corn broom weighs 32 ÷ 12 = 2 2/3 lbs. ≈ 2 lbs. 11 oz.

8. Number of bulbs at the beginning of the year = (7)(12) + (14)(12) = 252. Number of bulbs replaced over an entire year = (5)(3)(12) = 180. The number of unused bulbs = 252 - 180 = 72 = 6 dozen.

9. Total number of apartments = (4)(14)(10) = 560. The number of apartments with at least 4 rooms = (.65)(560) = 364.

10. 30 ÷ 1 1/2 = 20. Then, (20)(30) = 600 flights of stairs

11. The number of windows washed by A, B, C were 30, 120, and 60. Their total is 210.

12. The two missing dimensions are 26 - 14 = 12 ft. and 33 - 9 = 24 ft. Perimeter = 9 + 12 + 33 + 26 + 24 + 14 = 118 ft. Thus, total cost of fencing = (118)($7.50) = $885.00

13. $.625 = \dfrac{625}{1000} = \dfrac{5}{8}$

14. (12)(6)(4) = 288 cu.ft. Now, 1 cu.yd. = 27 cu.ft.; 288 cu.ft. is equivalent to 10 2/3 or about 11 cu.yds.

15. 144 sq.in. = 1 sq.ft. The room measures (8 ft.)x(10 ft.) = 80 sq.ft. = 11,520 sq.in. Each tile measures (9)(9) = 81 sq.in. The number of tiles needed = 11,520 ÷ 81 = 142.2 or about 142.

16. 20 ft. by 6 in. = (20 ft.)(1/2 ft.) = 10 sq.ft. Then, (10X.90) = $9.00

17. There will be 3 cuts in making 3 lengths of pipe, and these 3 cuts will use (3)(1/8) = 3/8 in. of pipe. The amount of pipe remaining after the 3 pieces are removed = 36 - 12 1/4 - 6 1/2 - 8 5/8 - 3/8 = 8 1/4 in.

18. The maintenance bond = (.10)($8,000,000) = $800,000

19. (100)(200) = 20,000 sq.ft. = 20,000 ÷ 9 ≈ 2222 sq.yds. Then, 2222 ÷ 700 ≈ 3.17. Since a core must be taken for each 700 sq.yds. plus any left over fraction, 4 cores will be needed.

20. Six inches means (6)(40) = 240 ft. of actual length.

21. (100 ft.)(110 ft.) = 11,000 sq.ft. ≈ 1222 sq.yds. Then, since 1 acre = 4840 sq.yds., 1222 sq.yds. is equivalent to about 1/4 acre.

22. 1 in. = 1/12 ft. ≈ .08 ft.

23. Area of △EFG = (1/2)(8)(6) + (1/2)(4)(6) = 36 sq.ft.

24. The amount to be retained = (.05)($300,000) = $15,000

25. (210)(30) = 6300 sq.ft. Since 1 sq.yd. = 9 sq.ft., 6300 sq.ft. equals 700 sq.yds.

TEST 2

DIRECTIONS: Each question or incomplete statement is followed by several suggested answers or completions. Select the one that BEST answers the question or completes the statement. *PRINT THE LETTER OF THE CORRECT ANSWER IN THE SPACE AT THE RIGHT.*

1. The TOTAL length of four pieces of 2" pipe, whose lengths are 7'3 1/2", 4'2 3/16", 5'7 5/16", and 8'5 7/8", respectively, is

   A. 24'6 3/4"
   B. 24'7 15/16"
   C. 25'5 13/16"
   D. 25'6 7/8"

   1.____

2. Under the same conditions, the group of pipes that gives the SAME flow as one 6" pipe is (neglecting friction) _____ pipes.

   A. 3 3" B. 4 3" C. 2 4" D. 3 4"

   2.____

3. A water storage tank measures 5' long, 4' wide, and 6' deep and is filled to the 5 1/2' mark with water.
   If one cubic foot of water weighs 62 pounds, the number of pounds of water required to COMPLETELY fill the tank is

   A. 7,440 B. 6,200 C. 1,240 D. 620

   3.____

4. A hot water line made of copper has a straight horizontal run of 150 feet and, when installed, is at a temperature of 45°F. In use, its temperature rises to 190°F.
   If the coefficient of expansion for copper is 0.0000095" per foot per degree F, the total expansion, in inches, in the run of pipe is given by the product of 150 multiplied by 0.0000095 by

   A. 145
   B. 145 x 12
   C. 145 divided by 12
   D. 145 x 12 x 12

   4.____

5. To dig a trench 3'0" wide, 50'0" long, and 5'6" deep, the total number of cubic yards of earth to be removed is MOST NEARLY

   A. 30 B. 90 C. 140 D. 825

   5.____

6. If it costs $65 for 20 feet of subway rail, the cost of 150 feet of this rail will be

   A. $487.50 B. $512.00 C. $589.50 D. $650.00

   6.____

7. The number of cubic feet of concrete it takes to fill a form 10 feet long, 3 feet wide, and 6 inches deep is

   A. 12 B. 15 C. 20 D. 180

   7.____

8. The sum of 4 1/16, 5 1/4, 3 5/8, and 4 7/16 is

   A. 17 3/16 B. 17 1/4 C. 17 5/16 D. 17 3/8

   8.____

9. If you earn $10.20 per hour and time and one-half for working over 40 hours, your gross salary for a week in which you worked 42 hours would be

   A. $408.00 B. $428.40 C. $438.60 D. $770.80

   9.____

10. A drill bit, used to drill holes in track ties, has a diameter of 0.75 inches. When expressed as a fraction, the diameter of this drill bit is

    A. 1/4"   B. 3/8"   C. 1/2"   D. 3/4"

11. Three dozen shovels were purchased for use.
    If the shovels were used at the rate of nine a week, the number of weeks that the three dozen lasted was

    A. 3   B. 4   C. 9   D. 12

12. Assume that you earn $20,000 per year.
    If twenty percent of your pay is deducted for taxes, social security, and pension, your weekly take-home pay will be MOST NEARLY

    A. $280   B. $308   C. $328   D. $344

13. If a measurement scaled from a drawing is one inch, and the scale of the drawing is 1/8 inch to the foot, then the one inch measurement would represent an ACTUAL length of

    A. 8 feet   B. 2 feet
    C. 1/8 of a foot   D. 8 inches

14. Tiles 12" x 12" are used to lay a floor having the dimensions 10'0" x 12'0".
    The MINIMUM number of tiles needed to completely cover the floor is

    A. 60   B. 96   C. 120   D. 144

15. The volume of concrete in a strip of sidewalk 30 feet long by 4 feet wide by 3 inches thick is _____ cubic feet.

    A. 30   B. 120   C. 240   D. 360

16. To change a quantity of cubic feet into an equivalent quantity of cubic yards, _____ the quantity by _____.

    A. multiply; 9   B. divide; 9
    C. multiply; 27   D. divide; 27

17. If a pump can deliver 50 gallons of water per minute, then the time needed for this pump to empty an excavation containing 5,800 gallons of water is _____ hour(s) _____ minutes.

    A. 2; 12   B. 1; 56   C. 1; 44   D. 1; 32

18. The sum of 3 1/6", 4 1/4", 3 5/8", and 5 7/16" is

    A. 15 9/16"   B. 16 1/8"   C. 16 23/48"   D. 16 3/4"

19. If a measurement scaled from a drawing is 2 inches, and the scale of the drawing is 1/8 inch to the foot, then the two inch measurement would represent an ACTUAL length of

    A. 8 feet   B. 4 feet
    C. 1/4 of a foot   D. 16 feet

20. A room is 7'6" wide by 9'0" long with a ceiling height of 8'0". One gallon of flat paint will cover approximately 400 square feet of wall.
The number of gallons of this paint required to paint the walls of this room, making no deductions for windows or doors, is MOST NEARLY

   A. 1/4   B. 1/2   C. 2/3   D. 1

20._____

21. The cost of a certain job is broken down as follows:

   Materials $3,750
   Rental of equipment 1,200
   Labor   3,150

   The percentage of the total cost of the job that can be charged to materials is MOST NEARLY

   A. 40%   B. 42%   C. 44%   D. 46%

21._____

22. By trial, it is found that by using two cubic feet of sand, a 5 cubic foot batch of concrete is produced. Using the same proportions, the amount of sand required to produce 2 cubic yards of concrete is MOST NEARLY _____ cubic feet.

   A. 20   B. 22   C. 24   D. 26

22._____

23. It takes 4 men 6 days to do a certain job.
Working at the same speed, the number of days it will take 3 men to do this job is

   A. 7   B. 8   C. 9   D. 10

23._____

24. The cost of rawl plugs is $27.50 per gross. The cost of 2,448 rawl plugs is

   A. $467.50   B. $472.50   C. $477.50   D. $482.50

24._____

25. In a certain district, the area of a building may be no longer than 55% of the area of the lot on which it stands. On a rectangular lot 75 ft. by 125 ft., the maximum permissible area of building is, in square feet, MOST NEARLY

   A. 5,148   B. 5,152   C. 5,156   D. 5,160

25._____

KEY (CORRECT ANSWERS)

1.	D	11.	B
2.	B	12.	B
3.	D	13.	A
4.	A	14.	C
5.	A	15.	A
6.	A	16.	D
7.	B	17.	B
8.	D	18.	C
9.	C	19.	D
10.	D	20.	C

21. D
22. B
23. B
24. A
25. C

SOLUTIONS TO PROBLEMS

1. $3\frac{1}{6}" + 4\frac{1}{4}" + 3\frac{5}{8}" + 5\frac{7}{16}" = 3\frac{8}{48}" + 4\frac{12}{48}" + 3\frac{30}{48}" + 5\frac{21}{48}" = 15\frac{71}{48}" = 16\frac{23}{48}"$

2. The flow of a 6" pipe is measured by the cross-sectional area. Since diameter = 6", radius = 3", and so area = 9π sq.in. A single 3" pipe would have a cross-sectional area of $(3/2)\pi$ sq.in. = 2.25π sq.in. Now, $9 \div /2.25 = 4$. Thus, four 3" pipes is equivalent, in flow, to one 6" pipe.

3. $(5 \times 4 \times 6) - (5 \times 4 \times 5\ 1/2) = 10$. Then, $(10)(62) = 620$ pounds.

4. The total expansion = $(150')(.0000095"/1\ ft.)(190° - 45°)$. So, the last factor is 145.

5. $(3')(50')(5\ 1/2') = 825$ cu.ft. Since 1 cu.yd. = 27 cu.ft., 825 cu.ft. cu.yds.

6. $150 \div 20 = 7.5$. Then, $(7.5)(\$65) = \$487.50$

7. $(10')(3')(1/2') = 15$ cu.ft.

8. $4\frac{1}{16} + 5\frac{4}{16} + 3\frac{10}{16} + 4\frac{7}{16} = 16\frac{22}{16} = 17\frac{3}{8}$

9. Gross salary = $(\$10.20)(40) + (\$15.30)(2) = \$438.60$

10. $75" = \frac{75}{100}" = \frac{3}{4}"$

11. 3 dozen = 36 shovels. Then, $36 \div 9 = 4$ weeks

12. Since 20% is deducted, the take-home pay = $(\$20,000)(.80) = \$16,000$ for the year, which is $\$16,000 \div 52 \approx \$308$ per week.

13. A scale drawing where 1/8" means an actual size of 1 ft. implies that a scale drawing of 1" means an actual size of $(1')(8) = 8'$

14. $(10')(12') = 120$ sq.ft. Since each tile is 1 sq.ft., a total of 120 tiles will be used.

15. $(30')(4')(1/4') = 30$ cu.ft.

16. To convert a given number of cubic feet into an equivalent number of cubic yards, divide by 27.

17. $5800 \div 50 = 116$ min. = 1 hour 56 minutes

18. $3\frac{1}{6}" + 4\frac{1}{4}" + 3\frac{5}{8}" + 5\frac{7}{16}" = 3\frac{8}{48}" + 4\frac{12}{48}" + 3\frac{30}{48}" + 5\frac{21}{48}" = 15\frac{71}{48}" = 16\frac{23}{48}"$

19. $2 \div 1/8 = 16$, so a 2" drawing represents an actual length of 16 feet.

20. The area of the 4 walls = 2(7 1/2')(8') + 2(9')(8') = 264 sq.ft. Then, 264 ÷ 400 = .66 or about 2/3 gallon of paint.

21. $3750 + $1200 + $3150 = $8100. Then, $3750/$8100 ≈ 46%

22. 2 cu.yds. ÷ 5 cu.ft. = 54 ÷ 5 = 10.8. Now, (10.8)(2 cu.ft.) ≈ 22 cu.ft. Note: 2 cu.yds. = 54 cu.ft.

23. (4)(6) = 24 man-days. Then, 24 ÷ 3 = 8 days

24. 2448 ÷ 144 = 17. Then, (17)($27.50) = $467.50

25. (75')(125') = 9375 sq.ft. The maximum area of the building = (.55)(9375 sq.ft.) * 5156 sq.ft.

TEST 3

DIRECTIONS: Each question or incomplete statement is followed by several suggested answers or completions. Select the one that BEST answers the question or completes the statement. *PRINT THE LETTER OF THE CORRECT ANSWER IN THE SPACE AT THE RIGHT.*

1. A steak weighed 2 pounds, 4 ounces. How much did it cost at $4.60 per pound?

    A. $7.80   B. $8.75   C. $9.90   D. $10.35

2. twenty pints of water just fill a pail. the capacity of the pail, in gallons, is

    A. 2   B. 2 1/4   C. 2 1/2   D. 2 3/4

3. The sum of 5/12 and 1/4 is

    A. 7/12   B. 2/3   C. 3/4   D. 5/6

4. The volume of earth, in cubic yards, excavated from a trench 4'0" wide by 5'6" deep by 18'6" long is MOST NEARLY

    A. 14.7   B. 15.1   C. 15.5   D. 15.9

5. 5/8 written as a decimal is

    A. 62.5   B. 6.25   C. .625   D. .0625

6. The number of cubic feet in a cubic yard is

    A. 9   B. 12   C. 27   D. 36

7. If it costs $16.20 to lay one square yard of asphalt, to lay a patch 15' by 15', it will cost MOST NEARLY

    A. $405.00   B. $3,645.00   C. $134.50   D. $243.00

8. You are assigned thirty (30) asphalt workers to be divided into two crews so that one crew will have 2/3 as many men as the other.
The number of men you would put into the SMALLER crew is

    A. 10   B. 12   C. 14   D. 20

9. It takes 12 asphalt workers, working 6 hours a day, 5 days to complete a certain job. The number of days it will take 10 men, working 8 hours a day, to do the same job, assuming all work at the same rate, is

    A. 2 1/2   B. 3   C. 4 1/2   D. 6

10. A street is laid to a 3% grade. This means that in 150 ft., the street grade will rise

    A. 4 1/2 inches   B. 45 inches
    C. 4 1/2 feet   D. 45 feet

11. The sum of the following dimensions, 3 4/8, 4 1/8, 5 1/8, and 6 1/4, is 11.____
    A. 19   B. 19 1/8   C. 19 1/4   D. 19 1/2

12. A worker is paid $9.30 per hour. 12.____
    If he works 8 hours each day on Monday, Tuesday, and Wednesday, 3 1/2 hours on Thursday, and 3 hours on Friday, the TOTAL amount due him is
    A. $283.65   B. $289.15   C. $276.20   D. $285.35

13. The price of metal lath is $395.00 per 100 square yards. The cost of 527 square yards of this lath is MOST NEARLY 13.____
    A. $2,076.50   B. $2,079.10   C. $2,081.70   D. $2,084.30

14. The total cost of applying 221 square yards of plaster board is $3,430. 14.____
    The cost per square yard is MOST NEARLY
    A. $14.00   B. $14.50   C. $15.00   D. $15.50

15. In a three-coat plaster job, the scratch coat is 1/8 in. thick in front of the lath, the brown coat is 3/16 in. thick, and the finish coat is 1/8 in. thick. 15.____
    The TOTAL thickness of this plaster job, measured from the face of the lath, is
    A. 7/16"   B. 1/2"   C. 9/16"   D. 5/8"

16. If an asphalt worker earns $38,070 per year, his wages per month are MOST NEARLY 16.____
    A. $380.70   B. $735.00   C. $3,170.00   D. $3,807.00

17. The sum of 4 1/2 inches, 3 1/4 inches, and 7 1/2 inches is 1 foot _____ inches. 17.____
    A. 3   B. 3 1/4   C. 3 1/2   D. 4

18. The area of a rectangular asphalt patch, 9 ft. 3 in. by 6 ft. 9 in., is _____ square feet. 18.____
    A. 54   B. 54 1/4   C. 54 1/2   D. 62 7/16

19. The number of cubic feet in a cubic yard is 19.____
    A. 3   B. 9   C. 16   D. 27

20. A 450 ft. long street with a grade of 2% will have one end of the street higher than the other end by _____ feet. 20.____
    A. 2   B. 44   C. 9   D. 20

21. If the drive wheel of a roller is 6 ft. in diameter and the tiller wheel is 4 ft. in diameter, whenever the drive wheel makes a complete revolution on a straight pass, the tiller wheel makes _____ revolution(s). 21.____
    A. 1   B. 1 1/4   C. 1 1/2   D. 2

22. A point on the centerline of a street is marked: Station 42 + 51. Another point on the centerline 30 feet from the first is marked Station 42+81. 22.____
    A third should be marked Station
    A. 12+51   B. 42+21   C. 45+51   D. 72+51

23. In twenty minutes, a truck moving with a speed of 30 miles an hour will cover a distance   23._____
    of _____ miles.

    A. 3   B. 5   C. 10   D. 30

24. The number of pounds in a ton is   24._____

    A. 500   B. 1,000   C. 2,000   D. 5,000

25. During his summer vacation, a boy earned $45.00 per day and saved 60% of his earn-   25._____
    ings.
    If he worked 45 days, how much did he save during his vacation?

    A. $15.00   B. $18.00   C. $1,215.00 D. $22.50

KEY (CORRECT ANSWERS)

1.	D	11.	A
2.	C	12.	A
3.	B	13.	C
4.	B	14.	D
5.	C	15.	A
6.	C	16.	C
7.	A	17.	B
8.	B	18.	D
9.	C	19.	D
10.	C	20.	C

21.	C
22.	B
23.	C
24.	C
25.	C

SOLUTIONS TO PROBLEMS

1. ($4.60)(2 1/4 lbs.) = $10.35

2. 1 gallon = 8 pints, so 20 pints = 20/8 = 2 1/2 gallons

3. $\dfrac{5}{12}+\dfrac{1}{4}=\dfrac{5}{12}+\dfrac{3}{12}=\dfrac{8}{12}=\dfrac{2}{3}$

4. (4')(5 1/2')(18 1/2') = 407 cu.ft. Since 1 cu.yd. = 27 cu.ft., 407 cu.ft. ≈ 15.1 cu.yds.

5. 5/8 = 5 ÷ 8.000 = .625

6. There are (3)(3)(3) = 27 cu.ft. in a cu.yd.

7. (15')(15') = 225 sq.ft. = 25 sq.yds. Then, ($16.20)(25) = $405.00

8. Let 2x = size of smaller crew and 3x = size of larger crew. Then, 2x + 3x = 30. Solving, x = 6. Thus, the smaller crew consists of 12 workers.

9. (12)(6)(5) = 360 worker-days. Then, 360 ÷ [(10)(8)] = 4 1/2 days

10. (.03)(150') = 4 1/2 ft.

11. $3\dfrac{4}{8}+4\dfrac{1}{8}+5\dfrac{1}{8}+6\dfrac{2}{8}=18\dfrac{8}{8}=19$

12. ($9.30)(8+8+8+3 1/2+3) = ($9.30)(30 1/2) = $283.65

13. The cost of 527 sq.yds. = (5.27)($395.00) = $2081.65 ≈ $2081.70

14. $3430 ÷ 221 ≈ $15.50

15. $\dfrac{1}{8}"+\dfrac{3}{16}"+\dfrac{1}{8}"=\dfrac{2}{16}"+\dfrac{3}{16}"+\dfrac{2}{16}"=\dfrac{7}{16}"$

16. $38,070 ÷ 12 = $3172.50 ≈ $3170.00 per month

17. 4 1/2" + 3 1/4" + 7 1/2" = 15 1/4" = 1 ft. 3 1/4 in.

18. 9 ft. 3 in. = 9 1/4 ft., 6 ft. 9 in. = 6 3/4 ft. Area = (9 1/4)(6 3/4) = 62 7/16 sq.ft.

19. A cubic yard = (3)(3)(3) = 27 cubic feet

20. (450')(.02) = 9 ft.

21. 6/4 = 1 1/2 revolutions

22. Station 42 + 51
    30 ft away would be 51 + 30 = 81 OR 51 - 30 = 21
    Station 42 + 81 or 42 + 21 (ANSWER: B)

23. 30 miles in 60 minutes means 10 miles in 20 minutes.

24. There are 2000 pounds in a ton.

25. ($45.00)(.60) = $27.00 savings per day. For 45 days, his savings is (45)($27.00) = $1215.00

MASONRY

TABLE OF CONTENTS

	Page
SECTION 1 – Masons' Tools and Equipment	1
2 – Mortar	4
3 – Scaffolding	7

MASONRY
General

Section I. MASONS' TOOLS AND EQUIPMENT

7-1. Tools

The mason's tools are shown in figure 7-1.

a. Trowels. The trowel is usually triangular, the largest size being 9 to 11 inches long and from 4 to 8 inches wide. The length and weight 6f the trowel used depends on the mason. He should select the one he can handle the best. Generally, the short wide trowels are best since the weight is nearer the wrist and does not put as much strain on the wrist. Trowels used for pointing and striking joints are smaller in size: 3 to 6 inches long and 2 to 3 inches wide. The trowel is used to -
  (1) Mix and pick up mortar from the board.
  (2) Throw mortar on the block.
  (3) Spread mortar.
  (4) Tap the block down into its bed when necessary.

b. Chisel or Bolster. The tool is used to cut concrete block. It is 2 1/2 to 4 1/2 inches wide.

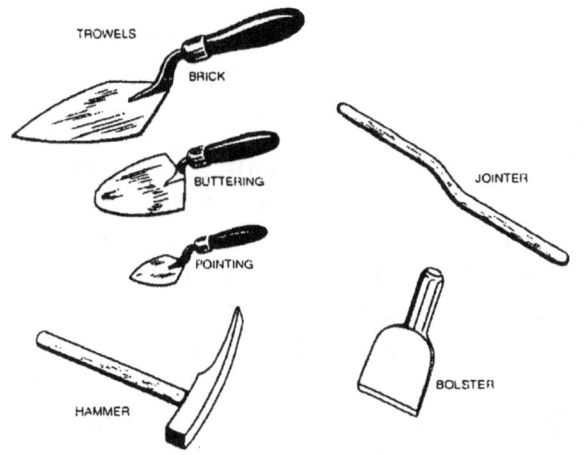

Figure 7-1. Mason's tools.

c. Hammer. The hammer has a square face on one end and a long chisel peen on the other. It weighs from 1 1/2 to 3 1/2 pounds. It is used for splitting and rough-breaking of blocks.

d. Jointer. This tool is used for making various types of joints. There are several different types. They are rounded, flat, or pointed depending on the shape of the mortar joint desired.

e. Square. The square (1, fig. 7-2) is used to measure right angles and lay out corners.

f. Mason's Level. The level enables the mason to plumb and level walls. It is from 36 to 48 inches long and is made of wood or metal. Two, figure 7-2 illustrates a level. When the level is placed horizontally on the masonry and the bubble in the center tube is exactly in the middle of the center tube, the masonry is level. When the level is placed vertically against the masonry and the bubble in the end tube is exactly in the middle of the tube, the masonry is plumb. For long, high walls or tall columns an offset line from the face of the work should be established. To assure straightness and plumbness, offset checks between this line and the face should be made frequently.

g. Straightedge. A straightedge, as shown in 3, figure 7-2, may be of any length up to 16 feet and should be 1 1/8 inches thick and 6 to 10 inches wide. The top and bottom edges must be parallel. The straightedge can be used as an extension of the level to cover distances longer than the length of the level.

h. Miscellaneous Tools. Additional equipment required includes shovels, mortar hoes, wheelbarrows, chalk, plumb bobs, and a 200-foot ball of No. 18 to 21 hard-twisted cotton cord of the same type used as chalkline by carpenters.

i. Care of Tools. Wheelbarrows, mortar box, and mortar tools should be kept clean

2

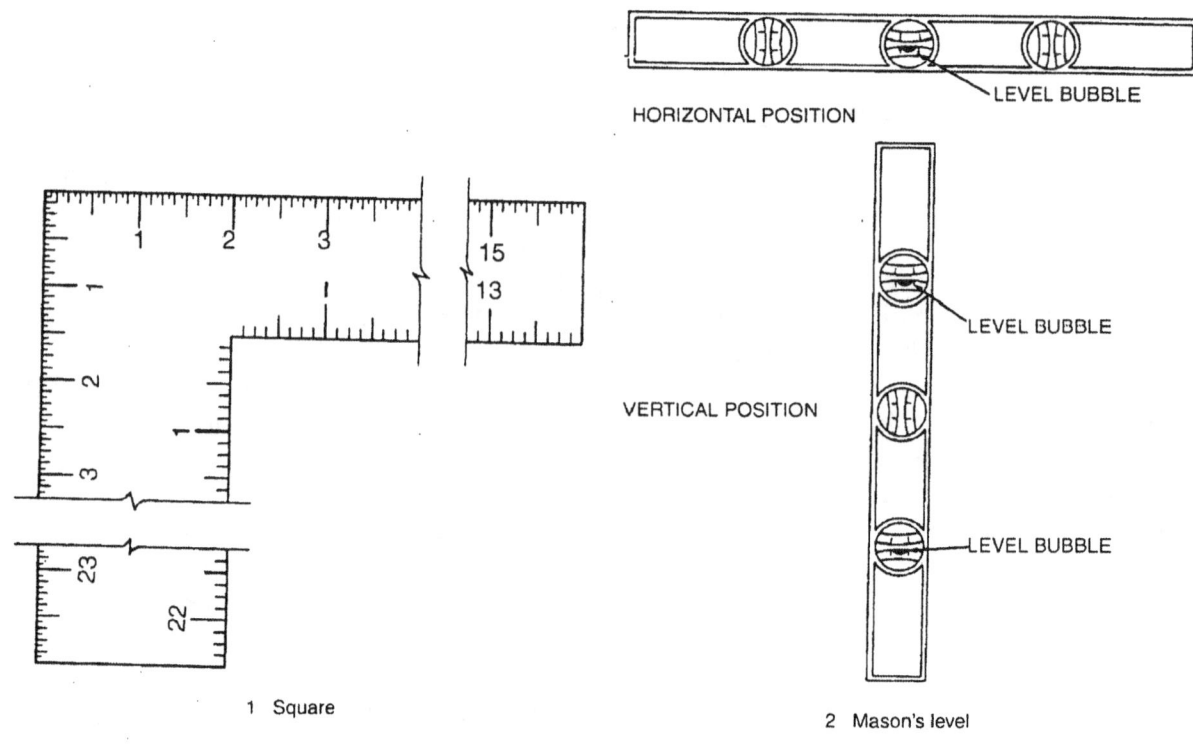

1 Square   2 Mason's level

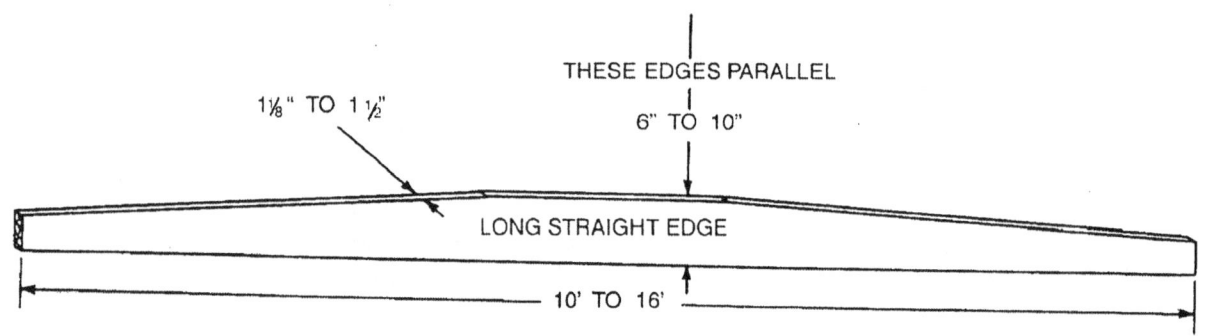

3 Straightedge

since hardened mortar is difficult to remove. All tools and equipment should be cleaned thoroughly at the end of each day, or when the job is finished, as appropriate.

7-2. Equipment

a. Mortar Box. The mortar box (1, fig. 7-3) is used to mix mortar by hand. It should be as water tight as possible.

b. Mortar Board. The mortar board is constructed as shown in 2, figure 2-3. It can be from 3- to 4-feet square. The mortar board should be thoroughly wetted down before any mortar is placed on it to prevent the wood from absorbing moisture and causing the mortar to dry out. The mortar should be kept rounded up in the center of the board and the outer edges kept clean. If spread in a thin layer, the mortar will dry out quickly and there will be a tendency for lumps to form. Proper consistency must be maintained at all times. Three, figure 7-3 indicates the proper way to fill a mortar board.

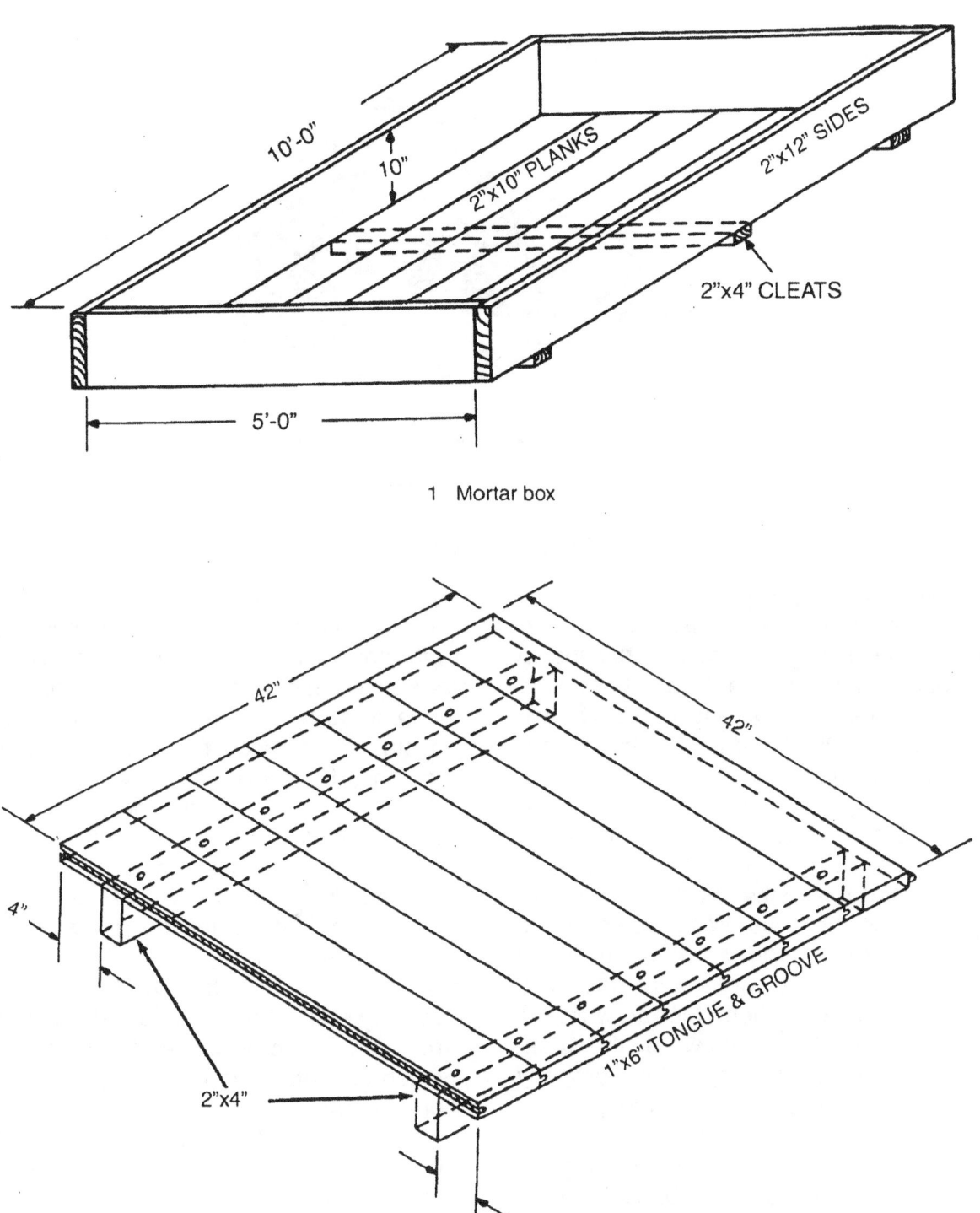

Figure 7-3. Mortar board and mortar box.

3   Filling a mortar doard

Figure 7-3.- Continued.

Section II. MORTAR

7-3. Desirable Properties

a. Basic Considerations. Good mortar which is necessary to good workmanship and good wall service must bond the masonry units into a strong, well-knit wall. The strength of the bond is affected by various factors including the type and quantity of the cementing material, the workability or plasticity of the mortar, the surface texture of the mortar bedding areas, the water retentivity of the mortar, and the quality of workmanship in laying the units. Water retentivity is that property of mortar which resists rapid loss of water to masonry units which may possess high absorption. Mortar which is used to bond brick together will be the weakest part of brick masonry unless properly mixed and applied. Both the strength and resistance to rain penetration of brick masonry walls are dependent to a great degree on the strength of the bond. Water in the mortar is essential to the development of bond and if the mortar contains insufficient water the bond will be weak and spotty. When brick walls leak it is usually through the mortar joints. Irregularities in dimensions and shape of bricks are corrected by the mortar joint.

b. Mortar Properties. Mortar should be plastic enough to work with a trowel. The properties of mortar depend largely upon the type of sand used in it. Clean, sharp sand produces excellent mortar. Too much sand in mortar will cause it to segregate, drop off the trowel, and weather poorly. Workability, an important requirement of mortar, should be obtained through the proper grading of the sand, the use of mortar with good water retentivity, and through thorough mixing rather than through the use of excessive amounts of cementitious material.

c. Water Retentivity. Loss of moisture due to poor water retention results in rapid loss of plasticity and may seriously reduce the effectiveness of the bond. As concrete masonry units should be kept dry until they are built into the wall, they should never be wetted to control suction before the application of mortar.

d. Strength and Durability. The strength and durability requirements of a mortar depend upon the type of service the wall is to give. Walls subjected to severe stresses or to severe weathering naturally need to be laid in more durable, stronger mortars than walls for ordinary service. Table 7-1 lists mortar mixes that provide adequate mortar strength and durability for the conditions indicated. The volumetric proportions shown may be converted to weight proportions by multiplying the unit volumes by the weight per cubic foot of the materials, which may be assumed to be as follows:

Masonry cement------------------Weight printed on bag
Portland cement -------------------- 94 lb
Hydrated lime ---------------------- 40 lb
Mortar sand, damp and loose-85 lb (approximately)

The section of mortar for brick construction depends on the use requirements of the structure. For example, the recommended mortar for use in laying up interior non-load-bearing partitions would not be satisfactory for foundation walls. In many cases, the builder relies upon a fixed proportion of cement, lime and sand to provide a satisfactory mortar.

e. Bond. Bond is the property of a hardened mortar that knits the masonry units together. The strength of bond is affected by a number of factors such as the kind and quantity of cementitious material, the workability of the mortar, the surface texture of the mortar bedding areas, the rate of suction of the masonry unit's and the quality of workmanship in making the joints.

f. Types of Mortar. The following types of mortar are proportioned on a volume basis:

(1) *Type M.* 1 part portland cement, 1/4 part hydrated lime or lime putty, 3 parts sand, or 1 part portland cement, 1 part type II masonry cement, and 6 parts sand. This mortar is suitable for general use and is recommended specifically for masonry below grade and in contact with earth, such as foundations, retaining walls, and walks.

Table 7-1. Recommended Mortar Mixes Proportions by volume.

Type of service	Cement	Hydrated lime	Mortar sand, in damp, loose condition
FOR ORDINARY SERVICE.	1-masonry cement* or		2 1/4 to 3.
	1-Portland cement	1/2 to 1 1/4	4 1/2 to 6.
SUBJECT TO EXTREMELY HEAVY LOADS, VIOLENT WINDS, EARTHQUAKES, OR SEVERE FROST ACTION ISOLATED PIERS.	1-masonry cement* plus 1-Portland cement or		4 1/2 to 6
	1-Portland cement.	0 to 1/4	2 1/4 to 3.

*ASTM Specification C 91 Type II.

(2) *Type S.* 1 part portland cement, 1/2 part hydrated lime or lime putty, 4 1/2 parts sand, or 1/2 part portland cement, 1 part type II masonry cement and 4 1/2 parts sand. This mortar is also suitable for general use and is recommended where high resistance to lateral forces is required.

(3) *Type N.* 1 part portland cement, 1 part hydrated lime or lime putty, 6 parts sand, or 1 part type II masonry cement and 3 parts sand. This mortar is suitable for general use in exposed masonry above grade and is recommended specifically for exterior walls subjected to severe exposures as, for example, on the Atlantic Seaboard.

(4) *Type O.* 1 part Portland cement, 2 parts hydrated lime or lime putty, and 9 parts sand, or 1 part type I or type II masonry cement and 3 parts sand. This mortar is recommended for load-bearing walls of solid units where the compressive stresses do not exceed 100 pounds per square inch and the masonry will not be subjected to freezing and thawing in the presence of excessive moisture.

g. Storage of Mortar Materials. All mortar materials except sand and slaked quicklime must be stored in a dry place.

7-4. Mixing Mortar

a. Machine Mixing. If a large quantity of mortar is required, it should be mixed in a drum-type mixer similar to those used for mixing concrete. The mixing time should not be less than 3 minutes. All dry ingredients should be placed in the mixer first and mixed for 1 minute before adding the water.

b. Hand Mixing. Unless large amounts of mortar are required, the mortar is mixed by hand using a mortar box shown in figure 7-3. Care must be taken to mix all the ingredients thoroughly to obtain a uniform mixture. As in machine mixing, all dry material should be mixed first. A steel drum full of water should be kept close to the mortar box for the water supply. A second drum of water should be available for shovels and hoes when not in use.

c. Mixing Mortar With Lime Putty. When a machine mixer is used, the lime putty should be measured with a GI pail and loaded in the skip on top of the sand. If the mortar is to be mixed by hand, sand is added to the lime putty. Pails should be wet before mortar is placed in them and should be cleaned immediately after they have been emptied.

d. Water. Water used in mixing mortar should meet the same requirements as water used in mixing concrete. Water containing large amounts of dissolved salts should not be used as they will cause efflorescence and weaken the mortar.

e. Retempering Mortar. Mortar that has stiffened on the mortar board because of evaporation should be reworked to restore its workability by thorough remixing and by the addition of water as required. Mortar stiffened by initial setting should be discarded. A practical guide in determining the suitability of mortar, since it is difficult to determine the cause of stiffening, is that it should be used within 2 1/2 hours after original mixing when the air temperature is 80 F. or higher and within 3 1/2 hours when the air temperature is below 80F. Mortar not used within the above limits should be discarded.

f. Antifreeze Materials. The use of an admixture to lower the freezing point of mortars during winter construction should be avoided. The quantity of such material necessary to lower the freezing point of mortar to any appreciable degree would be so large that the mortar strength and other desirable properties would be seriously impaired. If mortar freezes, it must not be used; freezing destroys its bonding ability.

g. Accelerators. Calcium chloride is sometimes added to mortar to accelerate the rate of hardening and to increase early strengths. Not more than 2 percent calcium chloride by weight of the port-land cement should be used for this purpose. Not more than 1 percent of calcium chloride should be used with masonry cements. A trial mix will indicate the percentage of calcium chloride that will give the desired rate of hardening of the mortar. High early strengths in mortars can also be obtained by the use of high-early-strength portland cement.

h. Repair and Tuckpointing. The mortar mixes shown in table 7-1 can be used in repairing and tuckpointing old masonry walls. After the mortar has partially stiffened, the joints should be thoroughly compacted by tooling.

Section III. SCAFFOLDING

7-5. Basic Considerations

A scaffold is a temporary platform built for the support of workman and materials. Scaffolds are necessary after the bricklayer has completed work at the height he can reach by standing on the floor or ground. Extreme care is taken in building scaffolds because workmen's lives depend upon them. No scaffolding is temporarily nailed for it may be forgotten and never adequately nailed. When the scaffold planks at one level are no longer needed, they should be removed; falling mortar will hit them and splash on the wall. Rough lumber should be used for wood scaffolding.

7-6. Types of Scaffolding

Several types of scaffolds are described below.

a. Trestle Scaffold. When construction is such that the brick can be laid from the inside of the wall, a trestle scaffold as shown in figure 7-4 may be used. The trestles should be from 4 to 4 feet 6 inches high. The scaffold planks rest on the trestles and should be 2 by 10's. After the wall has been built to a height of 4 or 5 feet, the trestle scaffold should be erected. The wall can then be completed to the next floor level while the bricklayer works from the scaffold. As soon as the rough flooring for the next floor is in place, the above procedure is repeated. The trestle should remain at least 3 inches from the wall in order to make sure it will not push against the newly laid brick and force them out of line.

b. Foot Scaffold. At times it may be necessary to reach higher than the trestle scaffold permits. Then a foot scaffold such as the one shown in figure 7-5 can be used. The 2 by 10 planks rest on bricks which can be supported by the trestle scaffold. This type of scaffold should not exceed 18 inches in height.

c. Putlog Scaffold.

(1) When it is necessary to erect the scaffold from the ground to the height required, a putlog scaffold can be used to advantage. The uprights should be 4 by 4's supported on a 2- by 12-inch plank 12 inches long for bearing on the soil. These upright's should be spaced on 8-foot centers. There should be 4 feet 6 inches between the wall and the uprights. The ledgers should be made from 1- by 8-inch lumber nailed to the uprights, as shown in figure 7-6. The putlog is a 3- by 4-inch piece of lumber that rests on top of the ledger and against the upright. The other end of the 3 by 4 rest's on the wall; a brick is omitted to provide an opening for it. The putlog is not fastened to the ledger. On top of the putlog, five 2 by 12's are placed to form the scaffold platform. The planks are not nailed to the putlog.

(2) The uprights must be tied to the wall by stays. These stays may be passed through a window opening and fastened to the structure inside the building or spring stays may be used as shown in figure 7-6. Spring stays are made by placing two 2- by 6-inch boards in an opening in the wall formed by omitting a brick. After the boards are inserted into the hole, a brick is placed between them and forced to a position close to the wall. The boards are then sprung together and securely nailed to the ledger.

(3) The putlog may also be used as a stay in which case a wooden wedge should be driven above the putlog and into its hole in the wall. The wedge should then be nailed to the putlog and the putlog nailed to the ledger. Longitudinal cross bracing must be installed as shown in figure 7-6.

d. Outrigger Scaffold. This scaffold consists of 2- by 10-inch planks supported on a wooden beam projecting from the building. The beam is supported as shown in figure 7-7. If a steel outrigger beam is used, the beam is fastened to the form work of the structure by means of threaded U-shaped bolts.

e. Steel Scaffolding. When prefabricated steel scaffolding such as that shown in figure 7-8 is available, it should be used. It is more easily erected and dismantled and can be reused many times.

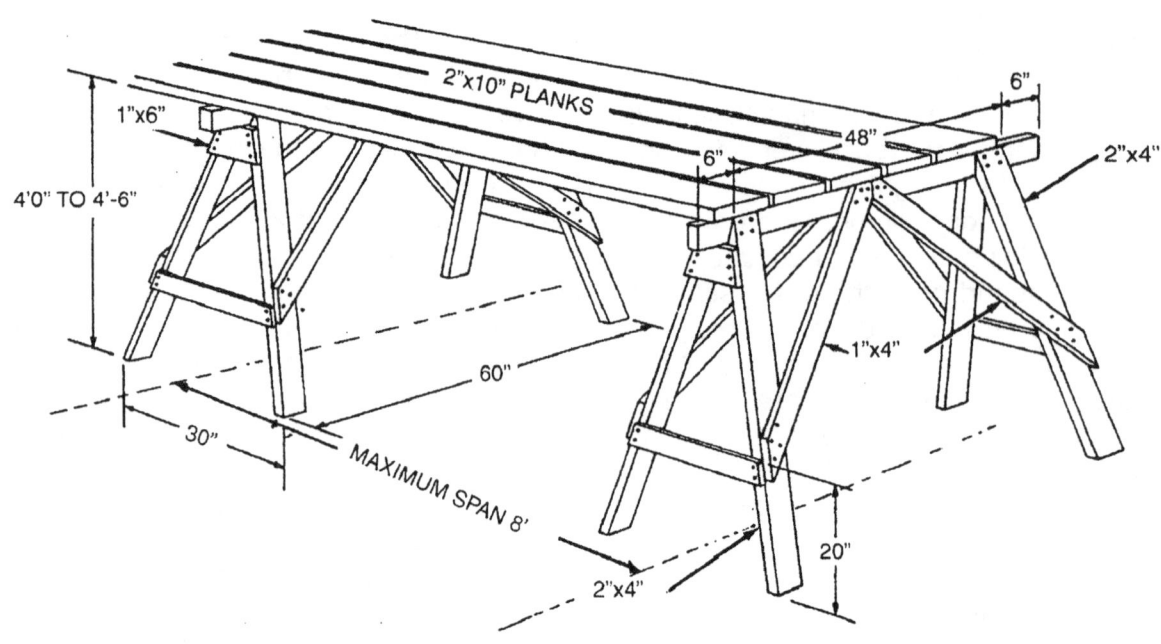

Figure 7-4. Trestle scaffold.

7-7. Material Hoist

a. Details. On a large number of jobs, a material hoist is necessary. This hoist should be constructed as shown in 1, figure 7-9. It should be located in such a way that materials may be moved to it with the shortest possible haul. The material tower should be located far enough away from the structure to clear any outside scaffold to be used. A distance of 6 feet 8 inches is enough for

Figure 7-5. Foot scaffold.

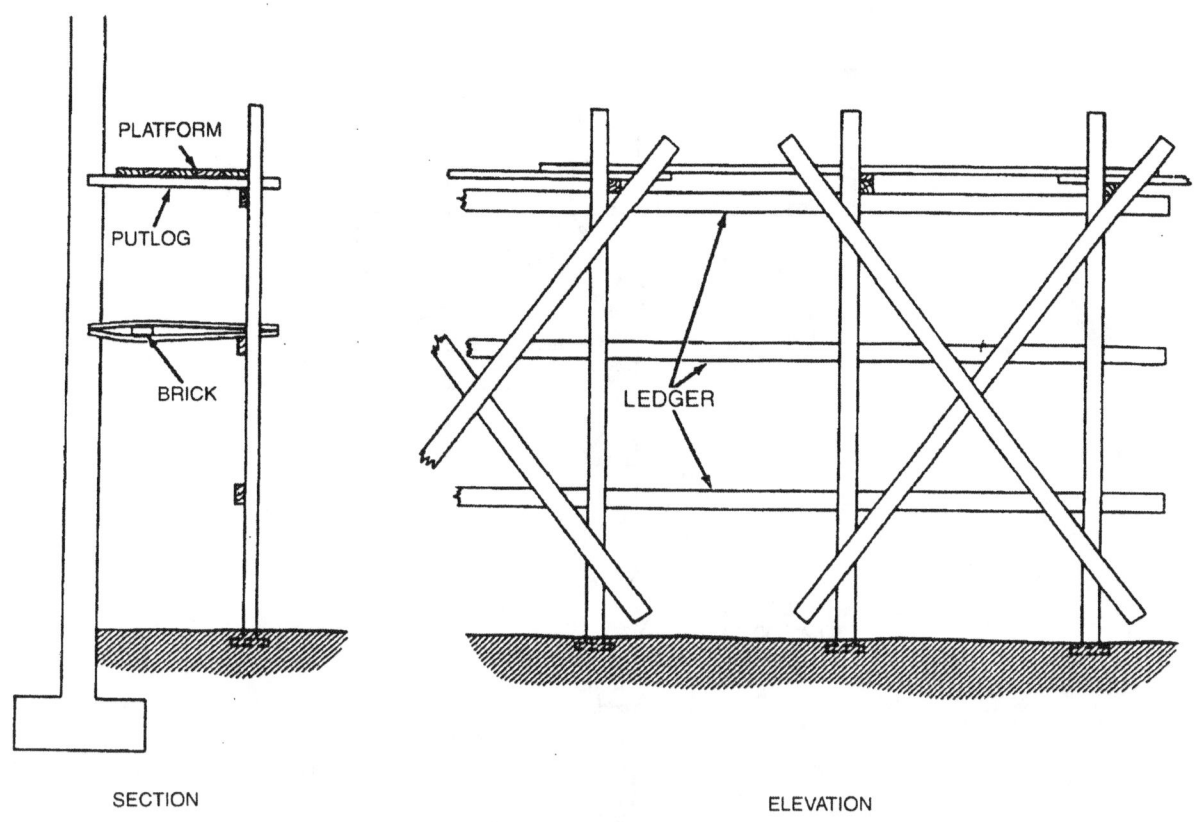

Figure 7-6. Putlog scaffold.

scaffolds that have a platform made up of five 2 by 12's. Landings that extend from the material tower to the floors and scaffold platforms are constructed as needed. These landings should be made using 2- by 10- or 2- by 12-inch lumber. The tower should extend to a height of at least 15 feet above the highest point at which a landing is needed. The footing for the tower should be constructed of two 2 by 12's, 2 feet long, placed under each of the posts.

b. *Elevator.* The elevator for the material tower is shown in 2, figure 7-9. Note how the elevator fits into the guides fastened to the material tower. The rope and pulley arrangement to be used is given in 2, figure 7-9. If a steel tower is available, it should be used. Steel towers are more easily erected and generally safer.

10

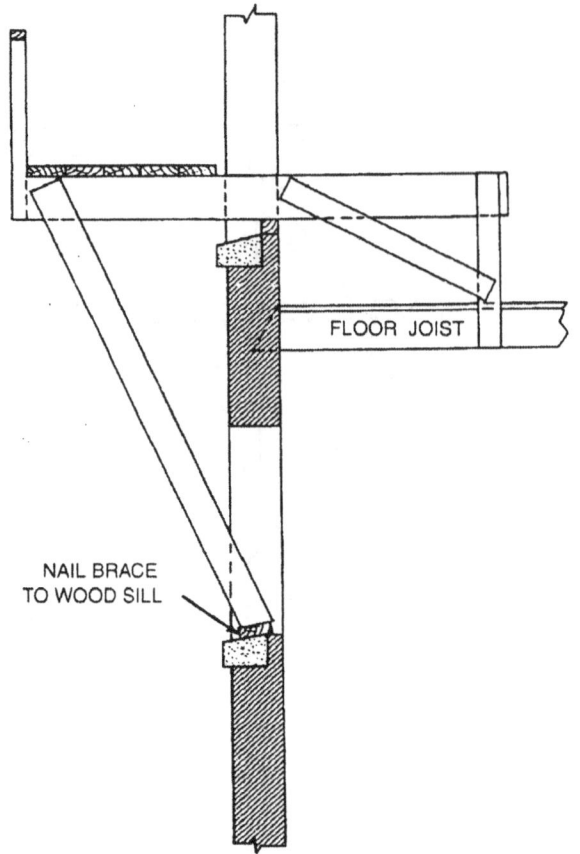

Figure 7-7. Outrigger scaffold.

Figure 7-8. Steel scaffold

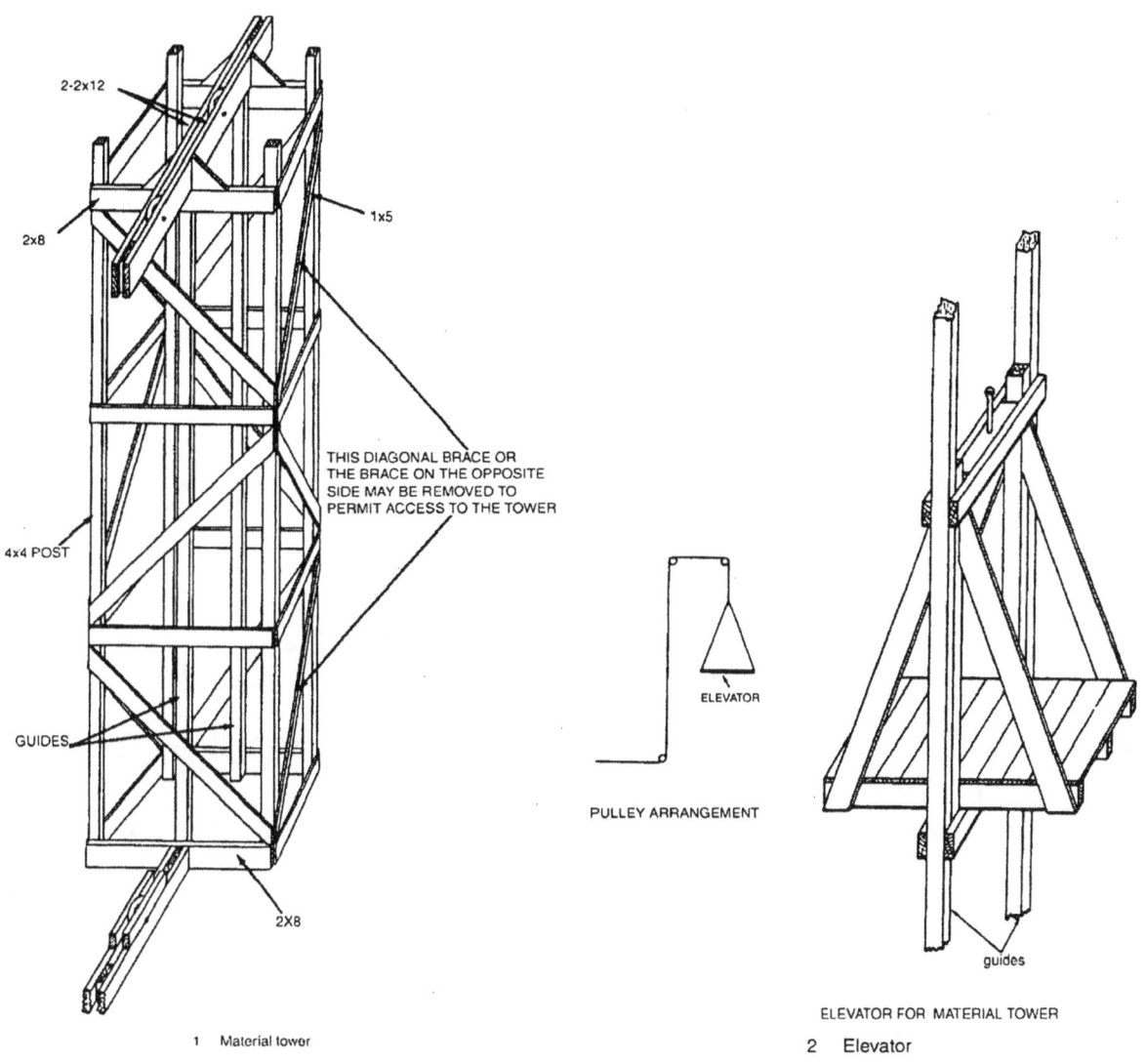

Figure 7-9. Material tower and elevator

BASIC FUNDAMENTALS OF
BRICK AND TILE MASONRY

CONTENTS

	Page
SECTION I - Characteristics of Brick and Brick Masonry	9-1
II - Bricklaying Methods	9-4
III - Brick Construction	9-13

BASIC FUNDAMENTALS OF BRICK AND TILE MASONRY

Section I. CHARACTERISTICS OF BRICK AND BRICK MASONRY

9-1. Terminology

a. Definition. Brick masonry is that type of construction in which units of baked clay or shale of uniform size, small enough to be placed with one hand, are laid in courses with mortar joints to form walls of virtually unlimited length and height. Brick are kiln-baked from various clay and shale mixtures. The chemical and physical characteristics of the ingredients vary considerably; these and the kiln temperatures combine to produce brick in a variety of colors and hardnesses. In some regions, pits are opened and found to yield clay or shale which, when ground and moistened, can be formed and baked into durable brick; in other regions, clays or shales from several pits must be mixed.

b. Brick Sizes. Standard bricks manufactured in the United States are 2¼ by 3¾ by 8 inches. English bricks are 3 by 4½ by 9 inches, Roman bricks are 1½ by 4 by 12 inches, and Norman bricks are 2¾ by 4 by 12 inches. The actual dimensions of brick vary a little because of shrinkage during burning.

c. Cut Brick. Frequently the bricklayer cuts the brick into various shapes. The more common of these are shown in figure 9-1. They are called half or bat, three-quarter closure, quarter closure, king closure, queen closure, and split. They are used to fill in the spaces at corners and such other places where a full brick will not fit.

d. Names of Brick Surfaces. The six surfaces of a brick are called the face, the side, the cull, the end, and the beds, as shown in figure 9-2.

e. Brick Classification. There are three general types of structural clay masonry units: solid masonry units, hollow masonry units and architectural terra cotta. These units may serve a structural function only, as a decorative finish, or a combination of both. Structural clay products include brick, hollow tile of all types and architectural terra cotta. They do not include thin wall tile, sewer pipe, flue linings, drain tile and the like.

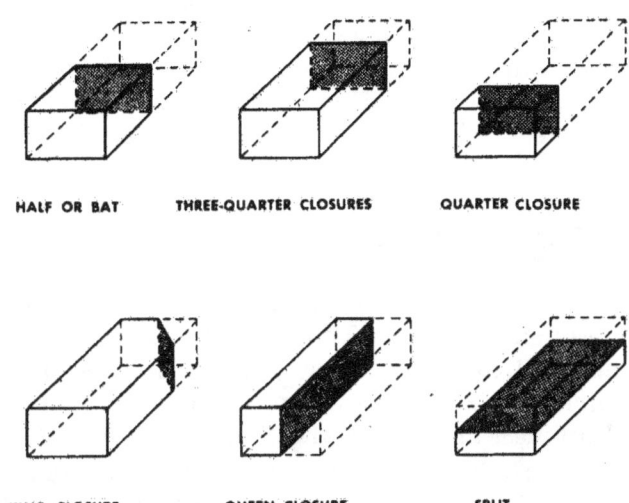

Figure 9-1. Shapes of cut brick.

f. Types of Bricks. There are many types of brick. Some are different in formation and composition while others vary according to their use. Some commonly used types of bricks are:

(1) *Building brick.* The term building brick, formerly called common brick, is applied to brick made of ordinary clays or shales and burned in the usual manner in the kilns. These bricks do not have special scorings or markings and are not produced in any special color or surface texture. Building brick is also known as hard and kiln run brick. It is used generally for the backing courses in solid or cavity brick walls. The harder and more durable kinds are preferred for this purpose.

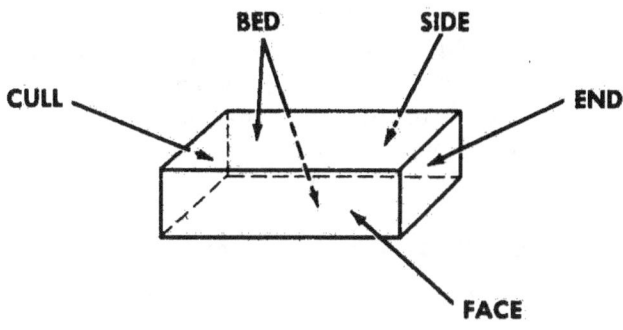

Figure 9-2. Names of brick surfaces.

(2) *Face brick.* Face brick are used in the exposed face of a wall and are higher quality units than backup brick. They have better durability and appearance. The most common colors of face brick are various shades of brown, red, gray, yellow, and white.

(3) *Clinker brick.* When bricks are overburned in the kilns, they are called clinker brick. This type of brick is usually hard and durable and may be irregular in shape. Rough hard corresponds to the clinker classification.

(4) *Pressed brick.* The dry press process is used to make this class of brick which has regular smooth faces, sharp edges, and perfectly square corners. Ordinarily all press brick are used as face brick.

(5) *Glazed brick.* This type of brick has one surface of each brick glazed in white or other color. The ceramic glazing consists of mineral ingredients which fuse together in a glass-like coating during burning. This type of brick is particularly suited for walls or partitions in hospitals, dairies, laboratories or other buildings where cleanliness and ease of cleaning is necessary.

(6) *Fire brick.* This type of brick is made of a special type of fire clay which will withstand the high temperatures of fireplaces, boilers and similar usages without cracking or decomposing. Fire brick is generally larger than regular structural brick and often it is hand molded.

(7) *Cored brick.* Cored brick are brick made with two rows of five holes extending through their beds to reduce weight. There is no significant difference between the strength of walls constructed with cored brick and those constructed with solid brick. Resistance to moisture penetration is about the same for both types of walls. The most easily available brick that will meet requirements should be used whether the brick is cored or solid.

(8) *European brick.* The strength and durability of most European clay brick, particularly English and Dutch, compares favorably with the clay brick made in the United States.

(9) *Sand-lime brick.* Sand-lime bricks are made from a lean mixture of slaked lime and fine silicious sand molded under mechanical pressure and hardened under steam pressure. They are used extensively in Germany.

9–2. Strength of Brick Masonry

a. The principal factors governing the strength of brick masonry are:

(1) Strength of the brick.

(2) Strength and elasticity of the mortar.

(3) Workmanship of the bricklayer.

(4) Uniformity of the brick used.

(5) Method used in laying the brick.

b. The strength of an individual brick varies widely, depending upon the material and manufacturing method. Brick with ultimate compressive strengths as low as 1,600 pounds per square inch have been made, whereas some well-burned bricks have compressive strengths exceeding 15,000 pounds per square inch.

c. The strength of portland-cement-lime mortar is normally higher than the strength of the brick. Because of this, the strength of brick masonry laid in cement-lime mortar is higher than the strength of the individual brick. The use of plain lime mortar reduces the load-carrying capacity of a wall or column to considerably less than half the load-carrying capacity of the same type construction in which portland-cement-lime mortar has been used. The compressive working strength of a brick wall or column that has been laid up with cement-lime mortar is normally from 500 to 600 pounds per square inch.

d. High suction brick, if laid dry, will absorb water from the mortar before the bond has developed and, for this reason, such brick must be thoroughly wetted before laying to obtain good masonry construction. In wetting brick, sprinkling is not sufficient. A hose stream should be played on the pile until water runs from all sides, after which the brick should be allowed to surface dry before they are laid. Water on the surface of the brick will cause floating on the mortar bed. A rough but effective on-the-job test for determining whether the brick should be wet before laying is to sprinkle a few drops of water on the flat side of the brick. If these drops of water are absorbed completely in less than 1 minute, the brick should be wet when laid.

9–3. Resistance to Weathering

a. The resistance of masonry walls to weathering depends almost entirely upon their resistance to water penetration because freezing and thawing action is virtually the only type of weathering that affects brick masonry. With the best workmanship, it is possible to build brick walls that will resist the penetration of rain water during a storm lasting as long as 24 hours accompanied by a 50- to 60-mile-per-hour wind. In most construction, it is unreasonable to expect the type of workmanship required to build a wall that will allow no water pentration. It is advisable to provide some means of taking care of moisture after it has penetrated the brick masonry. Properly designed flashing and cavity walls are two ways of handling moisture that has entered the wall.

b. Important factors in preventing the entrance of water are tooled mortar joints and caulking around windows and door frames.

c. The joints between the brick must be solidly filled, especially in the face tier. Slushing or grouting the joints after the brick has been laid does not completely fill the joint. The mortar joint should be tooled to a concave surface before the mortar has had a chance to set up. In tooling, sufficient force should be used to press the mortar tight against the brick on both sides of the mortar joint.

d. Mortar joints that are tightly bonded to the brick have been shown to have greater resistance to moisture penetration than joints not tightly bonded to the brick.

9-4. Fire Resistance

Fire-resistance tests conducted upon brick walls laid up with portland-cement-lime mortar have made it possible to give fire-resistance periods for various thicknesses of brick walls. A summary is given in table 9-1. The tests were made using the American Society for Testing Materials standard method for conducting fire tests.

9-5. General characteristics of Brick Masonry

a. Heat-Insulating Properties. Solid brick masonry walls provide very little insulation against heat and cold. A cavity wall or a brick wall backed with hollow clay tile has much better insulating value.

b. Sound-Insulating Properties. Because brick walls are exceptionally massive, they have good sound-insulating properties. In general, the heavier the wall, the better will be its sound-insulating value; however, there is no appreciable increase in sound insulation by a wall more than 12 inches thick as compared to a wall between 10 and 12 inches thick. The expense involved in constructing a thicker wall merely to take advantage of the slight increase is too great to be worthwhile. Dividing the wall into two or more layers, as in the case of a cavity wall, will increase its resistance to the transmission of sound from one side of the wall to the other. Brick walls are poor absorbers of sound originating within the walls and reflect much of it back into the structure. Sounds caused by impact, as when the wall is struck with a hammer, will travel a great distance along the wall.

c. Expansion and Construction. Brick masonry expands and contracts with temperature change. Walls up to a length of 200 feet do not need expansion joints. Longer walls need an expansion joint for every 200 feet of wall. The joint can be made as shown in figure 4-26. A considerable amount of the expansion and contraction is taken up in the wall itself. For this reason, the amount of movement that theoretically takes place does not actually occur.

d. Abrasion Resistance. The resistance of brick to abrasion depends largely upon its compressive strength, related to the degree of burning. Well-burned brick have excellent wearing quantities.

e. Weight of Brick. The weight of brick varies from 100 to 150 pounds per cubic foot depending upon the nature of the materials used in making the brick and the degree of burning. Well-burned brick are heavier than under-burned brick.

Table 9-1. Fire Resistance of Brick Load-Bearing Walls Laid with Portland Cement Mortar

Normal wall thickness (inches)	Type of wall	Material	Ultimate fire-resistance period. Incombustible members framed into wall or not framed in members		
			No plaster (hours)	Plaster on one side* (hours)	Plaster on two sides* (hours)
4	Solid	Clay or shale	1¼	1¾	2½
8	Solid	Clay or shale	5	6	7
12	Solid	Clay or shale	10	10	12
8	Hollow rowlock	Clay or shale	2½	3	4
12	Hollow rowlock	Clay or shale	5	6	7
9 to 10	Cavity	Clay or shale	5	6	7
4	Solid	Sand-lime	1¾	2½	3
8	Solid	Sand-lime	7	8	9
12	Solid	Sand-lime	10	10	12

*Not less than ½ inch of 1:3 sanded gypsum plaster is required to develop these ratings.

Section II. BRICKLAYING METHODS

9-6. Fundamentals

Good bricklaying procedure depends on good workmanship and efficiency. Means of obtaining good workmanship are treated below. Efficiency involves doing the work with the fewest possible motions. The bricklayer studies his own operations to determine those motions that are unnecessary. Each motion should have a purpose and should accomplish a definite result. After learning the fundamentals, every bricklayer develops his own methods for achieving maximum efficiency. The work must be arranged in such a way that the bricklayer is continually supplied with brick and mortar. The scaffolding required must be planned before the work begins. It must be built in such a way as to cause the least interference with other workmen. Masons' tools and equipment which are generally the same or similar to those used in bricklaying are discussed in paragraphs 7-1 and 7-2.

9-7. Types of Bonds

The word bond, when used in reference to masonry, may have three different meanings:

a. Structural Bond. Structural bond is the method by which individual masonry units are interlocked or tied together to cause the entire assembly to act as a single structural unit. Structural bonding of brick and tile walls may be accomplished in three ways. First, by overlapping (interlocking) the masonry units, second by the use of metal ties imbedded in connecting joints, and third by the adhesion of grout to adjacent wythes of masonry.

b. Mortar Bond. Mortar bond is the adhesion of the joint mortar to the masonry units or to the reinforcing steel.

c. Pattern Bond. Pattern bond is the pattern formed by the masonry units and the mortar joints on the face of a wall. The pattern may result from the type of structural bond used or may be purely a decorative one in no way related to the structural bond. There are five basic pattern bonds in common use today (fig. 9-3): running bond, common or American bond, Flemish bond, English bond, and block or stack bond.

  (1) *Running bond.* This is the simplest of the

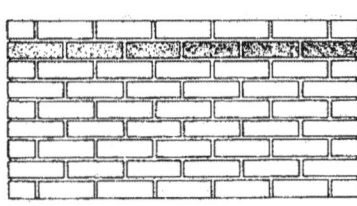
RUNNING

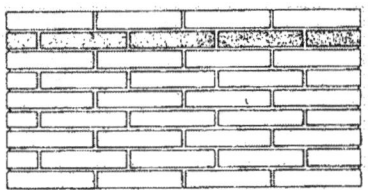
1/3 RUNNING

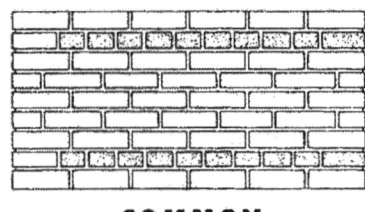
COMMON

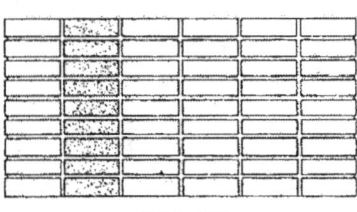
STACK

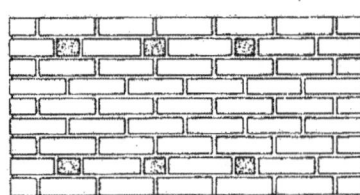
FLEMISH COMMON

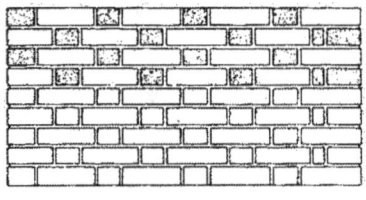
FLEMISH

ENGLISH

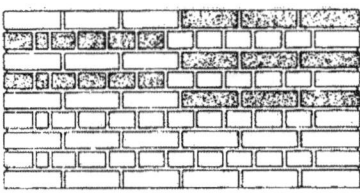
ENGLISH CROSS

Figure 9-3. Some types of brick masonry bond.

basic pattern bonds, the running bond consists of all stretchers. Since there are no headers used in this bond, metal ties are usually used. Running bond is used largely in cavity wall construction and veneered walls of brick, and often in facing tile walls where the bonding may be accomplished by extra width stretcher tile.

(2) *Common or American bond.* Common bond is a variation of running bond with a course of full length headers at regular intervals. These headers provide structural bonding as well as pattern. Header courses usually appear at every fifth, sixth, or seventh course depending on the structural bonding requirements. In laying out any bond pattern it is very important that the corners be started correctly. For common bond, a "three-quarter" brick must start each header course at the corner. Common bond may be varied by using a Flemish header course.

(3) *Flemish bond.* Each course of brick is made up of alternate stretchers and headers, with the headers in alternate courses centered over the stretchers in the intervening courses. Where the headers are not used for the structural bonding, they may be obtained by using half brick, called "blind-headers." There are two methods used in starting the corners. Figure 9–3 shows the so called "Dutch" corner in which a three-quarter brick is used to start each course and the "English" corner in which 2 inch or quarter-brick closures must be used.

(4) *English bond.* English bond is composed of alternate courses of headers and stretchers. The headers are centered on the stretchers and joints between stretchers in all courses line up vertically. Blind headers are used in courses which are not structural bonding courses.

(5) *Block or stack bond.* Stack bond is purely a pattern bond. There is no overlapping of the units, all vertical joints being alined. Usually this pattern is bonded to the backing with rigid steel ties, but when 8 inch thick stretcher units are available, they may be used. In large wall areas and in load-bearing construction, it is advisable to reinforce the wall with steel pencil rods placed in the horizontal mortar joints. The vertical alinement requires dimensionally accurate units, or carefully prematched units, for each vertical joint alinement. Variety in pattern may be achieved by numerous combinations and modifications of the basic patterns shown.

(6) *English cross or Dutch bond.* This bond is a variation of English bond and differs only in that vertical joints between the stretchers in alter-

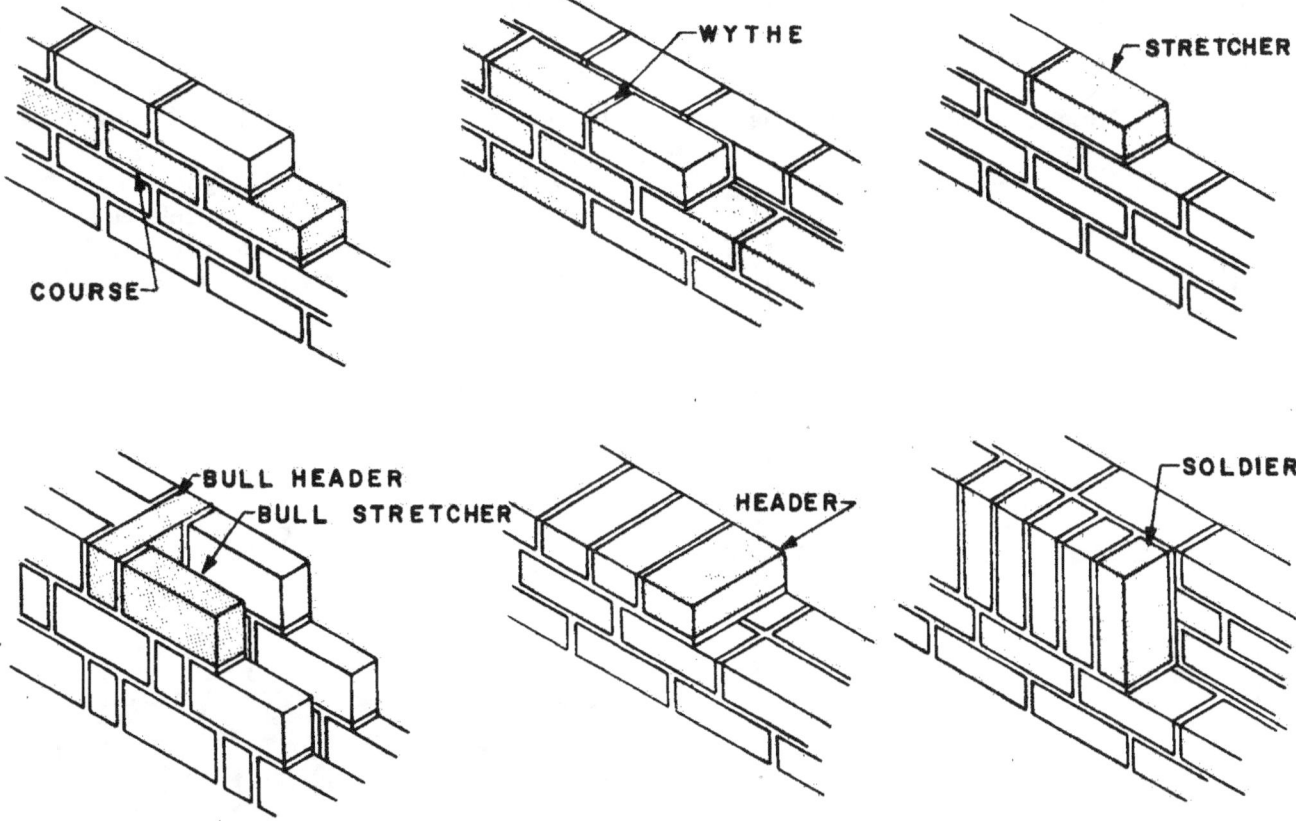

Figure 9–4. Masonry units and mortar joints.

nate courses do not line up vertically. These joints center on the stretchers themselves in the courses above and below.

d. Masonry Terms. Specific terms are used to describe the various positions of masonry units and mortar joints in a wall (fig. 9–4):

(1) *Course.* One of the continuous horizontal layers (or rows) of masonry which, bonded together, form the masonry structure.

(2) *Wythe.* A continuous vertical 4-inch or greater section or thickness of masonry as the thickness of masonry separating flues in a chimney.

(3) *Stretcher.* A masonry unit laid flat with its longest dimension parallel to the face of the wall.

(4) *Header.* A masonry unit laid flat with its longest dimension perpendicular to the face of the wall. It is generally used to tie two wythes of masonry together.

(5) *Rowlock.* A brick laid on its edge (face).

(6) *Bull-Stretcher.* A rowlock brick laid with its longest dimension parallel to the face of the wall.

(7) *Bull-Header.* A rowlock brick laid with its longest dimension perpendicular to the face of the wall.

(8) *Soldier.* A brick laid on its end so that its longest dimension is parallel to the vertical axis of the face of the wall.

e. Metal Ties. Metal ties can be used to tie the brick on the outside face of the wall to the backing courses. These are used when no header courses are installed. They are not as satisfactory as header courses. Typical metal ties are shown in figure 9–5.

f. Flashing. Flashing is installed in masonry construction to divert moisture, which may enter the masonry at vulnerable spots, to the outside. Flashing should be provided under horizontal masonry surfaces such as sills and copings, at intersections of masonry walls with horizontal surfaces such as roof and parapet or roof and chimney, over heads of openings such as doors and windows, and frequently at floor lines, depending upon the type of construction. To be most effective, the flashing should extend through the outer face of the wall and be turned down to form a drop. Weep holes should be provided at intervals of 18 inches to 2 feet to permit the water which accumulates on the flashing to drain to the outside. If, because of appearance, it is necessary to stop the flashing back of the face of the wall, weep holes are even more important than when the flashing extends through the wall. Concealed flashing with tooled mortar joints frequently will retain water in the wall for long periods and, by concentrating moisture at one spot, may do more harm than good.

9–8. Mortar Joints and Pointing

a. Holding the Trowel. The trowel should be held firmly in the position shown in figure 9–6. The thumb should rest on top of the handle and should not encircle it.

b. Picking up Mortar. A right-handed bricklayer picks up mortar with the left edge of the trowel from the outside of the pile (1, fig. 9–7). He picks up the correct amount of spread for one

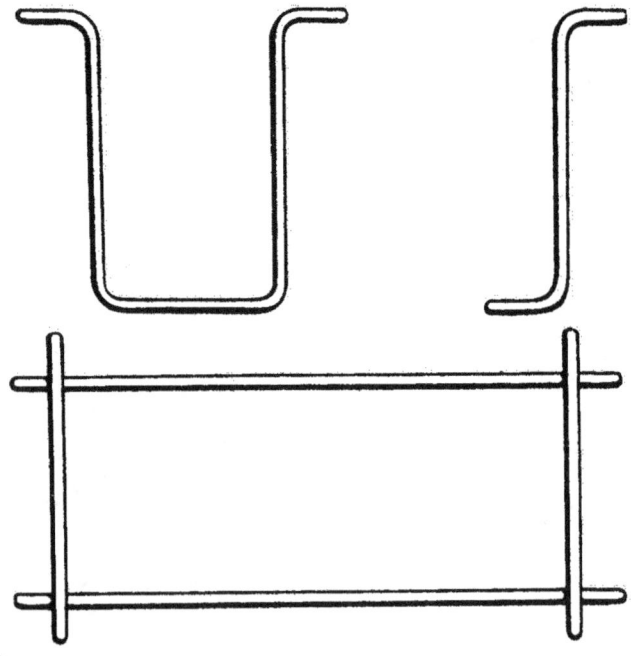

Figure 9–5. Metal ties.

Figure 9–6. Correct way to hold a trowel.

to five bricks, according to the wall space and his skill. A pickup for one brick forms a small windrow along the left edge of the trowel. A pickup for five bricks is a full load for a large trowel (2, fig. 9-7).

c. Spreading Mortar. Holding the trowel with its left edge directly over the centerline of the previous course, the bricklayer tilts the trowel slightly and moves it to the right, dropping a windrow of mortar along the wall unit until the trowel is empty (3, fig. 9-7). In some instances mortar will be left on the trowel when the spreading of mortar on the course below has been completed. When this occurs the remaining mortar is returned to the board. A right-handed bricklayer works from left to right along the wall.

d. Cutting Off Mortar. Mortar projecting beyond the wall line is cut off with the trowel edge (step 1, fig 9-8) and thrown back on the mortar board, but enough is retained to "butter" the left end of the first brick to be laid in the fresh mortar.

e. Bed Joint. With the mortar spread about 1 inch thick for the bed joint as shown in step 1, figure 9-8, a shallow furrow is made (step 2, figure 9-8) and the brick pushed into the mortar (step 3, figure 9-8). If the furrow is too deep, there will be a gap left between the mortar and the brick bedded in the mortar. This gap will reduce the resistance of the wall to water penetration. The mortar for a bed joint should not be spread out too far in advance of the laying. A distance of 4 or 5 bricks is advisable. Mortar that has been spread out too far will dry out before the brick is bedded in it. This results in a poor bond as can be seen by figure 9-9. The mortar must be soft and plastic so that the brick can be easily bedded in it.

f. Head Joint. The next step after the bed joint mortar has been spread is the laying of the brick. The brick to be laid is picked up as shown in figure

1 Proper way to pick up mortar

3 Mortar thrown on brick

2 Trowel full of mortar

4 Mortar spread for a distance of 3 to 5 brick

Figure 9-7. Picking up and spreading mortar.

Step 1

Step 2

Step 3

Figure 9-8. Bed joint and furrow.

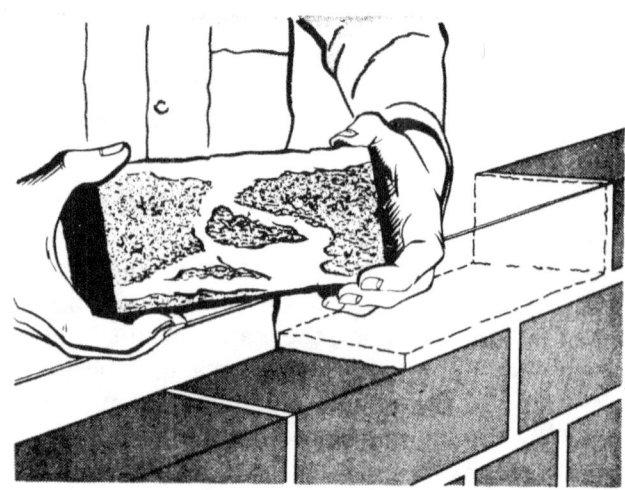

Figure 9-9. A poorly bonded brick.

9-10 with the thumb on one side of the brick and the fingers on the other. As much mortar as will stick is placed on the end of the brick. The brick should then be pushed into place so that excess mortar squeezes out at the head joint and at the sides of the wall as indicated in figure 9-11. The head joint must be completely filled with mortar. This can only be done by placing plenty of mortar on the end of the brick. After the brick is bedded, the excess mortar is cut off and used for the next end joint. Surplus mortar should be thrown to the back of the mortar board for retempering if necessary. The proper position of the brick is determined by the use of a cord which can be seen in step 1, figure 9-14.

Figure 9-10. Proper way to hold a brick.

Figure 9-11. Head joint in a stretcher course.

g. *Method of Inserting Brick in Wall.* The method of inserting a brick in a space left in a wall is shown in figure 9-12. A thick bed of mortar is spread (step 1, fig. 9-12) and the brick shoved into this deep bed of mortar (step 2, fig. 9-12) until squeezes out at the top of the joint at the face tier, and at the header joint (step 3, fig. 9-12) so that the joints are full of mortar at every point.

h. *Cross Joints in Header Courses.* The position of a cross joint is illustrated in figure 9-13. These joints must be completely filled with mortar. The mortar for the bed joint should be spread several brick widths in advance. The mortar is spread over the entire side of the header brick before it is placed in the wall (step 1, fig. 9-13). The brick is then shoved into place so that the mortar is forced out at the top of the joint and the excess mortar cut off, as shown in step 2, figure 9-13.

i. *Closure Joints in Header Courses.* Figure 9-14 shows the method of laying a closure brick in a header course. Before laying the closure brick, plenty of mortar should be placed on the sides of the brick already in place (step 1, fig. 9-14). Mortar should also be spread on both sides of the closure brick to a thickness of about 1 inch (step 2, fig. 9-14). The closure brick should then be laid in position without disturbing the brick already in place (step 3, fig. 9-14).

j. *Closure Joints in Stretcher Courses.* Before laying a closure brick for a stretcher course, the ends of the brick on each side of the opening to be filled with the closure brick should be well covered with mortar (step 1, fig. 9-15). Plenty of mortar should then be thrown on both ends of the closure brick (step 2, fig. 9-15) and the brick laid without disturbing those already in place (step 3, fig. 9-15). If any of the adjacent brick are disturbed they must be removed and relaid. Otherwise,

Step 1

Step 2

Step 3

Figure 9-12. Laying inside brick.

9-10

Step 1

Step 2

Figure 9-13. Making cross joints in header courses.

cracks will form between the brick and mortar, allowing moisture into the wall.

k. Thickness of Mortar Joints. There is no hard and fast rule regarding the thickness of the mortar joint. Brick that are irregular in shape may require mortar joints up to ½-inch thick. All brick irregularities are taken up in the mortar joint. Mortar joints ¼ inch thick are the strongest and should be used when the bricks are regular enough to permit it.

l. Slushed Joints. Slushed joints are those made by depositing the mortar on the head joints in order that the mortar will run down between the brick to form a solid joint. *This should not be done.* Even when the space between the brick is completely filled, there is no way to compact the mortar against the faces of the brick and *a poor bond will result.*

m. Pointing. Filling exposed joints with mortar immediately after the wall has been laid is called pointing. Pointing is frequently necessary to fill

Step 1

Step 2

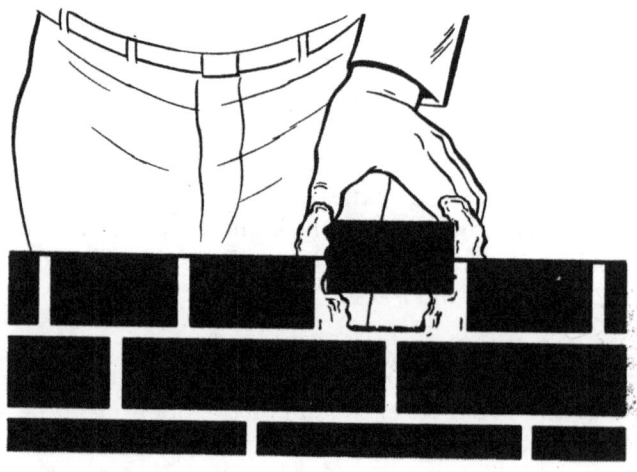

Step 3

Figure 9-14. Making closure joints in header courses.

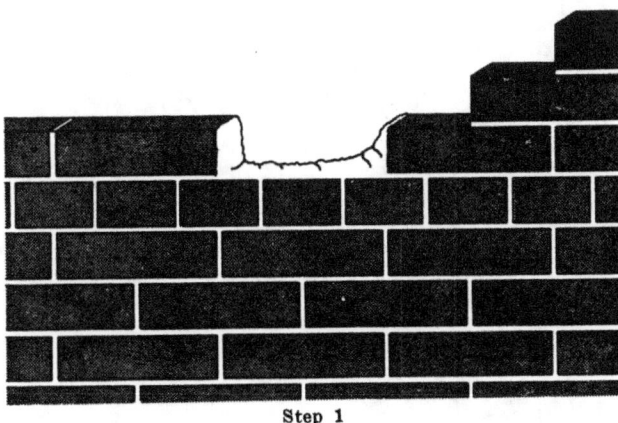

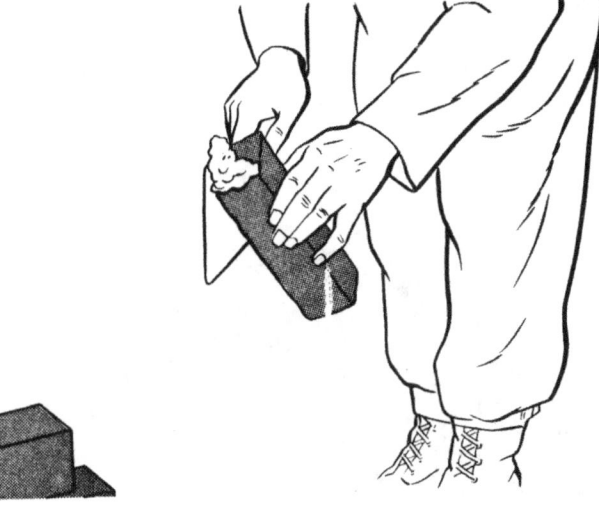

Figure 9–15. Making closure joints in stretcher courses.

holes and correct defective mortar joints. The pointing trowel is used for this purpose.

9–9. Cutting Brick

a. Cutting with Bolster or Brick Set. If a brick is to be cut to exact line the bolster or brick set should be used. When using these tools, the straight side of the cutting edge should face the part of the brick to be saved and also face the bricklayer. One blow of the hammer on the brick set should be enough to break the brick. Extremely hard brick will need to be cut roughly with the head of the hammer in such a way that there is enough brick left to be cut accurately with the brick set. See figure 9–16.

b. Cutting with the Hammer. For normal cutting work, such as is required for making the closures and bats required around openings in walls and for the completion of corners, the brick hammer should be used. The first step is to cut a line all the way around the brick with light blows of the hammer head (fig. 9–17). When the line is complete, a sharp blow to one side of the cutting line will split the brick at the cutting line. Rough places are trimmed using the blade of the hammer, as shown in figure 9–17. The brick can be held in the hand while being cut.

9–10. Joint Finishes

a. Exterior Surfaces. Exterior surfaces of mortar joints are finished to make the brickwork more waterproof and to improve the appearance. There are several types of joint finishes, as shown in figure 9–18. The more important of these are discussed below. When joints are cut flush with the brick and not finished, cracks are immediately apparent between the brick and the mortar. Although these cracks are not deep, they are undesirable and can be eliminated by finishing or tooling the joint. In every case, the mortar joint should be finished before the mortar has hardened to any appreciable extent. The jointing tool is shown in figure 7–1.

b. Concave Joint. The best joint from the standpoint of weather-tightness is the concave joint. This joint is made with a special tool after the excess mortar has been removed with the trowel. The tool should be slightly larger than the joint. Force is used to press the mortar tight against the brick on both sides of the mortar joint.

c. Flush Joint. The flush joint (fig. 9–18) is made by keeping the trowel almost parallel to the face of the wall while drawing the point of the trowel along the joint.

d. Weather Joint. A weather joint sheds water more easily from the surface of the wall and is formed by pushing downward on the mortar with the top edge of the trowel.

9-12

Figure 9-16. Cutting brick with a bolster.

1 Striking brick to one side of cutting line

2 Trimming rough spots

Figure 9-17. Cutting brick with a hammer.

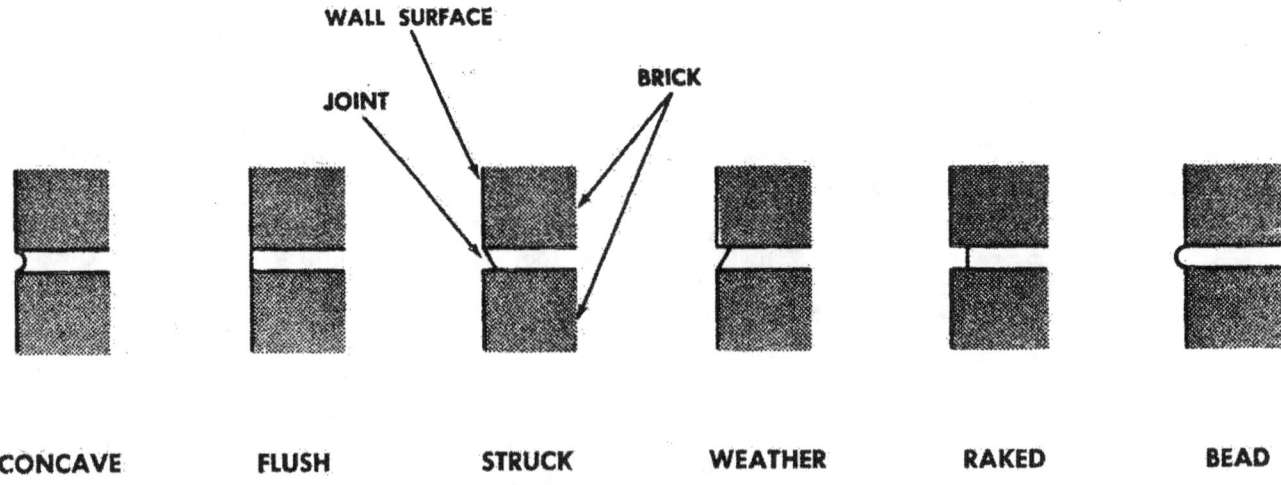

Figure 9-18. Joint finishes.

Section III. BRICK CONSTRUCTION

9–11. Bricktender's Duties

a. The bricktender mixes mortar, carries brick and mortar to the bricklayer, and keeps him supplied with these materials at all times. He fills the mortar board and places it in a position convenient for the bricklayer. He assists in the layout and, at times, such as during rapid backup bricklaying, he may lay out brick in a line on an adjacent course so that the bricklayer needs to move each brick only a few inches in laying backup work.

b. Wetting brick is also the duty of the bricktender. This is done when bricks are laid in warm weather. There are four reasons for wetting brick just before they are laid:

(1) There will be a better bond between the brick and the mortar.

(2) The water will wash dust and dirt from the surface of the brick. Mortar adheres better to a clean brick.

(3) If the surface of the brick is wet, the mortar spreads more evenly under it.

(4) A dry brick may absorb water from the mortar rapidly. This is particularly bad when mortar containing portland cement is used. In order for cement to harden properly, sufficient moisture must be present to complete the hydration of the cement. If the brick robs the mortar of too much water, there will not be enough left to hydrate the cement properly.

9–12. Bricklayer's Duties

The bricklayer does the actual laying of the brick. It is his responsibility to lay out the job so that the finished masonry will be properly done. In construction involving walls, he must see that the walls are plumb and the courses level.

FOURTH COURSE

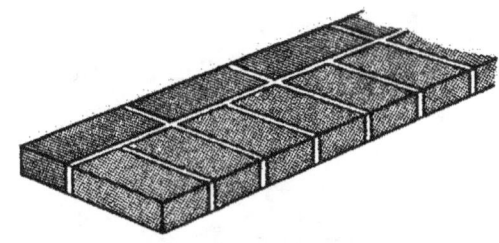
THIRD COURSE

FOOTING AND FOUNDATION COMPLETED

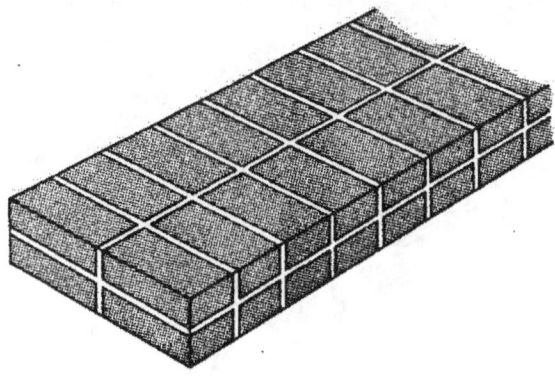
FIRST AND SECOND COURSE

Figure 9–19. Wall footing.

9-13. Footings

a. Wall Footing.

(1) A footing is required under a wall when the bearing capacity of the supporting soil is not sufficient to withstand the wall load without a further means of redistribution. The footing must be wider than the thickness of the wall, as illustrated in figure 9-19. The required footing width and thickness for walls of considerable height or for walls that are to carry a heavy load should be determined by a qualified engineer. Every footing should be below the frost line in order to prevent heaving and settlement of the foundation. For the usual one-story building with an 8-inch-thick wall, a footing 16 inches wide and approximately 8 inches thick as given in figure 9-19 is usually enough. Although brickwork footings are satisfactory, footings are normally concrete, leveled on top to receive the brick or stone foundation wall.

(2) As soon as the subgrade is prepared, the bricklayer should place a bed of mortar about 1 inch thick on the subgrade to take up all irregularities. The first course of the foundation is laid on this bed of mortar. The other courses are then laid on this first course (fig. 9-19).

b. Column Footing. A column footing for a 12- by 16-inch brick column is shown in figure 9-20. The construction method for this footing is the same as for the wall footing.

9-14. Eight-Inch Common Bond Brick Wall

a. Laying Out the Wall. For a wall of given

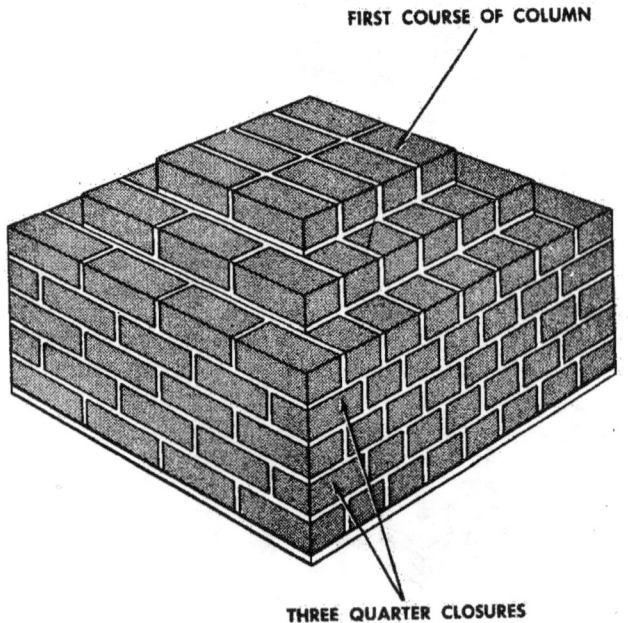

Figure 9-20. Column footing.

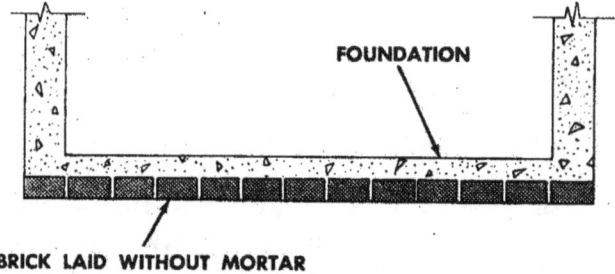

Figure 9-21. Determination of vertical brick joints and number of brick in one course.

length, the bricklayer makes a slight adjustment in the width of head joints so that some number of brick, or some number including one half-brick, will just make up the length. The bricklayer first lays the brick on the foundation without mortar (fig. 9-21). The distance between the bricks is equal to the thickness of the head mortar joints. Tables 9-2, 9-3, and 9-4 give the number of courses and horizontal joints required for a given wall height.

b. Laying Corner Leads. The corners are erected first. This is called "laying of leads." The bricklayer will use these leads as a guide in laying the remainder of the wall. Step 3, figure 9-23 shows a corner lead laid up and racked so that the center portion of the wall can be bonded into the corner lead. Only the face tier is laid in these corners and the corner lead is built up above the rest of the wall a distance of six or seven courses or to the height of the next header course above. Normally the first course is a header course.

(1) The first step in laying a corner lead is shown in first step, figure 9-22. Two three-quarter closures are cut and a 1-inch thick mortar bed is laid on the foundation. The three-quarter closure marked by *a* in second step, figure 9-22 is pressed down into the mortar bed until the bed joint becomes ½ inch thick. Next, mortar is placed on the end of three-quarter closure *b* and a head joint is formed as described in paragraph 9-8. The head joint between the two three-quarter closures should be ½ inch thick also. Excess mortar that has been squeezed out of the joints is cut off. The level of the two three-quarter closures should now be checked by means of the plumb rule placed in the positions indicated by the heavy dashed lines in second step, figure 9-22. The edges of both these closure bricks must be even with the outside face of the foundation.

(2) Next mortar is spread on the side of brick *c* and it is laid as shown in third step, figure 9-22. Its level is checked using the plumb rule in the

Table 9-2. Height of Courses: 2¼-Inch Brick, ⅜-Inch Joint

Courses	Height	Courses	Height	Courses	Height	Courses	Height	Courses	Height
1	0' 2⅝"	21	4' 7⅛"	41	8' 11⅝"	61	13' 4⅛"	81	17' 8⅝"
2	0' 5¼"	22	4' 9¾"	42	9' 2¼"	62	13' 6¾"	82	17' 11¼"
3	0' 7⅞"	23	5' 0⅜"	43	9' 4⅞"	63	13' 9⅜"	83	18' 1⅞"
4	0' 10½"	24	5' 3"	44	9' 7½"	64	14' 0"	84	18' 4½"
5	1' 1⅛"	25	5' 5⅝"	45	9' 10⅛"	65	14' 2⅝"	85	18' 7⅛"
6	1' 3¾"	26	5' 8¼"	46	10' 0¾"	66	14' 5¼"	86	18' 9¾"
7	1' 6⅜"	27	5' 10⅞"	47	10' 3⅜"	67	14' 7⅞"	87	19' 0⅜"
8	1' 9"	28	6' 1½"	48	10' 6"	68	14' 10½"	88	19' 3"
9	1' 11⅝"	29	6' 4⅛"	49	10' 8⅝"	69	15' 1⅛"	89	19' 5⅝"
10	2' 2¼"	30	6' 6¾"	50	10' 11¼"	70	15' 3¾"	90	19' 8¼"
11	2' 4⅞"	31	6' 9⅜"	51	11' 1⅞"	71	15' 6⅜"	91	19' 10⅞"
12	2' 7½"	32	7' 0"	52	11' 4½"	72	15' 9"	92	20' 1½"
13	2' 10⅛"	33	7' 2⅝"	53	11' 7⅛"	73	15' 11⅝"	93	20' 4⅛"
14	3' 0¾"	34	7' 5¼"	54	11' 9¾"	74	16' 2¼"	94	20' 6¾"
15	3' 3⅜"	35	7' 7⅞"	55	12' 0⅜"	75	16' 4⅞"	95	20' 9⅜"
16	3' 6"	36	7' 10½"	56	12' 3"	76	16' 7½"	96	21' 0"
17	3' 8⅝"	37	8' 1⅛"	57	12' 5⅝"	77	16' 10⅛"	97	21' 2⅝"
18	3' 11¼"	38	8' 3¾"	58	12' 8¼"	78	17' 0¾"	98	21' 5¼"
19	4' 1⅞"	39	8' 6⅜"	59	12' 10⅞"	79	17' 3⅜"	99	21' 7⅞"
20	4' 4½"	40	8' 9"	60	13' 1½"	80	17' 6"	100	21' 10½"

position given in third step, figure 9-22. Its end must also be even with the outside face of the foundation. Brick d is laid and its level and position checked. When brick d is in the proper position, the quarter closures e and f should be cut and placed according to the recommended procedure described for laying closure brick. All excess mortar should be removed and the tops of these quarter closures checked to see that they are at the same level as the tops of surrounding brick.

(3) Brick g (fourth step, fig. 9-22) is now shoved into position after mortar has been spread on its face. Excess mortar should be removed. Bricks h, i, j, and k are laid in the same manner. The level of the brick is checked by placing the plumb rule in the several positions indicated in fourth step, figure 9-22. All brick ends must be flush with the surface of the foundation. Bricks l, m, n, o, and p are then laid in the same manner. The number of leader bricks that must be laid in the first course of the corner lead can be determined from fifth step, figure 9-22. It will be noted that six header bricks are required on each side of the three-quarter closures a and b.

Table 9-3. Height of Courses: 2¼-Inch Brick, ½-Inch Joint

Courses	Height	Courses	Height	Courses	Height	Courses	Height	Courses	Height
1	0' 2¾"	21	4' 9¾"	41	9' 4¾"	61	13' 11¾"	81	18' 6¾"
2	0' 5½"	22	5' 0½"	42	9' 7½"	62	14' 2½"	82	18' 9½"
3	0' 8¼"	23	5' 3¼"	43	9' 10¼"	63	14' 5¼"	83	19' 0¼"
4	0' 11"	24	5' 6"	44	10' 1"	64	14' 8"	84	19' 3"
5	1' 1¾"	25	5' 8¾"	45	10' 3¾"	65	14' 10¾"	85	19' 5¾"
6	1' 4½"	26	5' 11½"	46	10' 6½"	66	15' 1½"	86	19' 8½"
7	1' 7¼"	27	6' 2¼"	47	10' 9¼"	67	15' 4¼"	87	19' 11¼"
8	1' 10"	28	6' 5"	48	11' 0"	68	15' 7"	88	20' 2"
9	2' 0¾"	29	6' 7¾"	49	11' 2¾"	69	15' 9¾"	89	20' 4¾"
10	2' 3½"	30	6' 10½"	50	11' 5½"	70	16' 0½"	90	20' 7½"
11	2' 6¼"	31	7' 1¼"	51	11' 8¼"	71	16' 3¼"	91	20' 10¼"
12	2' 9"	32	7' 4"	52	11' 11"	72	16' 6"	92	21' 1"
13	2' 11¾"	33	7' 6¾"	53	12' 1¾"	73	16' 8¾"	93	21' 3¾"
14	3' 2½"	34	7' 9½"	54	12' 4½"	74	16' 11½"	94	21' 6½"
15	3' 5¼"	35	8' 0¼"	55	12' 7¼"	75	17' 2¼"	95	21' 9¼"
16	3' 8"	36	8' 3"	56	12' 10"	76	17' 5"	96	22' 0"
17	3' 10¾"	37	8' 5¾"	57	13' 0¾"	77	17' 7¾"	97	22' 2¾"
18	4' 1½"	38	8' 8½"	58	13' 3½"	78	17' 10½"	98	22' 5½"
19	4' 4¼"	39	8' 11¼"	59	13' 6¼"	79	18' 1¼"	99	22' 8¼"
20	4' 7"	40	9' 2"	60	13' 9"	80	18' 4"	100	22' 11"

Table 9–4. Height of Courses: 2¼-Inch Brick, ⅝-Inch Joint

Courses	Height	Courses	Height	Courses	Height	Courses	Height	Courses	Height
1	0′ 2⅞″	21	5′ 0⅜″	41	9′ 9⅞″	61	14′ 7⅜″	81	19′ 4⅞″
2	0′ 5¾″	22	5′ 3¼″	42	10′ 0¾″	62	14′ 10¼″	82	19′ 7¾″
3	0′ 8⅝″	23	5′ 6⅛″	43	10′ 3⅝″	63	15′ 1⅛″	83	19′ 10⅝″
4	0′ 11½″	24	5′ 9″	44	10′ 6½″	64	15′ 4″	84	20′ 1½″
5	1′ 2⅜″	25	5′ 11⅞″	45	10′ 9⅜″	65	15′ 6⅞″	85	20′ 4⅜″
6	1′ 5¼″	26	6′ 2¾″	46	11′ 0¼″	66	15′ 9¾″	86	20′ 7¼″
7	1′ 8⅛″	27	6′ 5⅝″	47	11′ 3⅛″	67	16′ 0⅝″	87	20′ 10⅛″
8	1′ 11″	28	6′ 8½″	48	11′ 6″	68	16′ 3½″	88	21′ 1″
9	2′ 1⅞″	29	6′ 11⅜″	49	11′ 8⅞″	69	16′ 6⅜″	89	21′ 3⅞″
10	2′ 4¾″	30	7′ 2¼″	50	11′ 11¾″	70	16′ 9¼″	90	21′ 6¾″
11	2′ 7⅝″	31	7′ 5⅛″	51	12′ 2⅝″	71	17′ 0⅛″	91	21′ 9⅝″
12	2′ 10½″	32	7′ 8″	52	12′ 5½″	72	17′ 3″	92	22′ 0½″
13	3′ 1⅜″	33	7′ 10⅞″	53	12′ 8⅜″	73	17′ 5⅞″	93	22′ 3⅜″
14	3′ 4¼″	34	8′ 1¾″	54	12′ 11¼″	74	17′ 8¾″	94	22′ 6¼″
15	3′ 7⅛″	35	8′ 4⅝″	55	13′ 2⅛″	75	17′ 11⅝″	95	22′ 9⅛″
16	3′ 10″	36	8′ 7½″	56	13′ 5″	76	18′ 2½″	96	23′ 0″
17	4′ 0⅞″	37	8′ 10⅜″	57	13′ 7⅞″	77	18′ 5⅜	97	23′ 2⅞″
18	4′ 3¾″	38	9′ 1¼″	58	13′ 10¾″	78	18′ 8¼″	98	23′ 5¾″
19	4′ 6⅝″	39	9′ 4⅛″	59	14′ 1⅝″	79	18′ 11⅛″	99	23′ 8⅝″
20	4′ 9½″	40	9′ 7″	60	14′ 4½″	80	19′ 2″	100	23′ 11½″

(4) The second course, a stretcher course, is now laid. Procedure is shown in step 1, figure 9–23. A 1-inch thick layer of mortar should be spread over the first course and a shallow furrow made in the mortar bed. Brick *a* (step 2, figure 9–23) is then laid in the mortar bed and shoved down until the mortar joint is ½-inch thick. Brick *b* may now be shoved into place after mortar has been spread on its end. Excess mortar is removed and the joint checked for thickness. Bricks *c, d, e, f,* and *g* are laid in the same manner and checked to make them level and plumb. The level is checked by placing the plumb rule in the position indicated in step 2, figure 9–23. The bricks are plumbed by using the plumb rule in a vertical position as shown in figure 9–24. This should be done in several places. As may be determined from 3, figure 9–23, seven bricks are required for the second course. The remaining bricks in the corner lead are laid in the manner described for the bricks in the second course.

(5) Since the portion of the wall between the leads is laid using the leads as a guide, the level of the courses in the lead must be checked continually, and after the first few courses the lead is plumbed. If the brickwork is not plumb, bricks must be moved in or out until the lead is accurately plumb. It is not good practice to move brick much once they are laid in mortar; therefore, care is taken to place the brick accurately at the start. Before the mortar has set, the joints are tooled or finished.

(6) A corner lead at the opposite end of the wall is built in the same manner. It is essential that the level of the tops of corresponding courses be the same in each lead; that is, the top of the second course in one corner lead must be at the same height above the foundation as the second course in the other corner lead. A long 2-by 2-inch pole can be used to mark off the heights of the different courses above the foundation. This pole can be used to check the course height in the corner leads. The laying of leads is closely supervised and only skilled men are employed in this work.

c. Laying the Face Tier Between the Corner Leads.

(1) With the corner leads at each end of the wall completed, the face tier of brick for the wall between the leads is laid. It is necessary to use a line, as shown in figure 9–25. Nails are driven into the top of the mortar joint as shown in figure 9–25. The line is hung over the nails and pulled taut by means of weights attached to each end. The line is positioned $\frac{1}{16}$ inch outside the wall face level with the top of the brick.

(2) With the line in place, the first or header course is laid in place between the two corner leads, as described in paragraph 9–8. The brick is shoved into position so that its top edge is $\frac{1}{16}$ inch behind the line. Do not crowd the line. If the corner leads are accurately built, the entire wall will be level and plumb. It is not necessary to use

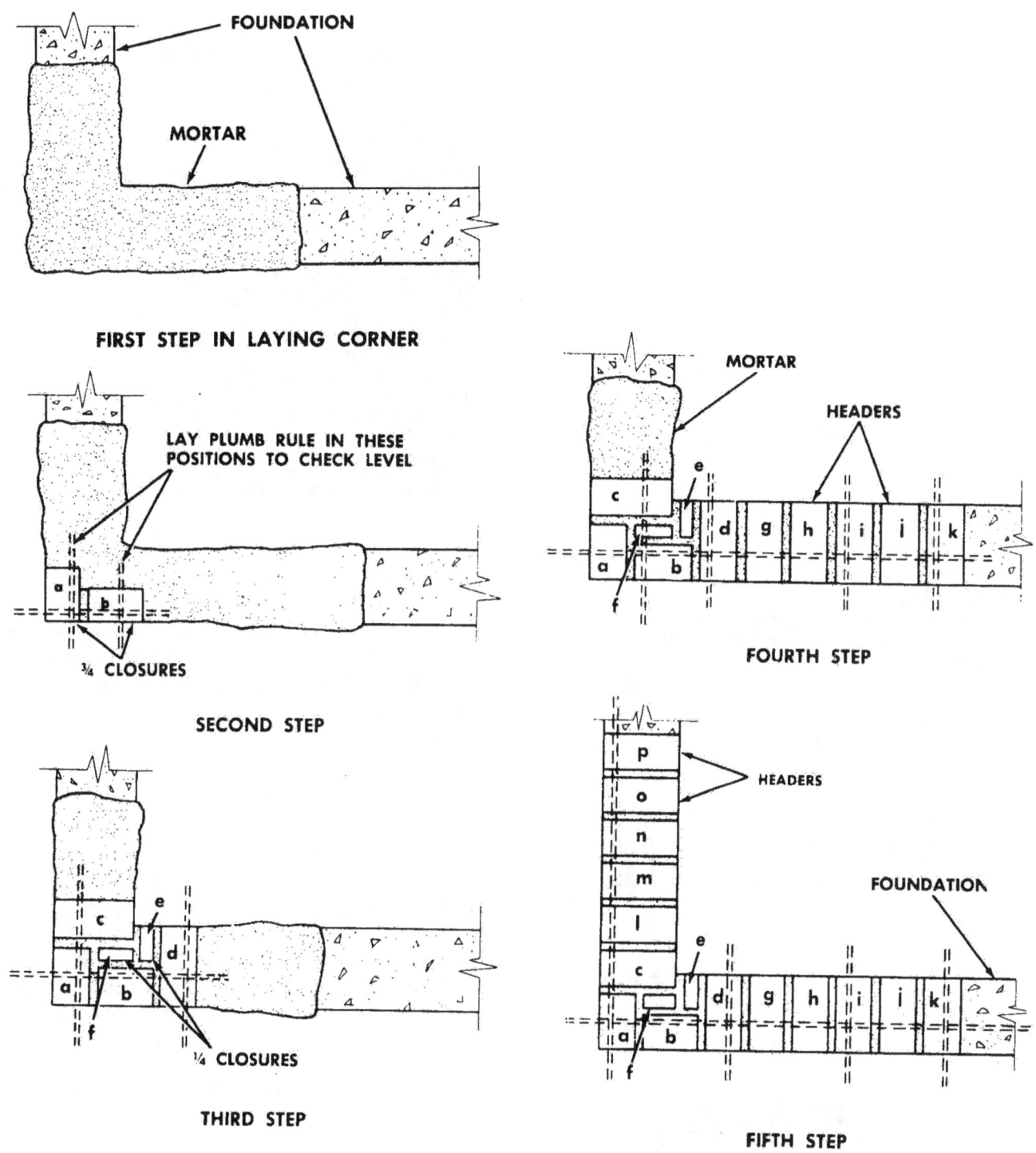

Figure 9-22. First course of corner lead for 8-inch common bond brick wall.

the level on the section of the wall between the leads; however, it is advisable to check it with the level at several points. For the next course, the line is moved to the top of the next mortar joint. The brick in the stretcher course should be laid as described in paragraph 9–8. Finish the face joints before the mortar hardens.

d. Laying the Back Tier.

(1) When the face tier of brick for the wall between the leads has been laid up to but not including the second header course, normally six courses, the backup tier is laid. Procedure for laying backup brick has already been described. The backup brick for the corner leads are laid first and the remaining brick afterwards (fig. 9–26). The line need not be used for the backup brick in an 8-inch wall. When the backup brick have been laid up to the height of the second header course, the second header course is laid.

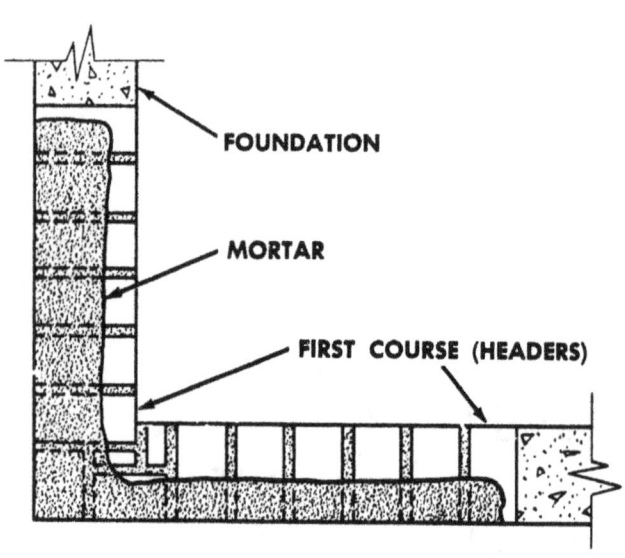

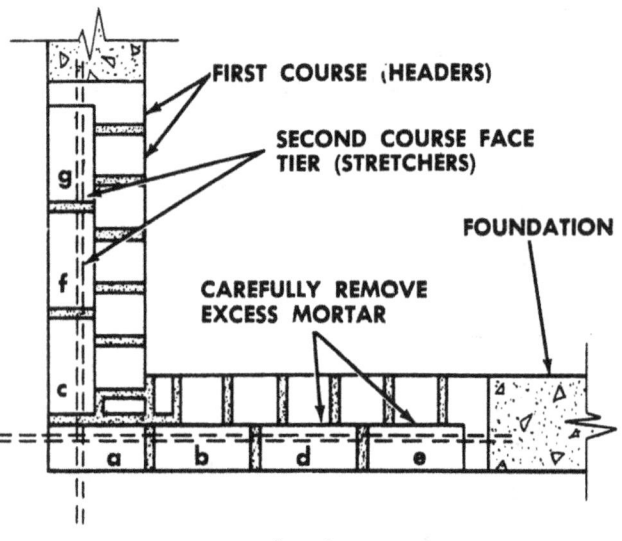

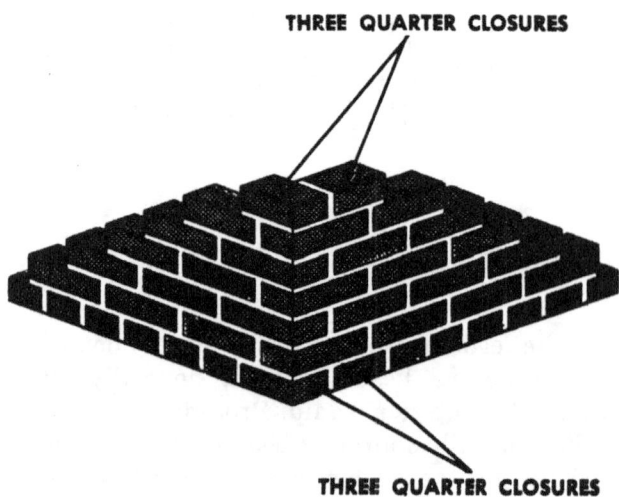

Figure 9-23. Second course of corner lead for 8-inch common bond brick wall.

Figure 9-24. Plumbing a corner.

(2) The wall for the entire building is built up to a height including the second header course at which time corner leads are continued six more courses. The wall between the leads is constructed as before and the entire procedure repeated until the wall has been completed to the required height.

9-15. Twelve-Inch Common Bond Brick Wall

The 12-inch-thick common bond brick wall is laid out as shown in 3, figure 9-27. Note that the construction is similar to that for the 8-inch wall with the exception that a third tier of brick is used. The header course is laid (1, fig. 9-27) first and the corner leads built. Two tiers of backing brick are required instead of one. The second course is shown in 2, figure 9-27 and the third course in 3, figure 9-27. Two header courses are required and they overlap as shown in 1, figure 9-27. A line should be used for the inside tier of backing brick for a 12-inch wall.

9-16. Protection of Brickwork and Use of a Trig

a. Protection the Brick. The tops of all brick walls should be protected each night from rain damage by placing boards or tarpaulins on top of the wall and setting loose bricks on them.

b. Use of a Trig. When a line is stretched on a long wall, a trig is used to prevent sagging and to keep it from being blown in or out from the face of the wall by the wind. The trig consists of a

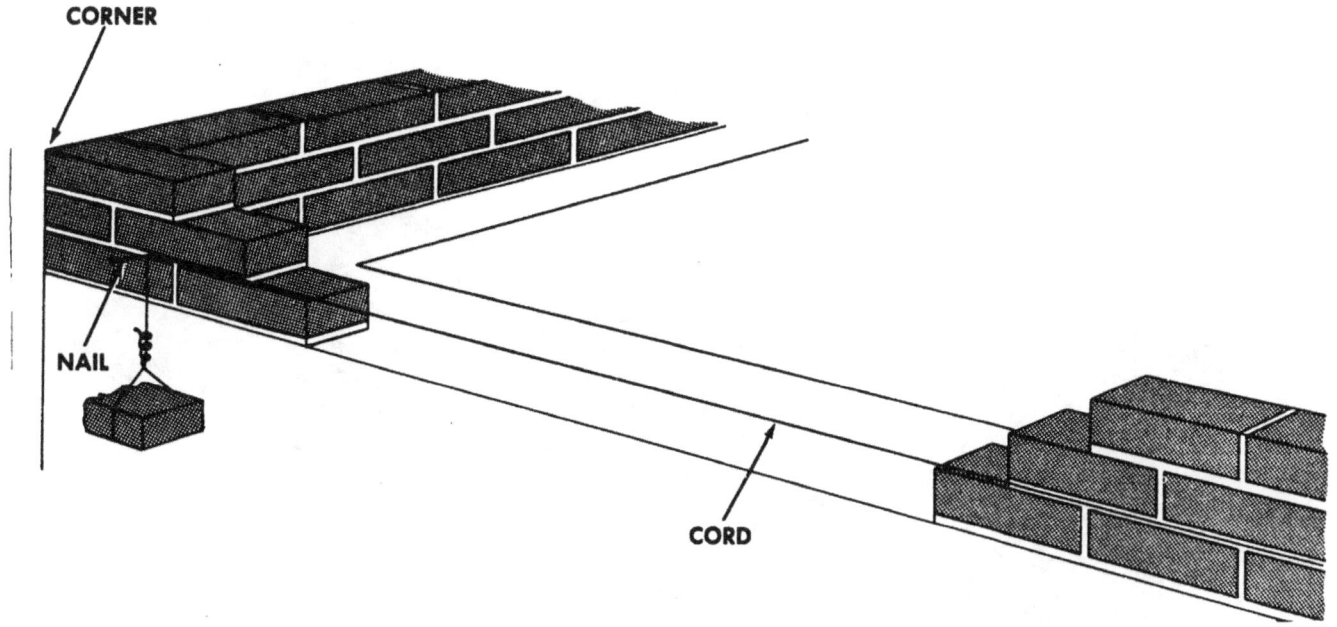

Figure 9-25. Use of the line.

short piece of line looped around the main line and fastened to the top edge of a brick that has been previously laid in proper position. A lead between the corner leads must be erected in order to place the trig brick in its proper location.

9-17. Window and Door Openings

a. Window Openings.

(1) If windows are to be installed in the wall, openings are left for them as the bricklaying proceeds. The height to the top of one full course should be exactly the height of the window sill. When the distance from the foundation to the bottom of the window sill is known, the bricklayer can determine how many courses are required to bring the wall up to that height. If the sill is to be

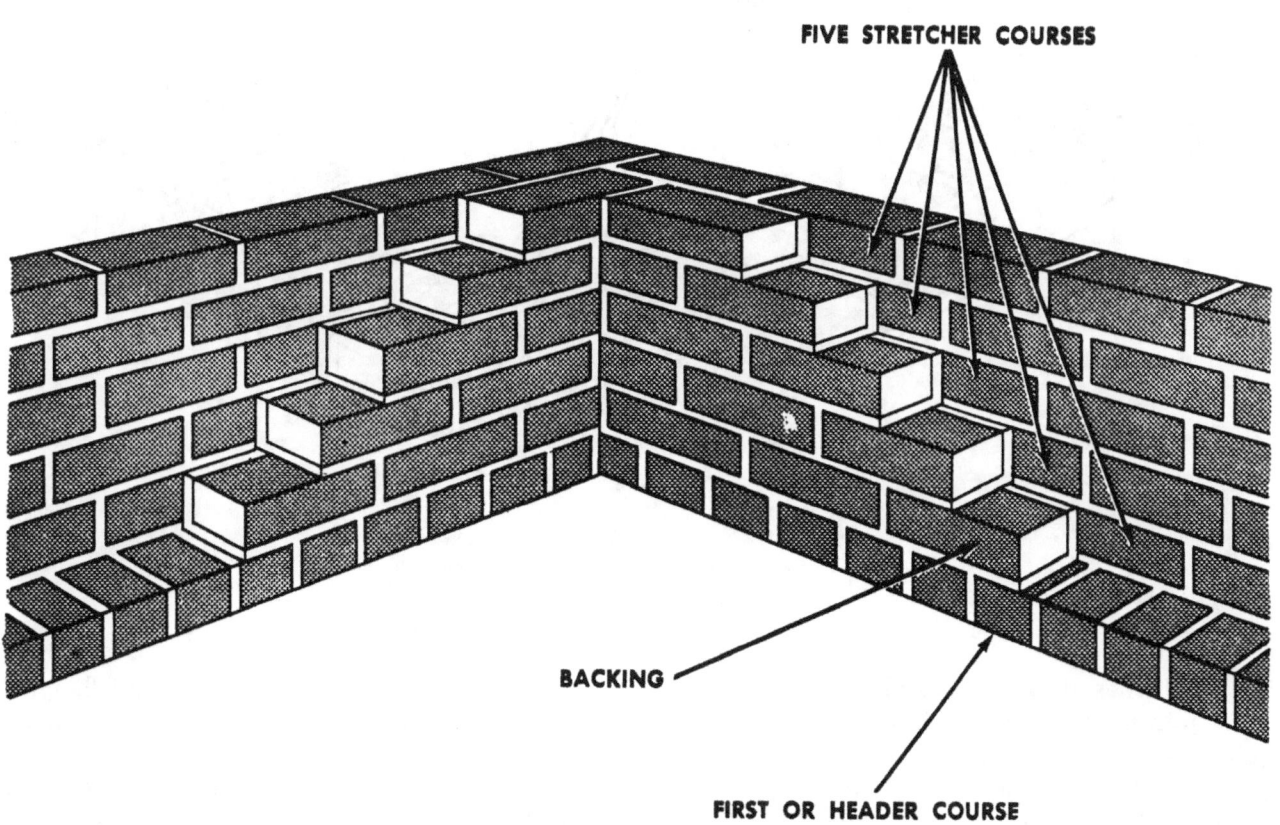

Figure 9-26. Backing brick at the corner—8-inch common bond brick wall.

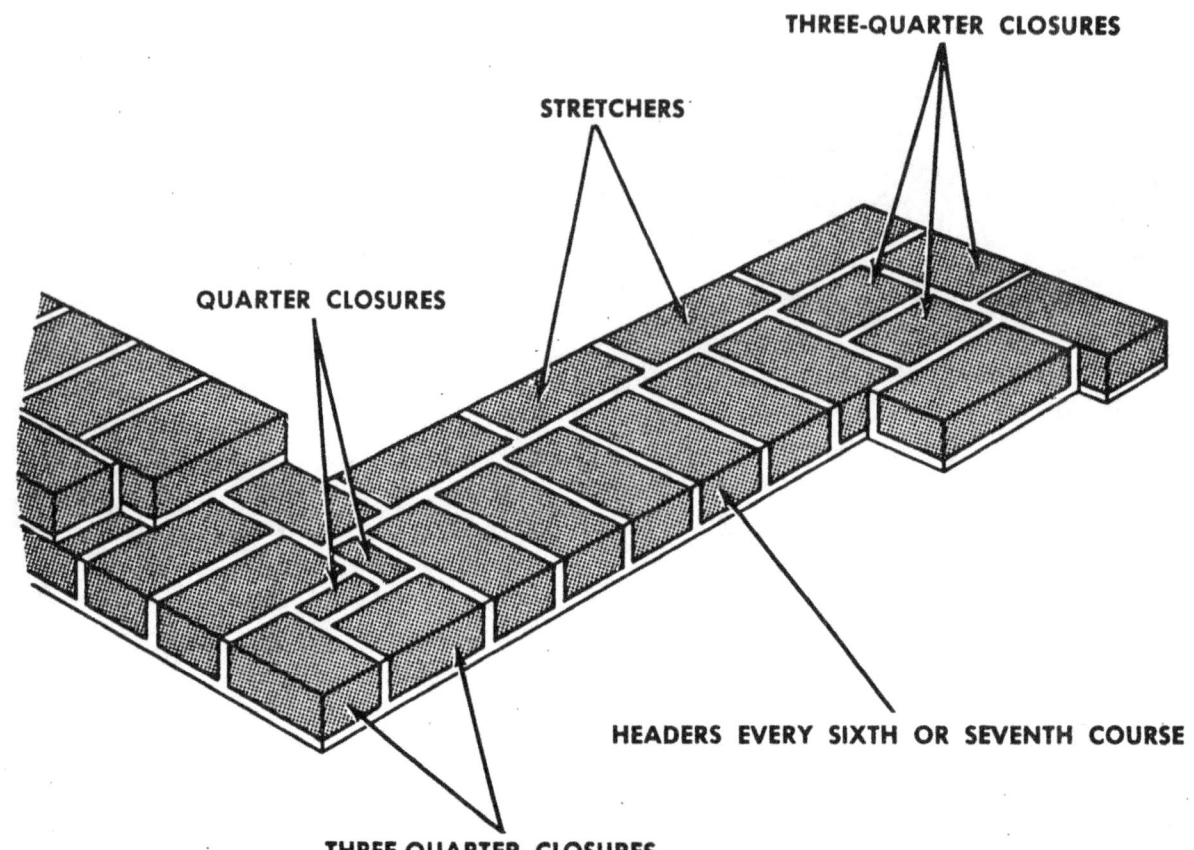

1 First course of 12-inch common bond wall

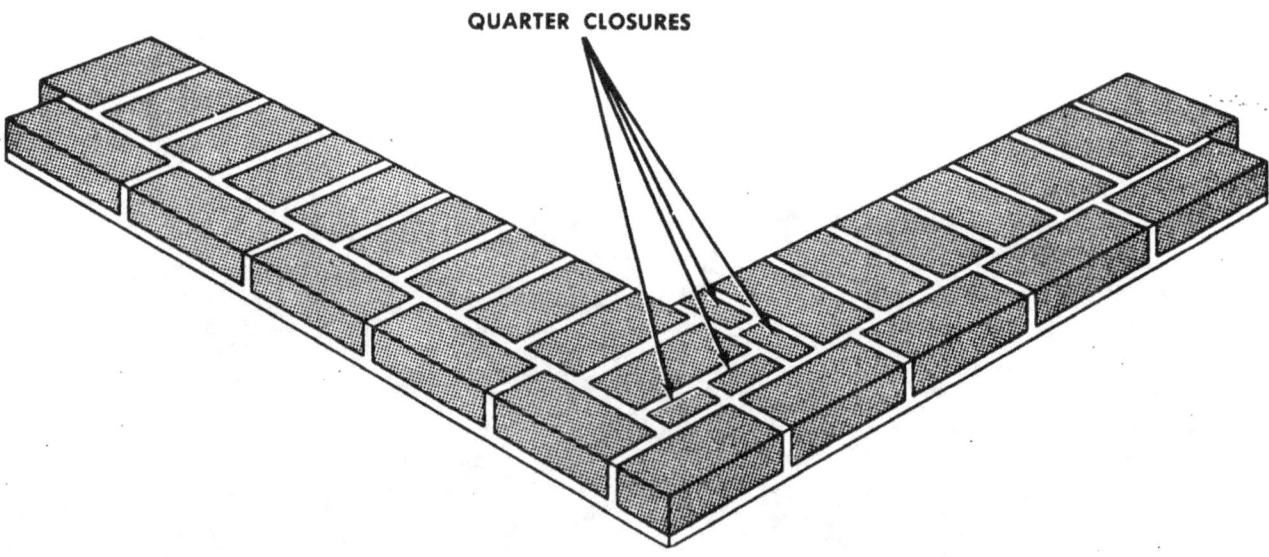

2 Second course of 12-inch common bond wall

Figure 9–27. Twelve-inch common bond wall.

4 feet 4¼ inches above the foundation and ½-inch mortar joints are to be used, 19 courses will be required. (Each brick plus one mortar joint is 2¼ + ½ = 2¾ inches. One course is thus 2¾ inches high. Four feet 4¼ inches divided by 2¾ is 19, the number of courses required.)

(2) With the brick laid up to sill height, the rowlock sill course is laid as shown in figure 9–28. The rowlock course is pitched downward. The slope is away from the window and the rowlock course normally takes up a vertical space equal to two courses of brick. The exterior surface of the

3   Third course of 12-inch common bond wall

Figure 9–27.—Continued.

joints between the brick in the rowlock course must be carefully finish to make them watertight.

(3) The window frame is placed on the rowlock sill as soon as the mortar has set. The window frame must be temporarily braced until the brickwork has been laid up to about one-third the height of the window frame. These braces are not removed for several days in order that the wall above the window frame will set properly. Now the bricklayer lays up the brick in the rest of the wall in such a way that the top of the brick in the course at the level of the top of the window frame is not more than $\frac{1}{4}$ inch above the frame. To do this, he marks on the window frame with a pencil the top of each course. If the top course does not come to the proper level, he changes the thickness of the joints slightly until the top course is at the proper level. The corner leads should be laid up after the height of each course at the window is determined.

(4) The mortar joint thickness for the corner leads is made the same as that determined at the window opening. With the corner leads erected, the line is installed as already described and is stretched across the window opening. The brick can now be laid in the rest of the wall. If the window openings have been planned properly, the brick in the face tier can be laid with a minimum of brick cutting.

b. Placing Lintel Over Window Opening. Lintels are placed above windows and doors to carry the weight of the wall above them. They rest on the brick course that is level or approximately level with the frame head, and are firmly bedded in mortar at the sides. Any space between the window frame and the lintel is closed with blocking and weatherstripped with bituminous materials. The wall is then continued above the window after the lintel is placed.

c. Door Openings. The same procedure can be used for laying brick around a door opening as was used for laying brick around a window opening, including placement of the lintel. The arrangement at a door opening is given in figure 9–29. Pieces of wood cut to the size of a half closure are laid in mortar as brick to provide for anchoring the door frame by means of screws or nails. These wood blocks are placed at several points along the top and sides of the door opening to allow for plumbing the frame.

9–18. Lintels

a. The brickwork above openings in walls must be supported by lintels. Lintels can be made of

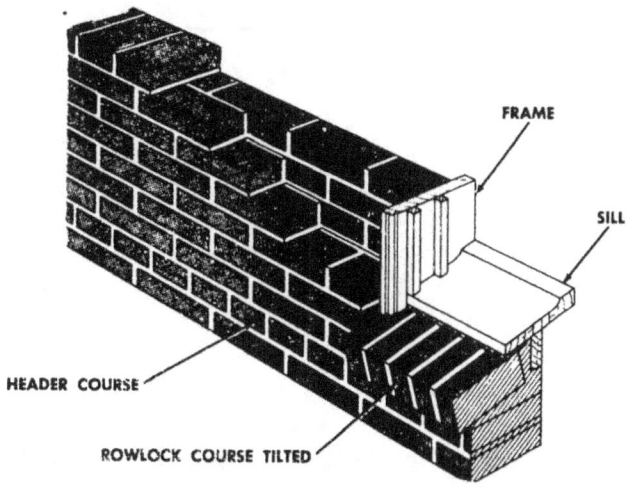

Figure 9–28. Construction of a window opening.

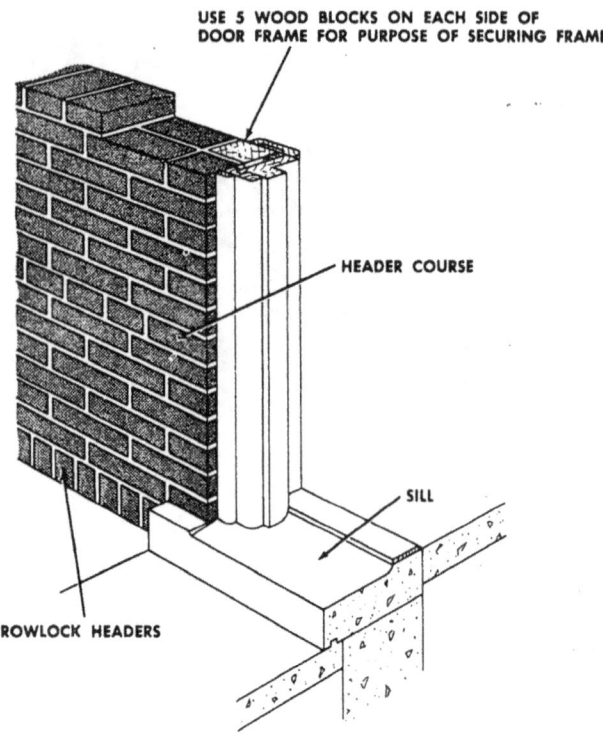

Figure 9-29. Construction at a door opening.

steel, precast reinforced concrete beams, or wood. The use of wood should be avoided as much as possible. If reinforced brick masonry is employed, the brick above the wall opening can be supported by the proper installation of steel reinforcing bars. This is discussed in paragraph 9-34. Figures 9-30 and 9-31 illustrate some of the methods of placing lintels for different wall thicknesses. The relative placement and position is determined both by wall thickness and the type of window being used.

b. Usually the size and type of lintels required are given on drawings for the structure. When not given, the size of double-angle lintels required for various width openings in an 8-inch and 12-inch wall can be selected from table 9-5. Wood lintels for various width openings are also given in table 9-5.

c. Installation of a lintel for an 8-inch wall is shown in figure 9-30. The thickness of the angle for a two-angle lintel should be ¼ inch. This makes it possible for the two-angle legs that pro-

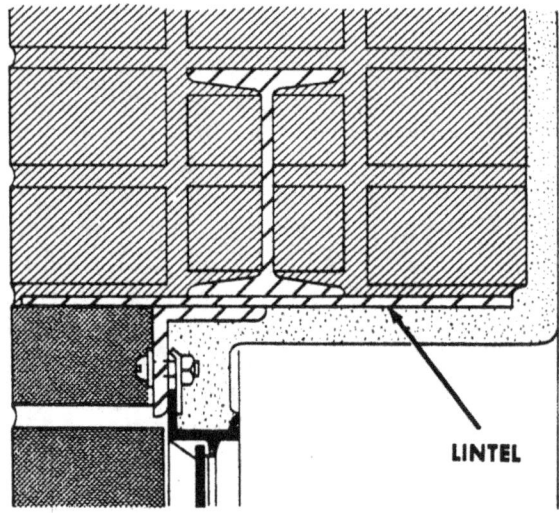

1. STEEL LINTEL

Figure 9-30. Lintels for an 8-inch wall.

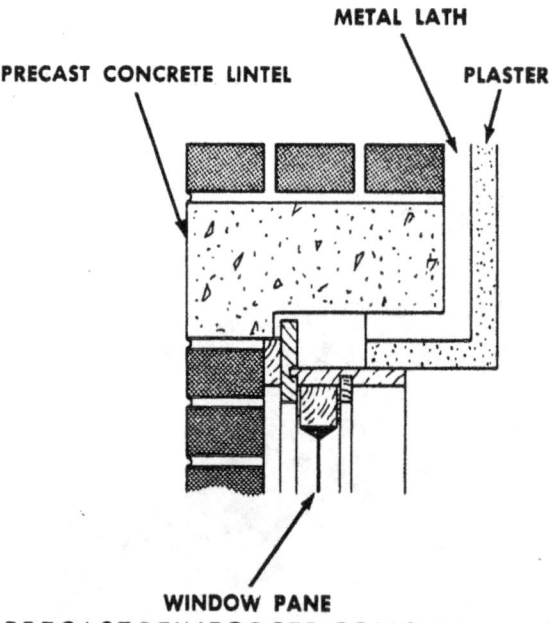

2. PRECAST REINFORCED CONCRETE LINTEL

Figure 9-31. Lintels for a 12-inch wall.

Table 9-5. Lintel Sizes

Wall thickness	Span				
	3 feet		4 feet* steel angles	5 feet* steel angles	6 feet* steel angles
	Steel angles	Wood			
8"	2-3 x 3 x ¼	2 x 8 2-2 x 4	2-3 x 3 x ¼	2-3 x 3 x ¼	2-3½ x 3½ x ¼
12"	2-3 x 3 x ¼	2 x 12 2-2 x 6	2-3 x 3 x ¼	2-3½ x 3½ x ¼	2-3½ x 3½ x ¼
				7 feet* steel angles	8 feet* steel angles
				2-3½ x 3½ x ¼	2-3½ x 3½ x ¼
				2-4 x 4 x ¼	2-4 x 4 x 4¼

*Wood lintels should not be used for spans over 3 feet since they burn out in case of fire and allow the brick to fall.

ject up into the brick to fit exactly in the ½-inch joint between the face and backing-up ties of an 8-inch wall.

9-19. Corbeling

a. Corbeling consists of courses of brick set out beyond the face of the wall in order to form a self-supporting projection. This type of construction is shown in figure 9-32. The portion of a chimney that is exposed to the weather is frequently corbeled out and increased in thickness to improve its weathering resistance. Headers should also be used as much as possible in corbeling. It is usually necessary to use various-sized bats. The first projecting course may be a stretcher course if necessary. No course should extend out more than 2 inches beyond the course below it and the total projection of the corbeling should not be more than the thickness of the wall.

b. Corbeling must be done carefully for the construction to have maximum strength. All mortar joints should be carefully made and completely filled with mortar. When the corbeled-out brick masonry is to withstand large loads, a qualified engineer should be consulted.

9-20. Brick Arches

a. *Characteristics.* If properly constructed, a brick arch can support a heavy load. The ability to support loads is derived primarily from its curved shape. Several arch shapes can be used; the circular and elliptical shapes are most common (fig. 9-33). The width of the mortar joint is less at the bottom of the brick than it is at the top, and it should not be thinner than ¼ inch at any point. Arches made of brick must be constructed with full mortar joints. As laying progresses, care must be taken to see that the arch does not bulge out of position.

b. *Use of Temporary Support.*

(1) A brick arch is constructed on a temporary support that is left in position until the mortar has set. The temporary support is made of wood as shown in figure 9-34. The dimensions required are obtained from drawings. For arches up to 6 feet in span, ¾-inch plywood should be used for temporary supports. Two pieces cut to the proper curved shape are made and nailed to 2 by 4's placed between them. This will provide a wide-enough surface to support the brick adequately.

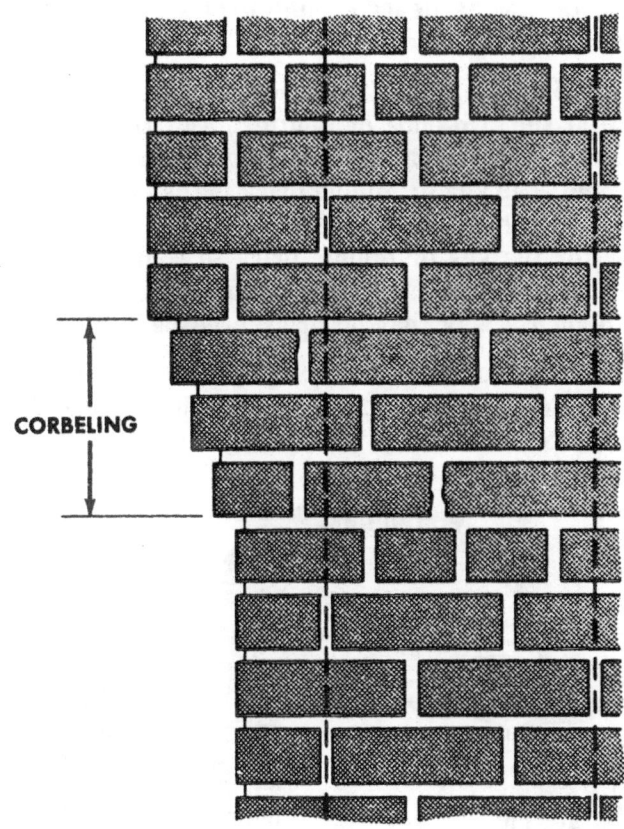

Figure 9-32. Corbeled brick wall.

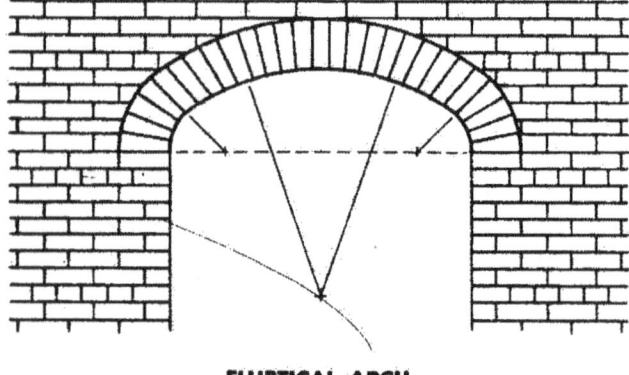

ELLIPTICAL ARCH

CIRCULAR ARCH

Figure 9-33. Types of arches.

(2) The temporary support should be held in position with wedges that can be driven out when the mortar has hardened enough for the arch to be self-supporting.

c. Laying the Arch. Construction of an arch is begun at the two ends or abutments of the arch. The brick is laid from each end toward the center or crown. The key or middle brick is the last to be placed. There should be an odd number of brick in order for the key or middle brick to come at the exact center of the arch. The arch should be laid out in such a way that no brick need be cut.

d. Determination of the Brick Spacing. The best way to determine the number of brick required for an arch is to lay a temporary support on its side on level ground and set brick around it. Adjust the spacing until the key brick comes at the exact center of the arch. When this has been done, the position of the brick can be marked on the temporary support to be used as a guide when the arch is actually built.

9-21. Watertight Walls

a. General.

(1) The water that passes through brick walls does not usually enter through the mortar or brick but through cracks between brick and mortar. Sometimes these cracks are formed because the bond between the brick and mortar is poor. They are more apt to occur in head joints than in bed joints. To prevent this, some brick must be wetted. If the position of the brick is changed after the mortar has begun to set, the bond between the brick and mortar will be destroyed and a crack will result. Shrinkage of the mortar is also frequently responsible for the formation of cracks.

(2) Both the size and number of cracks between the mortar and the brick can be reduced if the exterior face of all the mortar joints is tooled to a concave finish. All head joints and bed joints must be completely filled with mortar if watertightness is to be obtained.

b. Parging. A procedure found effective in producing a leakproof wall is shown in figure 9-35. The back of the brick in the face tier is plastered with not less than 3/8 inch of rich cement mortar before the backing bricks are laid. This is called parging or back plastering. Since parging should not be done over mortar protruding from the joints, all joints on the back of the face tier of bricks must be cut flush.

c. Membrane Waterproofing. Membrane waterproofing should be used if the wall is subject to considerable water pressure. The membrane, if

Figure 9-34. Use of a templet in arch construction.

Figure 9-35. Parging.

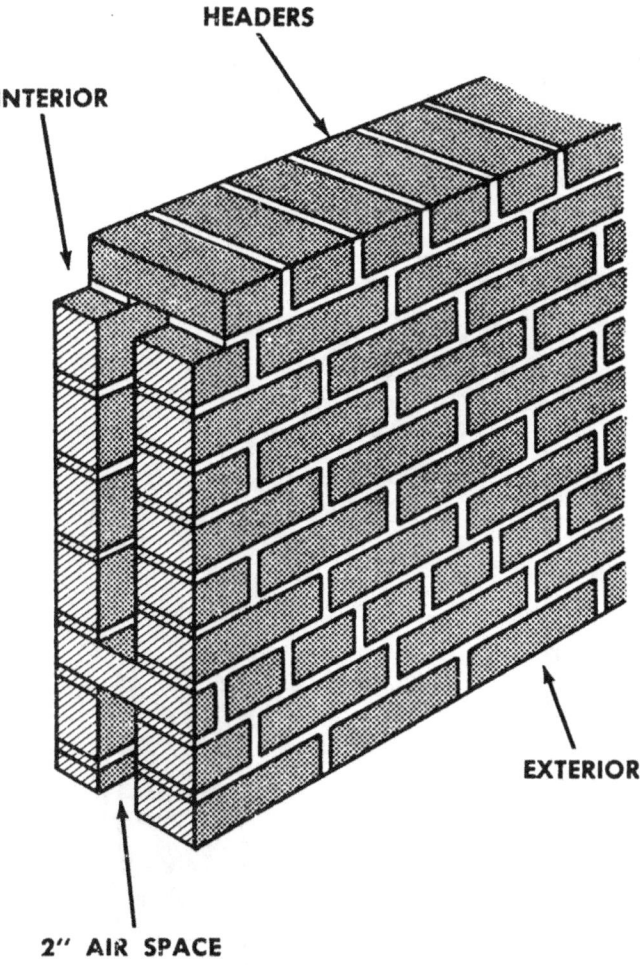

Figure 9-38. Details of a rowlock backwall.

are erected first and the wall between is built up afterward.

9-24. Manholes

a. Purpose.

(1) Manholes are required for sewers so they can be cleaned and inspected. The size of the manhole required depends largely upon the size of the sewer. Manholes should be circular or oval, since this reduces the stress arising from both water and soil pressure. For small sewers on a straight line, a 4-foot diameter manhole is satisfactory. Details of a typical manhole are given in figure 9-39.

(2) Both bottom and walls may be made of brick but normally the bottom is made of concrete because it is easier to cast the required shape in concrete rather than form it of brick. The walls of the manhole can be economically constructed if brick is used, eliminating the need for form work.

b. Required Wall Thickness. The thickness of walls required depends on the depth and the diameter of the manhole. An 8-inch thick wall should be used for manholes up to 8 feet in diameter and less than 15 feet deep. Manholes over 15 feet should be designed by a qualified engineer.

c. Manhole Construction.

(1) Only headers are used for an 8-inch wall. A line cannot be used in the construction of the manhole wall. The level is employed to make sure that all brick in a course are at the same level. The straightedge or a straight, surfaced 2 by 4 may be used to span the manhole and the plumb rule placed on the 2 by 4 to determine whether the brick rises at the same level all around the manhole. Since the manhole wall will not be seen, some irregularities in brick position and mortar joint thickness are permissible. All joints in this type of wall are bed joints, or closure joints, made as described in paragraph 9-8.

(2) Before the first course of brick is laid, a bed of mortar 1-inch thick should be placed on the foundation and the first course laid on this mortar bed.

(3) To reduce the size of the manhole to that required for the manhole frame and cover, the brick is corbeled inward as shown (2, fig. 9-39). One brick should not project more than 2 inches beyond the brick below it. Upon completion of the manhole wall, it is plastered on the outside with the same mortar used in laying the brick. The thickness of the mortar coating should be at least $3/8$ inch.

(4) The base of the manhole frame is placed in a 1-inch thick mortar bed spread on top of the manhole wall. The wrought-iron steps shown should be spaced at about 15 inches vertically and the embedded part placed in a cross mortar joint.

9-25. Method of Supporting Beams

a. When it is necessary to support a wood beam on a brick wall, it may be done as shown in 1, figure 9-40. Note the wall tie. If possible, the mortar should be kept away from the beam for dry rot may result if the wood is completely encased in mortar. This may be conveniently done by means of the wall box shown in 2, figure 9-40. The end of the beam should be cut at an angle which, in case of fire, will permit it to fall without damaging the wall above the beam. The beam should bear on the full width of the inside tier of brick for either an 8-inch or 12-inch wall.

b. If a steel beam is to be supported on a brick wall, a steel bearing plate set in mortar should be used under the beam. This bearing plate, when

9-28

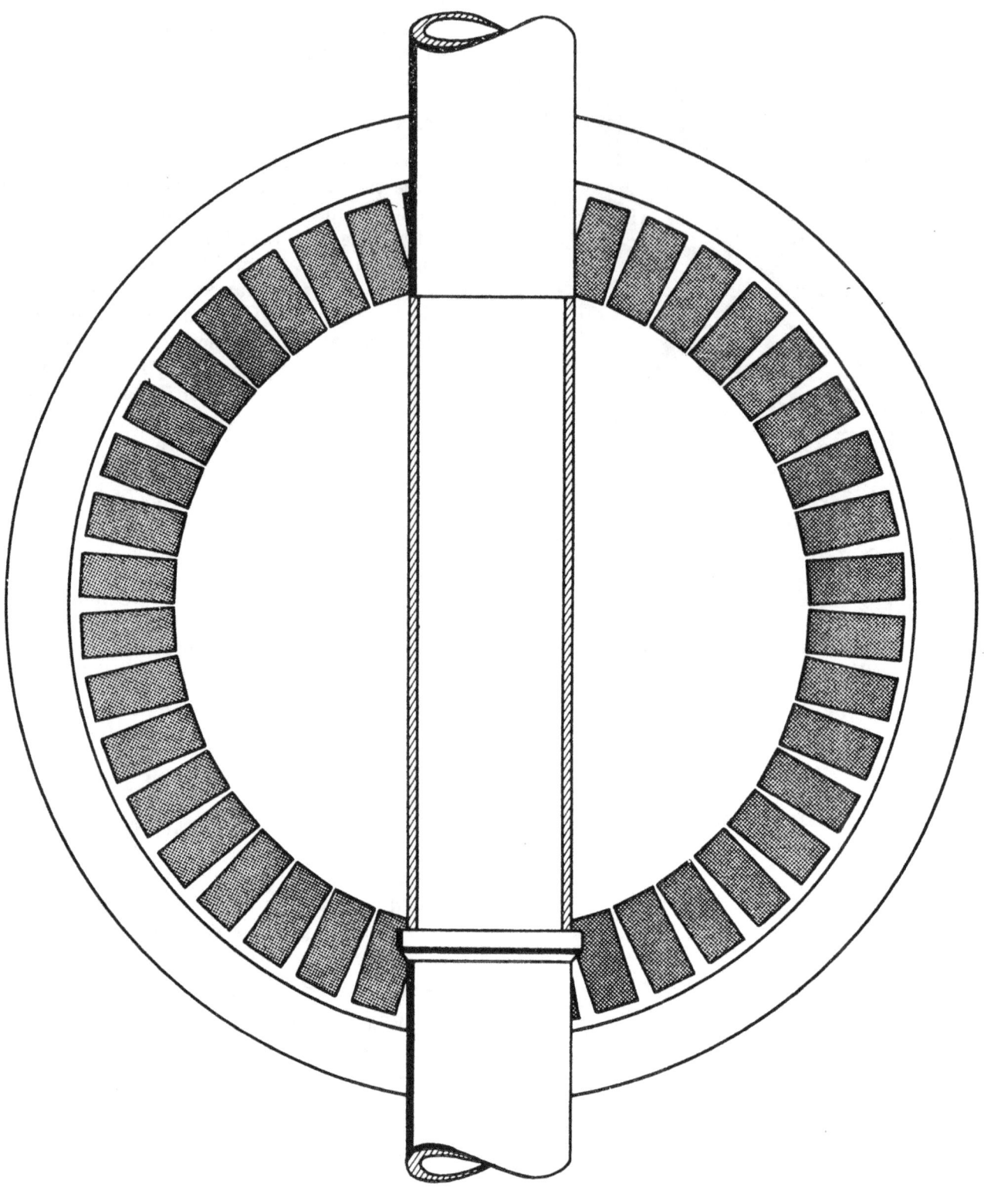

1   Plan of manhole

Figure 9-39. Details of a sewer manhole.

properly designed, reduces the tendency for the steel beam to crush the brick. The size of the bearing plate depends upon the size of beam and the load the beam carries. The method for determining the required thickness of bearing plates is beyond the scope of this manual.

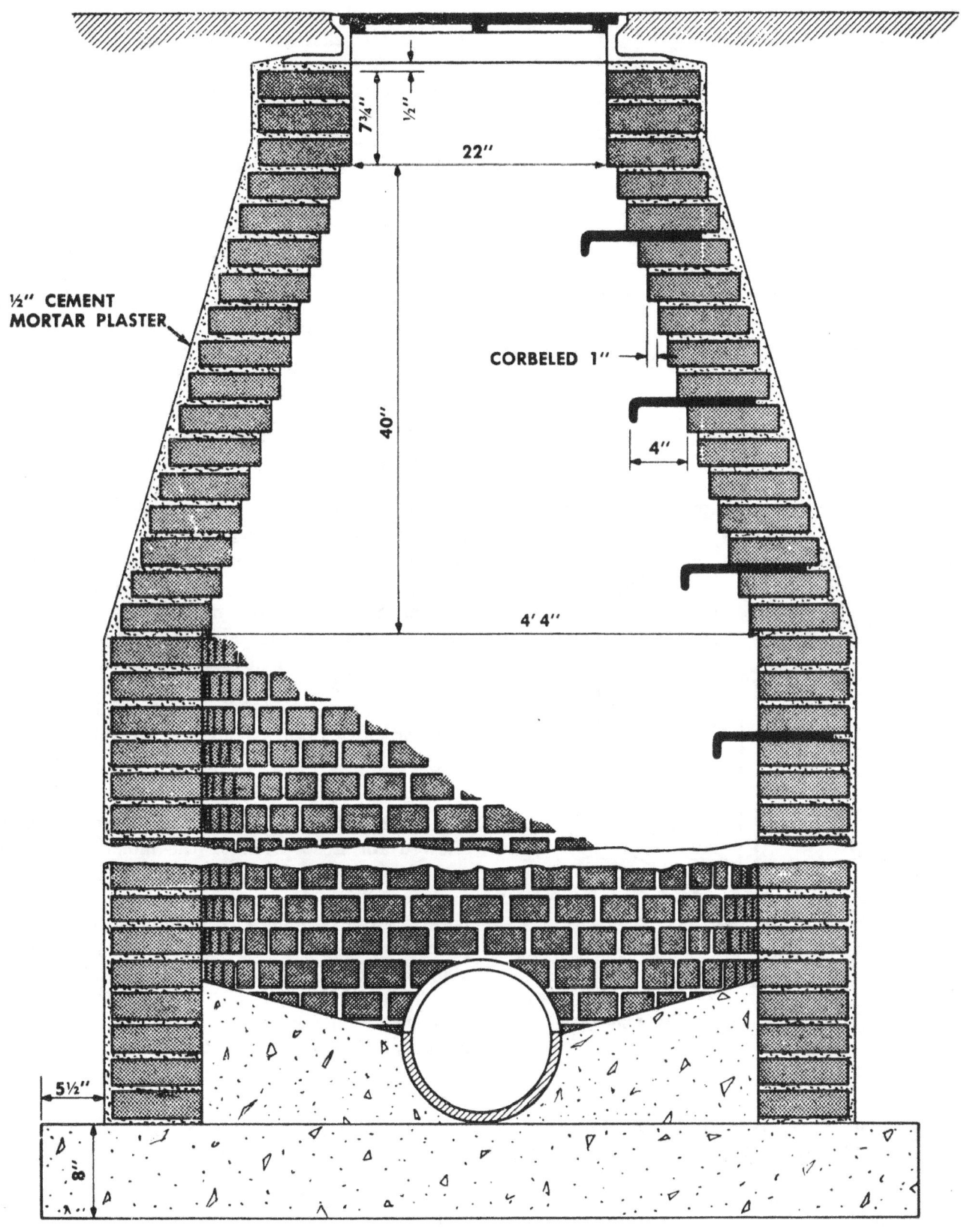

2 Brick manhole cross section

Figure 9-39.—Continued.

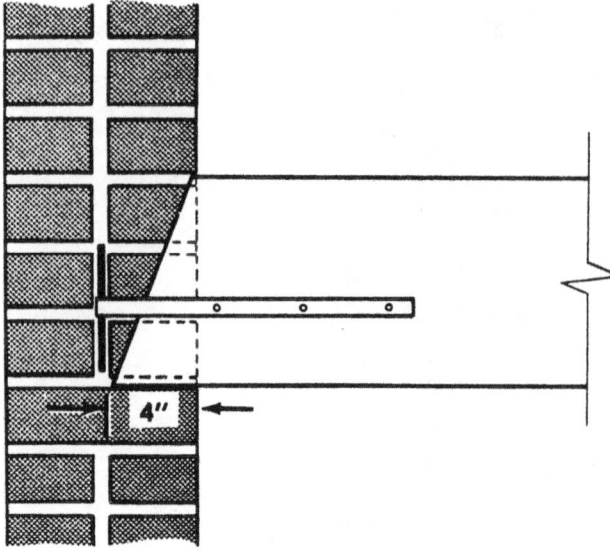

1 Wall tie

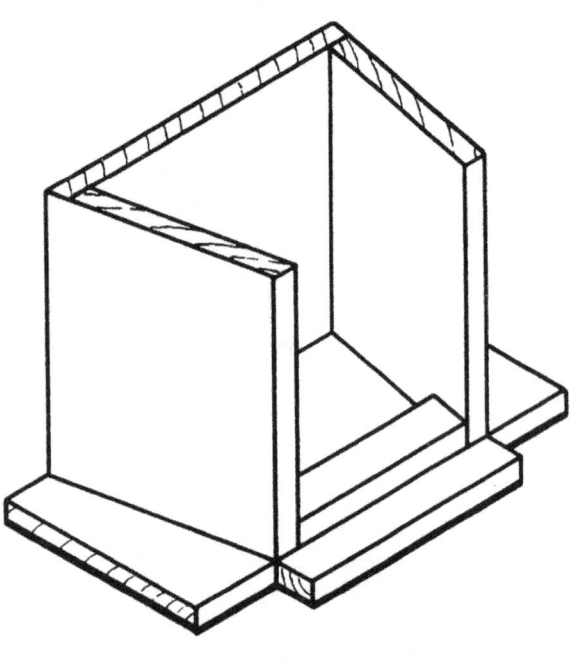

2 Beam box

Figure 9–40. Details of a wood beam supported by a brick wall.

9–26. Maintenance and Repair of Brick Walls

If a brick masonry wall is properly constructed, it requires little maintenance or repair. The proper repair of old masonry can be more expensive than the complete removal and replacement of the disintegrated portion. The use of good mortar, proper finishing of joints, and adequate flashing adds little to the initial cost and reduces the cost of maintenance throughout the life of the masonry.

a. Tuck-Pointing. Tuck-pointing consists of cutting out all loose and disintegrated mortar to a depth of at least ½ inch and replacing it with new. If leakage is to be stopped, all the mortar in the affected area should be cut out and new mortar placed according to instructions given in paragraph 9–21e. Tuck-pointing done as routine maintenance requires the removal of the defective mortar only.

b. Preparation of the Mortar Joint. All dust and loose material should be removed by brush or by means of a water jet after the cutting has been completed. A chisel with a cutting edge about ½-inch wide is suitable for cutting. If water is used in cleaning the joints, no further wetting is required. If not, the surface of the joint must be moistened.

c. Mortar for Tuck-Pointing. The mortar to be used for tuck-pointing should be portland-cement-lime, prehydrated type S mortar, or prehydrated prepared mortar made from type II masonary cement (para 7–3). The prehydration of mortar greatly reduces the amount of shrinkage. The procedure for prehydrating mortar is as follows: The dry ingredients for the mortar are mixed with just enough water to produce a damp mass of such consistency that it will retain its form when compressed into a ball with the hands. The mortar should then be allowed to stand for at least 1 hour and not more than 2 hours. After this has been done, it is mixed with the amount of water required to produce a stiff but workable consistency.

d. Filling the Joint. Sufficient time should be allowed for absorption of the moisture used in preparing the joint before the joint is filled with mortar. Filling the joint with mortar is called repointing and is done with a pointing trowel. The prehydrated mortar that has been prepared as above is packed tightly into the joint in thin layers about ¼ inch thick and finished to a smooth concave surface with a pointing tool. The mortar is pushed into the joint with a forward motion in one direction from a starting point to reduce the possibility of forming air pockets.

9–27. Cleaning New Brick Masonry and Removing Efflorescence

a. Cleaning New Brick Masonry. A skilled bricklayer is able to construct a masonry wall that is almost free of mortar stains. Most new brick walls, however, will need some cleaning.

(1) Upon completion of the work, the large particles of mortar adhering to the brick are re-

moved with a putty knife or chisel. Mortar stains are removed with acid prepared by mixing one part commercial muriatic acid with nine parts water. Pour the acid into the water. Before applying the acid, soak the surface thoroughly with water to prevent the mortar stain from being drawn into the pores of the brick.

(2) The acid solution is applied with a long-handled, stiff-fiber brush. Proper precautions must be taken to prevent the acid from getting on hands, arms, and clothing. Goggles are worn to protect the eyes. An area of 15 to 20 square feet is scrubbed with acid and then immediately washed down with clear water. All acid must be removed before it can attack the mortar joint. Door and window frames must be protected from the acid.

b. Removing Efflorescence. Efflorescence is a white deposit of soluble salts frequently appearing on the surface of brick walls. These soluble salts are contained in the brick. Water penetrating the wall dissolves out the salts and when the water evaporates the salt remains. Efflorescence cannot occur unless both water and the salts are present. The proper selection of brick and a dry wall will keep efflorescence to a minimum. It may be removed, however, with the acid solution recommended for cleaning new walls. Acid should be used only after it has been determined that scrubbing with water and stiff brushes will not remove the efflorescence.

9–28. Cleaning Old Brick Masonry

a. Methods. Sand blasting, steam with water jets, and the use of cleaning compounds are the principal methods of cleaning old brick masonry. The process used depends upon the materials used in the wall and the nature of the stain. Many cleaning compounds that have no effect upon brick will damage mortar. Rough-textured brick is more difficult to clean than smooth-textured brick. Often it cannot be cleaned without removing part of the brick itself, and changing the appearance of the wall.

b. Sand Blasting. This method consists of blowing hard sand through a nozzle against the surface to be cleaned. Compressed air forces the sand through the nozzle. A layer of the surface is removed to the depth required to remove the stain. This is a disadvantage in that the surface is given a rough texture upon which soot and dust collect. Sand blasting usually cuts deeply into the mortar joints and it is often necessary to repoint them. After the sand blasting has been completed, it is advisable to apply a transparent waterproofing paint to the surface to help prevent soiling of the wall by soot and dust. Sand blasting is never done on glazed surfaces. A canvas screen placed around the scaffold used for sand blasting will make it possible to salvage most of the sand.

c. Steam With Water Jets.

(1) Cleaning by this method is accomplished by projecting a finely divided spray of steam and water at a high velocity against the surface to be cleaned. Grime is removed effectively without changing the texture of the surface, which gives it an advantage over sand blasting.

(2) The steam may be obtained from a portable truck-mounted boiler. The pressure should be from 140 to 150 pounds per square inch and about 12 boiler horse-power per cleaning nozzle is required. The velocity with which the steam and water spray hits the wall is more important than the volume of spray used.

(3) A garden hose may be used to carry the water to the cleaning nozzle. Another garden hose supplies rinsing water. The operator experiments with the cleaning nozzle in order to determine the best angle and distance from the wall to hold the nozzle. The steam and water valves may also be regulated until the most effective spray is obtained. No more than a 3-foot-square area should be cleaned at one time. The cleaning should be done by passing the nozzle back and forth over the area, then rinsing it immediately with clean water before moving to the next space.

(4) Sodium carbonate, sodium bicarbonate, or trisodium phosphate may be added to the cleaning water entering the nozzle to aid the cleaning action. The amount of salt remaining can be reduced considerably by washing the surface down with water before and after cleaning.

(5) Hardened deposits that cannot be removed by steam cleaning should be removed with steel scrapers or wire brushes. Care must be taken not to cut into the surface. After the deposit has been removed, the surface should be washed down with water and steam cleaned.

d. Cleaning Compounds. There are a number of cleaning compounds that may be used, depending upon the stain to be removed. Most cleaning compounds contain material that will appear as efflorescence if allowed to penetrate the surface. This may be prevented if the surface to be cleaned is thoroughly wetted first. Whitewash, calcimine, and coldwater paints may be removed by the use of a solution of one part hydrochloric acid to five parts water. Fiber brushes are used to scrub the surface vigorously with the solution while the solution is still foaming. When the coating has been removed, the wall must be washed down with clean water until the acid is completely removed.

e. Paint Removers. Oil paint, enamels, varnishes, shellacs, and glue sizings should be removed with a paint remover applied with a brush and left on until the coating is soft enough to be scraped off with a putty knife. The following are effective paint removers:

(1) Commercial paint removers. If these are used, follow the manufacturer's instructions.

(2) Two pounds of trisodium phosphate in 1 gallon of hot water.

(3) One and one-half pounds of caustic soda in 1 gallon of hot water.

(4) Sand blasting or burning with a blowtorch.

f. Removal of Miscellaneous Stains.

(1) *Iron stains.* The cleaning solution is prepared by mixing seven parts of lime-free glycerine with a solution of one part sodium citrate in six parts lukewarm water. Whiting or kieselguhr is added to make a thick paste to be applied to the stain with a trowel and scraped off when dry. The procedure is repeated until the stain in removed. After this the surface must be washed down with water.

(2) *Tobacco stains.* The cleaning solution is prepared by dissolving 2 pounds of trisodium phosphate in 5 quarts of water. In an enameled pan, mix 12 ounces of chloride of lime in enough water to make a smooth thick paste. The trisodium phosphate solution is then mixed with the paste in a 2-gallon stoneware jar. When the lime has settled, the clear liquid is drawn off and diluted with an equal amount of water. A stiff paste is made by mixing the clear liquid with powdered talc; it is applied to the stain with a trowel and the surface washed.

(3) *Smoke stains.* A smooth stiff paste made from trichlorethylene and powdered talc is effective in removing smoke stains. The solution container should be covered to prevent evaporation. If after several applications a slight stain still remains, the surface should be washed down and the procedure recommended for the removal of tobacco stains used. This solution should not be used in an unventilated space for the fumes are harmful.

(4) *Copper and bronze stains.* These stains can be removed with a solution made by mixing one part of ammonium chloride (sal ammoniac) in dry form with four parts of powdered talc. Ammonia water is added and the solution stirred until a thick paste is obtained. This is applied to the stain with a trowel and allowed to dry. Several applications may be necessary after which the surface must be washed down with clear water.

(5) *Oil stains.* Oil stains are effectively removed with a solution consisting of one part trisodium phosphate and 1 gallon of water to which enough whiting has been added to form a paste. The paste should be troweled over the stain in a layer ½ inch thick and allowed to dry for 24 hours. The paste is removed and the surface washed with clean water.

9–29. Flashing

a. Description.

(1) Flashing is the impervious membrane placed at certain places in brick masonry for the purpose of excluding water or to collect any moisture that does penetrate the masonry and directing it to the outside of the wall. Flashing is installed at the head and sill of window openings and, in some buildings, at the intersection of the wall and roof. Where chimneys pass through the roof, the flashing should extend entirely through the chimney wall and turn up for a distance of 1 inch against the flue lining.

(2) The edges of the flashing are turned up as shown in figure 9–41 to prevent drainage into the wall. Flashing is always installed in mortar joints. Drainage for the wall above the flashing is provided by placing ¼-inch cotton-rope drainage wicks in the mortar joint just above flashing membrane at 18 inch spacings. Drainage may also be provided by holes left after dowels placed in the proper mortar joint are removed.

b. Flashing Materials. Copper, lead, aluminum, and bituminous roofing paper may be used for the flashing membrane. Copper is generally preferred but it will stain the masonry when it weathers. If this staining is undesirable, lead-coated copper should be used. Bituminous roofing papers are the cheapest but they are not as durable and may have to be replaced for permanent construction. The cost of replacement is many times the cost of installing high-quality flashing. Corrugated copper flashing sheets are available that produce a good bond with the mortar. These sheets have interlocking watertight joints at points of overlap.

c. Installation of Flashing.

(1) In placing flashing, a ½-inch thick bed of mortar is spread on top of the brick and the flash-

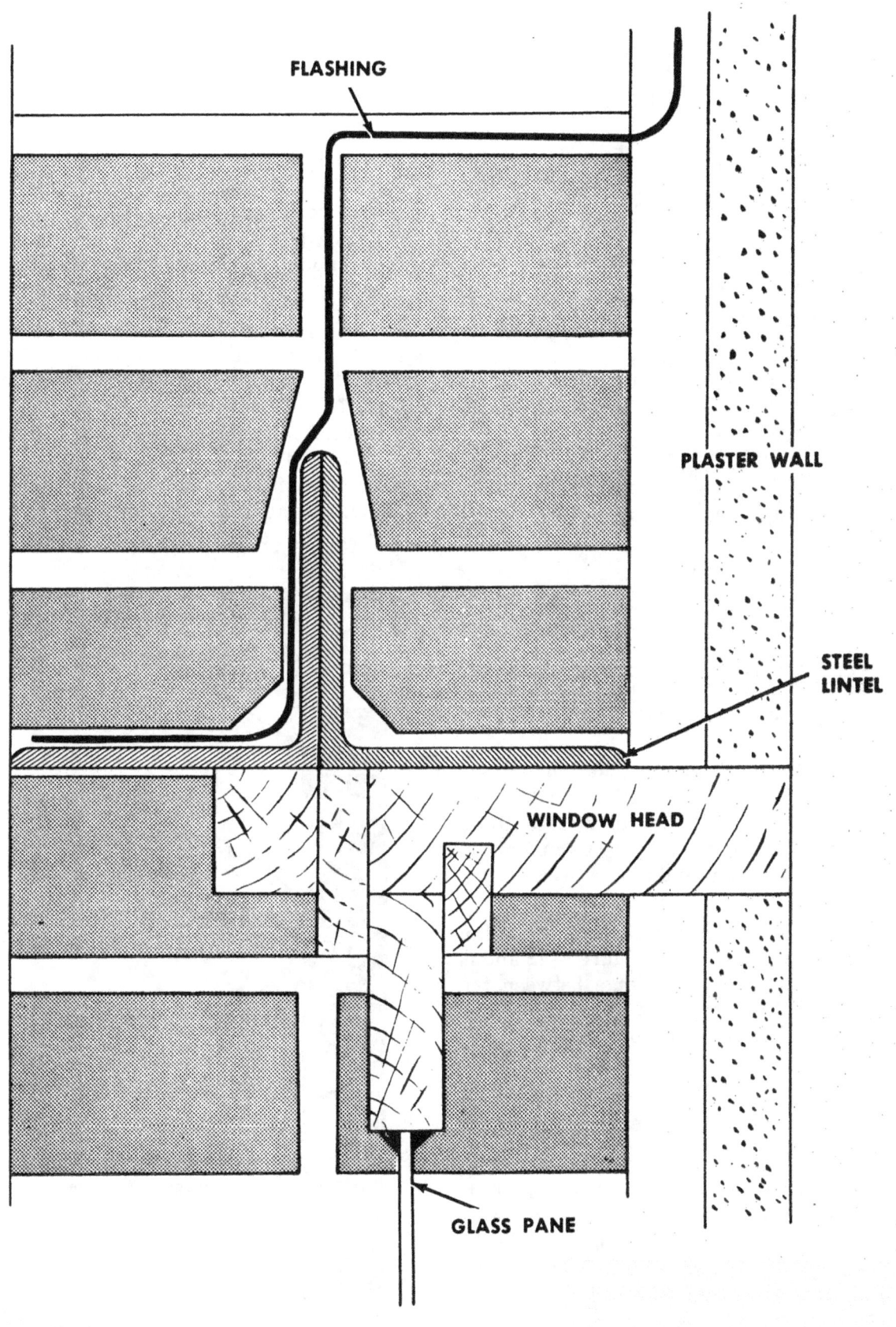

Figure 9-41. Flashing at window opening.

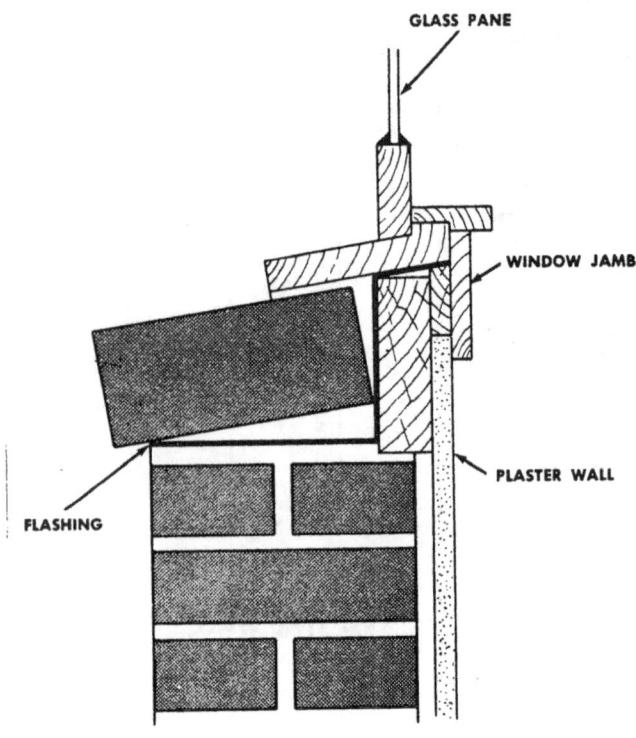

2 Window joint

Figure 9-41.—Continued.

ing sheet pushed firmly down into the mortar. The brick or sill that goes on top of the flashing is forced into a ½-inch thick mortar bed spread on the flashing.

(2) Details for the proper installation of flashing at the head and at the sill of a window are shown in figure 9-41. Note that at the steel lintel the flashing goes in under the face tier of brick, then back of the face tier, and finally over the top of the lintel.

(3) The flashing required at the intersection of the roof and wall is shown in figure 9-42 and is always installed to prevent leakage between the roof and the wall. The upper end of the flashing is fitted and caulked into the groove of the raggle block.

9-30. Protection Against Freezing During Constructoin

a. Precaution. Leaky masonry walls can be attributed to the freezing of mortar before it set or to the lack of protection of materials and walls during cold weather construction. During cold weather, all materials and walls should be protected against freezing temperatures by:

(1) Proper storage of materials.
(2) Proper preparation of mortar.
(3) Heating of masonry units.
(4) Laying precautions.
(5) Protection of work.

b. Storing of Materials. Carelessness in storing materials during cold weather construction encourages poor workmanship, since the removal of ice and snow and the thawing of masonry units are absolutely necessary before construction proceeds. All masonry units and mortar materials should be thoroughly covered with tarpaulins or building paper and stored on plank platforms thick enough or raised high enough to prevent absorption of moisture from the ground.

c. Preparation of Mortar. Water and sand should be heated not to exceed 160° F. and the temperature of the mortar when used should be at least 70° F. and not more than 120° F. On small jobs where mortar boxes are used, they should be of steel and raised about a foot above the ground so that provisions can be made to supply some sort of heat to keep the mortar warm after mixing. *Salt should never be added to mortar to lower its freezing point.*

d. Heating of Masonry Units. To prevent sud-

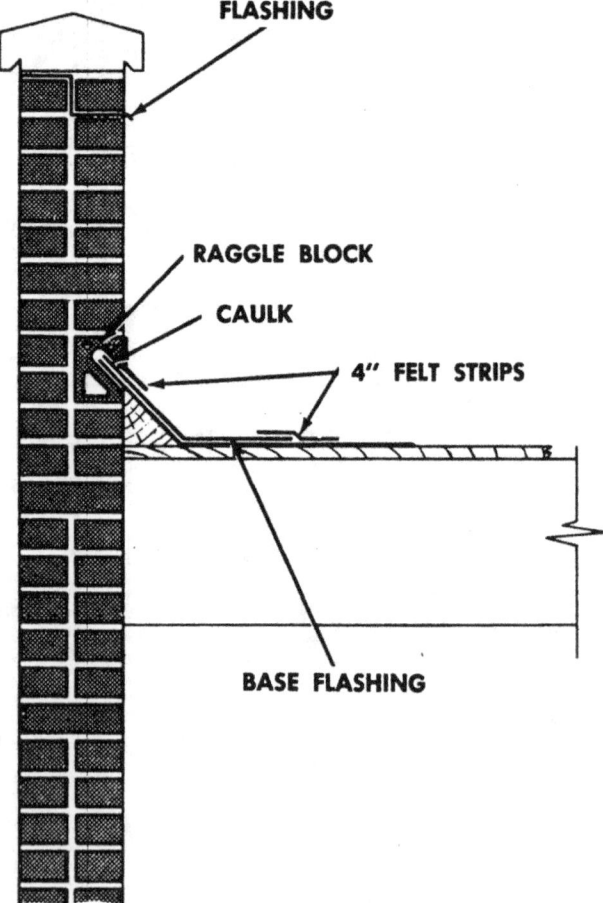

Figure 9-42. Flashing at intersection of roof and wall.

den cooling of the warm mortar in contact with cold units it is recommended that all masonry units be heated to a unit temperature of about 40° F. when the outside temperature is below 18° F. The heating of masonry units requires careful planning. Where required, inside storage should be provided so that heat may be supplied at minimum expense.

e. Laying Precautions. In below freezing weather, brick having high rates of absorption should be sprinkled with *warm* water *just* before laying. Masonry units should never be laid on snow- or ice-covered beds because there will be little or no bond between the mortar and masonry units when the base thaws. Tops of unfinished walls should be kept carefully covered when work is not proceeding. If the covering is displaced and ice or snow collects on the wall top, it should be removed with live steam before the work continues.

f. Protection of Work. Protection of the masonry from freezing is necessary and will vary with weather conditions. Each job is an individual problem. Job layout, desired rate of construction, and the prevailing weather conditions will determine the amount of protection and the type of heat necessary to maintain temperatures within the wall above freezing unit the mortar has set properly.

g. Temperature Variation. When the outside air temperature is below 40 °F., the temperature of the masonry when laid should be above 40° F. An air temperature of above 40° F. should be maintained on both sides of the masonry for at least 48 hours, if type M or S mortar is used, and for at least 72 hours if type N mortar is used. These periods may be reduced to 24 and 48 hours respectively, if high-early-strength cement is used. It is significant to note that the use of high-early-strength cement in mortars does not appreciably alter their rate of set. However, it does increase their rate of gaining strength, thereby providing greater resistance to further injury from freezing.

9-31. Quantities of Material Required for Brick Masonry

See table 9-6 for the quantity of brick and mortar required for various wall thicknesses.

Table 9-6. Quantities of Material Required for Brick Walls*

Wall area sq ft	Wall thickness in inches							
	4 inches		8 inches		12 inches		16 inches	
	Number of bricks	Cu ft mortar	Number of bricks	Cu ft mortar	Number of bricks	Cu ft mortar	Number of bricks	Cu ft mortar
1	6.17	.08	12.33	.2	18.49	.32	24.65	.44
10	61.7	.8	123.3	2	184.9	3.2	246.5	4.4
100	617	8	1,233	20	1,849	32	2,465	44
200	1,234	16	2,466	40	3,698	64	4,930	88
300	1,851	24	3,699	60	5,547	96	7,395	132
400	2,468	32	4,932	80	7,396	128	9,860	176
500	3,085	40	6,165	100	9,245	160	12,325	220
600	3,712	48	7,398	120	11,094	192	14,790	264
700	4,319	56	8,631	140	12,943	224	17,253	308
800	4,936	64	9,864	160	14,792	256	19,720	352
900	5,553	72	10,970	180	16,641	288	22,185	396
1,000	6,170	80	12,330	200	18,490	320	24,650	440

*Quantities are based on ½-inch-thick mortar joint. For ⅜-inch-thick joint use 80 percent of these quantities. For ⅝-inch-thick joint use 120 percent.

CONCRETE MASONRY

CONTENTS

	Page
SECTION I. CHARACTERISTICS OF CONCRETE BLOCKS	1
SECTION II. CONSTRUCTION PROCEDURES	3
SECTION III. RUBBLE STONE MASONRY	16

CONCRETE MASONRY

SECTION I. CHARACTERISTICS OF CONCRETE BLOCKS

8-1 Construction Material
Concrete masonry has become increasingly important as a construction material. Important technological developments in the manufacture and utilization of the units have accompanied the rapid increase in the use of concrete masonry. Concrete masonry walls properly designed and constructed will satisfy varied building requirements including fire, safety, durability, economy, appearance, utility, comfort, and good acoustics.

8-2 Concrete Masonry Units
a. *Uses.* Concrete masonry units are designed and made for use in all types of masonry construction. Some of the uses are:
   (1) Exterior load-bearing walls (below and above grade)
   (2) Interior load-bearing walls
   (3) Fire walls, curtain walls
   (4) Partition and panel walls
   (5) Backing for brick, stone, and other facings
   (6) Fireproofing over structural members
   (7) Firesafe walls around stair wells, elevators, and other enclosures
   (8) Piers and columns
   (9) Retaining walls
   (10) Chimneys
   (11) Concrete floor units

b. *Types of Units*: Concrete masonry building units are designated as:
   (1) Hollow load-bearing concrete block
   (2) Solid load-bearing concrete block
   (3) Hollow non-load-bearing concrete block
   (4) Concrete building tile
   (5) Concrete brick

c. *Heavyweight and Lightweight Units.* The different types of units are made with heavyweight or lightweight aggregates and are referred to as heavyweight and lightweight units, respectively. A hollow load-bearing concrete block of 8 x 8 x 16 inches nominal size will weigh from 40 to 50 pounds when made with heavyweight aggregate such as sand, gravel, crushed stone or air-cooled slag. Concrete bricks made with lightweight aggregate will weigh from 25 to 35 pounds each and are made with coal cinders, expanded shale, clay, slag, or natural lightweight materials such as volcanic cinders and pumice. Heavyweight and lightweight units are used for all types of masonry construction. The choice of units depends on availability and the requirements of the structure under consideration.

d. *Solid and Hollow Units.* A solid concrete block is defined in ASTM specifications as a unit in which the core area is not more than 25 percent of the gross cross-sectional area. Concrete blocks are generally solid and are sometimes available with a recessed pocket called a "frog". A hollow concrete block is a unit having a core area greater than 25 percent of its gross cross-sectional area. Generally, the core area of hollow units is 40 to 50 percent of the gross area.

e. *Sizes and Shapes.* Concrete building units are made in sizes and shapes to fit different construction needs. Units are made in full- and half-length sizes as shown in Figure 8-1. Concrete unit sizes are usually referred to by their nominal dimensions. A unit measuring $7^5/_8$ inches wide, $7^5/_8$ inches high, and 15. $^5/_8$ inches long is referred to as an 8 x 8 x 16 inch unit. When it is laid in a wall with $^3/_8$-inch mortar joints, the unit will occupy a space exactly 16 inches long and 8 inches high. Local manufacturers should be contacted for a schedule of sizes and shapes that are available. This information should be known prior to designing the proposed structure.

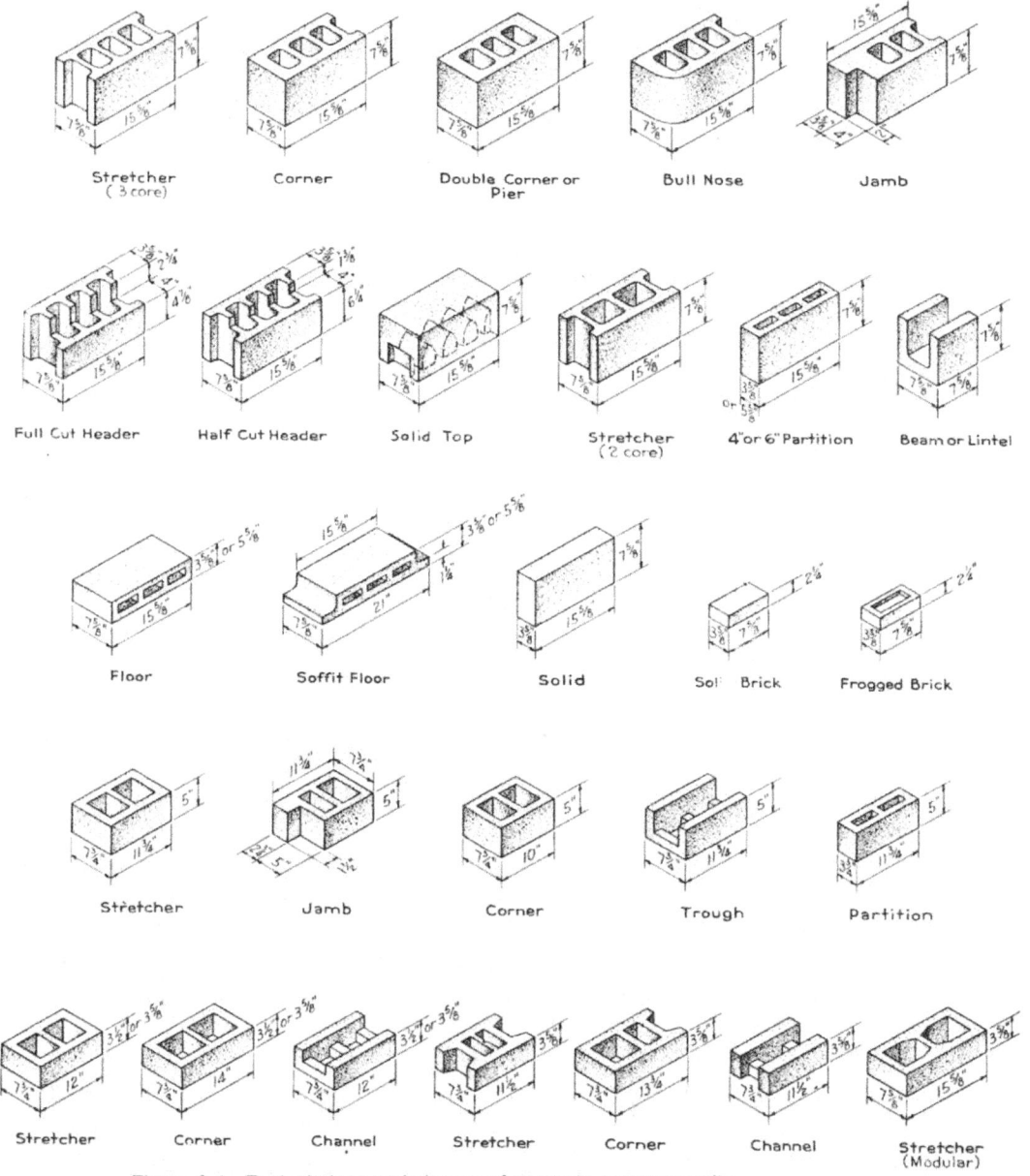

Figure 8-1.. Typical sizes and shapes of concrete masonry units.

f. *Block Machines.* Blocks are usually made in a power-tamping machine. Machines of this type are available from several manufacturers. The concrete is tamped into a mold and the mold immediately stripped off. In this way, blocks can be rapidly made using only one mold. The mix used is dry enough so that the block will retain its shape.

g. *Hand Method.* In this method, concrete of fluid consistency is placed into sets of iron molds. The molds are stripped after the concrete has hardened. By this process, dense block can be made with little labor. The disadvantage lies in the fact that a large number of molds is required.

h. *Curing.* Concrete blocks are usually steam-cured since less time is required. Concrete blocks cured in wet steam at 125°F. for a period of 15 hours will have 70 percent of their 28-day strength. If steam is not available, blocks may be cured by protecting them from the sun and keeping them damp for a period of 7 days.

i. *Exposed Blocks.* Concrete blocks exposed to weathering should be made with concrete having at least six sacks of cement per cubic yard of concrete. When lightweight porous aggregate is used, premixing with water for 2 minutes before adding the cement is advisable.

SECTION II. CONSTRUCTION PROCEDURES

8-3 Modular Planning

Concrete masonry walls should be laid out to make maximum use of full- and half-length units, thus minimizing cutting and fitting of units on the job. Length and height of wall, width and height of openings and wall areas between doors, windows, and corners should be planned to use full-size and half-size units which are usually available (Figure 8-2). This procedure assumes that window and door frames are of modular dimensions which fit modular full- and half-size units. Then, all horizontal dimensions should be in multiples of nominal full-length masonry units and both horizontal and vertical dimensions should be designed to be in multiples of 8 inches. Table 8-1 lists nominal length of concrete masonry walls by stretchers and Table 8-2 lists nominal height of concrete masonry walls by courses. When units 8x4x16 are used, the horizontal dimensions should be planned in multiples of 8 inches (half-length units) and the vertical dimensions in multiples of 4 inches. If the thickness of the wall is greater or less than the length of a half-unit, a special length is required at each corner in each course.

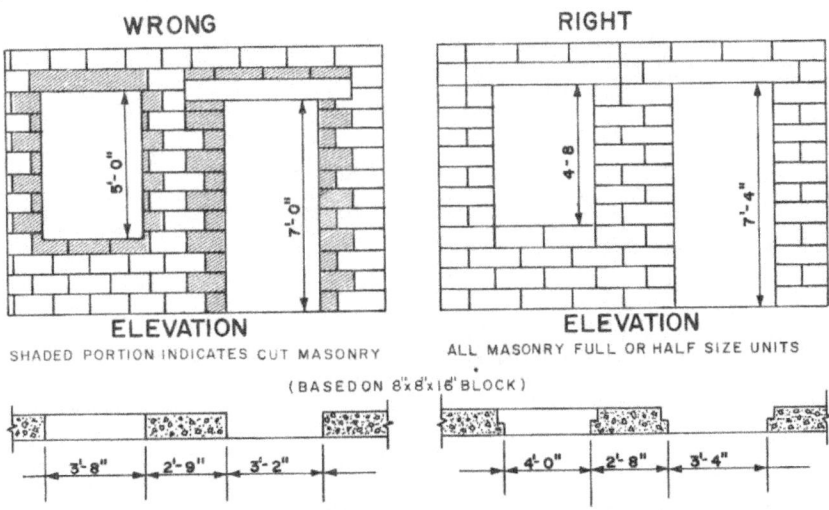

Figure 8-2. Planning concrete masonry wall openings

Table 8-1. Nominal Length of Concrete Masonry Walls by Stretchers

No. of stretchers	Nominal length of concrete masonry walls	
	Units 15⅝" long and half units 7⅝" long with ⅜" thick head joints.	Units 11⅝" long and half units 5⅝" long with ⅜" thick head joints.
1	1' 4"	1' 0".
1½	2' 0"	1' 6".
2	2' 8"	2' 0".
2½	3' 4"	2' 6".
3	4' 0"	3' 0".
3½	4' 8"	3' 6".
4	5' 4"	4' 0".
4½	6' 0"	4' 6".
5	6' 8"	5' 0".
5½	7' 4"	5' 6".
6	8' 0"	6' 0".
6½	8' 8"	6' 6".
7	9' 4"	7' 0".
7½	10' 0"	7' 6".
8	10' 8"	8' 0".
8½	11' 4"	8' 6".
9	12' 0"	9' 0".
9½	12' 8"	9' 6".
10	13' 4"	10' 0".
10½	14' 0"	10' 6".
11	14' 8"	11' 0".
11½	15' 4"	11' 6".
12	16' 0"	12' 0".
12½	16' 8"	12' 6".
13	17' 4"	13' 0".
13½	18' 0"	13' 6".
14	18' 8"	14' 0".
14½	19' 4"	14' 6".
15	20' 0"	15' 0".
20	26' 8"	20' 0".

(Actual length of wall is measured from outside edge to outside edge of units and is equal to the nominal length minus ⅜" (one mortar joint).)

Table 8-3. Nominal Height of Concrete Masonry Walls by Courses

No. of courses	Nominal height of concrete masonry walls	
	Units 7⅝" high and ⅜" thick bed joint	Units 3⅝" high and ⅜" thick bed joint
1	8"	4".
2	1' 4"	8".
3	2' 0"	1' 0".
4	2' 8"	1' 4".
5	3' 4"	1' 8".
6	4' 0"	2' 0".
7	4' 8"	2' 4".
8	5' 4"	2' 8".
9	6' 0"	3' 0".
10	6' 8"	3' 4".
15	10' 0"	5' 0".
20	13' 4"	6' 8".
25	16' 8"	8' 4".
30	20' 0"	10' 0".
35	23' 4"	11' 8".
40	26' 8"	13' 4".
45	30' 0"	15' 0".
50	33' 4"	16' 8".

(For concrete masonry units 7⅝" and 3⅝" in height laid with ⅜" mortar joints. Height is measured from center to center of mortar joints.)

8-4 Footings

Masonry wall footings should be placed on firm, undisturbed soil of adequate load-bearing capacity to carry the design load and they should be below frost penetration. Unless local requirements or codes stipulate otherwise, it is general practice to make footings for small buildings twice as wide as the thickness of the walls they support. Table 8-3 lists weights and quantities of materials for concrete masonry walls. The thickness of the footings is equal to one-half their width (Figure 8-3).

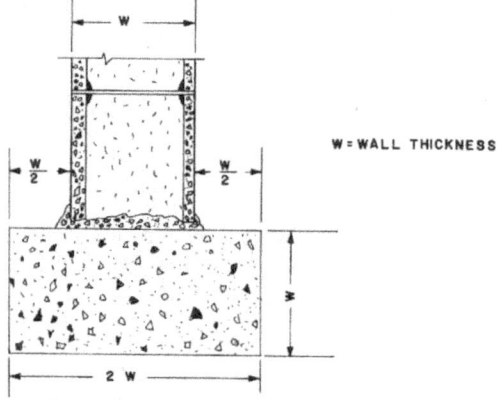

Figure 8-3. Dimensions of masonry wall footings.

Table 8-3. Weights and Quantities of Materials for Concrete Masonry Walls

Actual unit sizes (width x height x length) in.	Nominal wall thickness in.	For 100 sq ft of wall			For 100 concrete units	
		Number of units	Average weight of finished wall		Mortar** cu ft	Mortar*** cu ft
			Heavyweight aggregate lb*	Lightweight aggregate lb*		
3⅝ x 3⅝ x 15⅝	4	225	3050	2150	13.5	6.0
5⅝ x 3⅝ x 15⅝	6	225	4550	3050	13.5	6.0
7⅝ x 3⅝ x 15⅝	8	225	5700	3700	13.5	6.0
3⅝ x 7⅝ x 15⅝	4	112.5	2850	2050	8.5	7.5
5⅝ x 7⅝ x 15⅝	6	112.5	4350	2950	8.5	7.5
7⅝ x 7⅝ x 15⅝	8	112.5	5500	3600	8.5	7.5
11⅝ x 7⅝ x 15⅝	12	112.5	7950	4900	8.5	7.5

Table based on ⅜-in. mortar joints.
*Actual weight within ±7% of average weight.
**Actual weight within ±17% of average weight.
***With face-shell mortar bedding. Mortar quantities include 10% allowance for waste.
Actual weight of 100 sq ft of wall can be computed by formula $W(N) + 150(M)$ where:
W = actual weight of a single unit
N = number of units for 100 sq ft of wall
M = cu ft of mortar for 100 sq ft of wall

8.5 Subsurface Drainage

When the ground water level in the wet season can be expected to be at the elevation of the basement floor, a line of drain tile should be placed in the outer side of footings. The tile line should have a fall of at least ½ inch in 12 feet and should drain to a suitable outlet. Pieces of roofing felt placed over the joints prevent sediment from entering the tile during backfilling. The tile line should be covered to a depth of 12 inches with a permeable fill of coarse gravel or crushed stone ranging from 1 to 1½ inches in size. Then the rest of the trench can be filled with earth from the excavation after the first floor is in place.

8.6 Weathertight Walls

a. *Construction Details*. Good workmanship is always an important factor in building weathertight walls. Each masonry unit should be laid plumb and true. Both horizontal and vertical joints should be well filled and compacted by tooling when the mortar has partly stiffened. Flashing is necessary at vertical joints in copings and caps, at the joints between roofs and walls, and below cornices and other members projecting beyond the face of the wall. Drips should be provided for chimney caps, sills, and other projecting ledges to shed water away from the wall surface. Drains and gutters must be large enough to keep water from overflowing and running down over masonry surfaces.

b. *Exterior Masonry Joints*. Concave and V-shaped mortar joints (Figure 8-4) are recommended for walls of exterior concrete masonry in preference to struck or raked joints that form small lodges which may hold water. With modular-size masonry units, mortar joints will be approximately 3/8-inch thick. Experience has shown that this thickness of joint where properly made helps to produce a weathertight, neat, and durable concrete masonry wall.

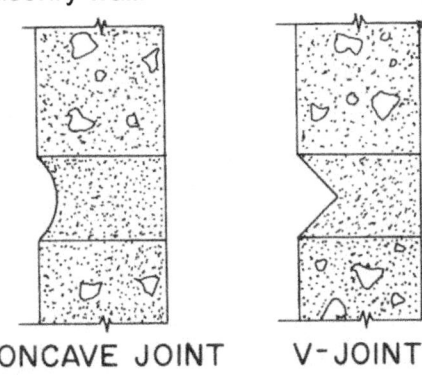

CONCAVE JOINT   V-JOINT

Figure 8-4. Tooled mortar joints for weathertight construction.

8-7 Basement Walls

a. *Plaster Coat.* The earth side of concrete masonry basement walls should always be given two ¼-inch thick coats of plaster. Either portland cement plaster (1-2½ mix by volume) or mortar used in laying the block should be used for this purpose. In hot dry weather, the wall surface should be very lightly dampened with a fog spray of water before application of the first coat of plaster. The first coat of plaster is roughened after it has partly hardened to provide a bond for the second coat, and allowed to harden 24 hours before the second coat is applied. The first coat is damped lightly just before the second coat is applied and the second coat should be kept damp for at least 48 hours after application. In very wet soils plastered surface below grade are frequently given two continuous coatings of bituminous material brushed on over a suitable priming coat. The plaster must be dry when the primer is applied to it and the primer coat must be dry when the bituminous material is applied. No backfilling against concrete masonry walls should be permitted until the first floor is in place.

b. *Supporting Floor and Roof Loads.* Masonry courses which support floor beams or floor slabs should be of solid masonry. This helps to distribute the loads over the wall and provides a barrier against termites. Such courses can be constructed by filling the cores of hollow block with concrete or mortar or by using solid masonry units without cores. Strips of expanded metal lath, laid in the bed joint below, support the concrete or mortar filling in the cores.

8-8 Concrete Masonry Walls

a. *First Course.* After locating the corners of the wall, the mason usually checks the layout by stringing out the blocks for the first course without mortar (1, Figure 8-5). A chalked snapline is useful to mark the footing and align the block accurately. A full bed of mortar is then spread and furrowed with the trowel to insure plenty of mortar along the bottom edges of the face shells of the block for the first course (2, Figure 8-5). The corner block should be laid first and carefully positioned (3, Figure 8-5). All blocks should be laid with the thicker end of the face shell up to provide a larger mortar-bedding area (4, Figure 8-5). Mortar is applied only to the ends of the face shells for vertical joints. Several blocks can be placed on end and the mortar applied to the vertical face shells in one operation. Each block is then brought over its final and pushed downward into the mortar bed and against the previously laid block to obtain a well-fitted vertical mortar joint (5, Figure 8-5). After three or four blocks have been laid, the mason's level is used as a straightedge to assure correct alignment of the blocks. Then the blocks are carefully checked with the level and brought to proper grade and made plumb by tapping with the trowel handle (1 and 2, Figure 8-6). The first course of concrete masonry should be paid with great care, to make sure it is properly aligned, leveled, and plumbed, and to assure that succeeding courses, and the finally the wall, are straight and true.

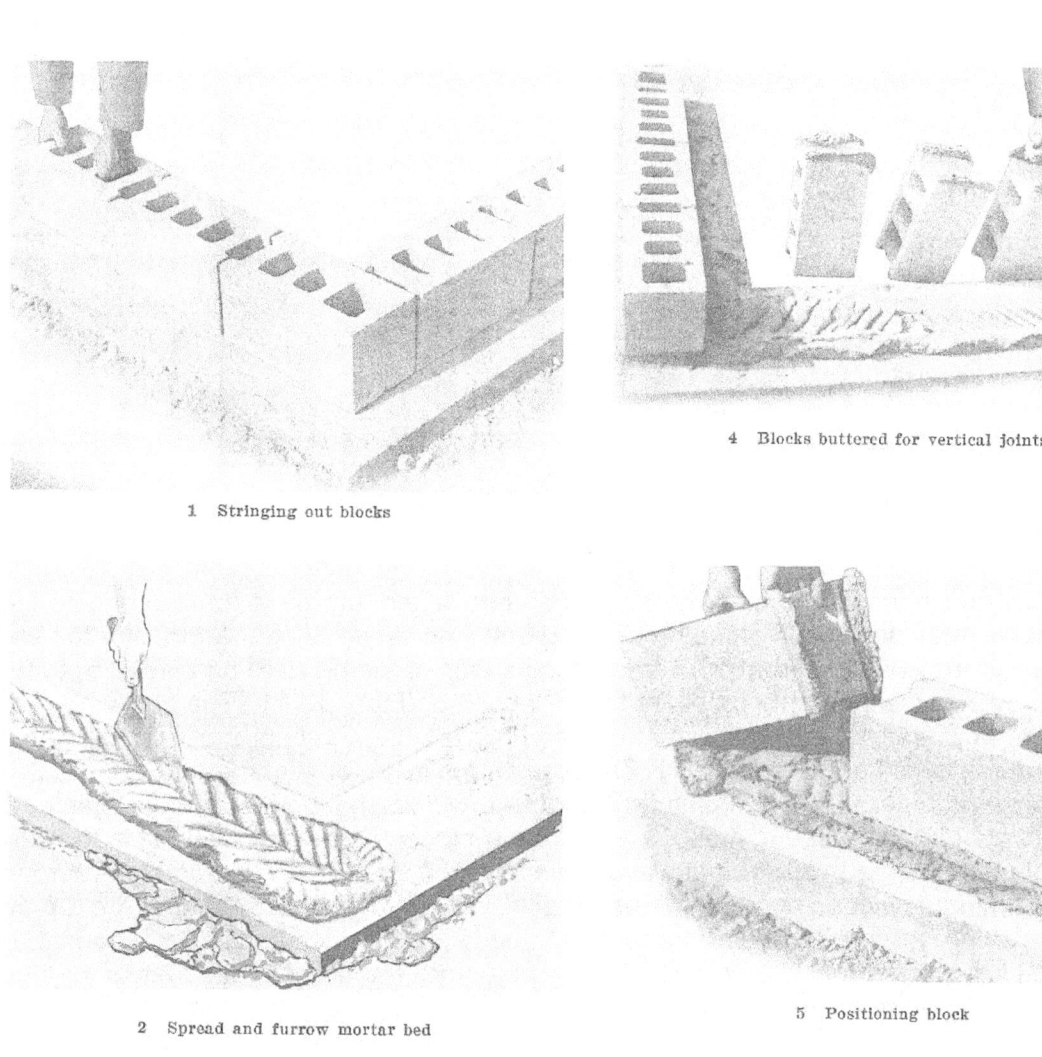

1 Stringing out blocks

4 Blocks buttered for vertical joints

2 Spread and furrow mortar bed

5 Positioning block

3 Position corner block

Figure 8-5. First course of blocks.

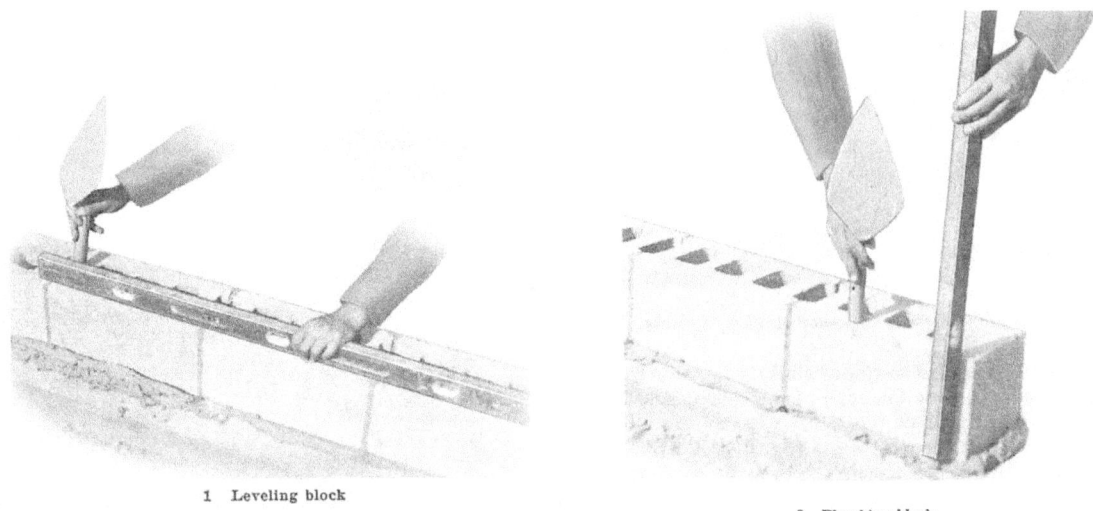

Figure 8-6. Checking first course of blocks.

b. *Laying Up the Corners.* After the first course is laid, mortar is applied only to the horizontal face shells of the block (face shell mortar bedding). Mortar for the vertical joints may be applied to the vertical face shells of the block to be placed or to the block previously laid or both, to insure well-filled joints (Figure 8-7). The corner of the wall are built first, usually four or five courses higher than the center of the wall. As each course is laid at the corner, it is checked with a level for alignment (1, Figure 8-8), for level (2, Figure 8-8), and plumb (3, Figure 8-8). Each block is carefully checked with a level of straightedge to make certain that the faces of the block are all in the same plane to insure true, straight walls. The use of a story or course-pole, a board with markings 8 inches apart, provides an accurate method of determining the top of the masonry for each course (Figure 8-9). Joints are 3/8-inch thick. Each course, in building the corners, is stepped back a half block and the mason checks the horizontal spacing of the block by placing his level diagonally across the corners of the block (Figure 8-10).

Figure 8-7. Vertical joints.

1 Aligning

2 Leveling

3 Plumbing
Figure 8-8. Checking each course

Figure 8-9. Use of story or course pole

Figure 8-10. Checking horizontal spacing of blocks

c. *Laying Block Between Corners.* When filling in the wall between the corners, a mason's line is stretched from corner to corner for each course and the top outside edge of each block is laid to this line. The manner of gripping the block is important. It should be tipped slightly towards the mason so he can see the edge of the course below, enabling him to place the lower edge of the block directly over the course below (Figure 8-11). All adjustments to final position must be made while the mortar is soft and plastic. Any adjustments made after the mortar has stiffened will break the mortar bond and allow the penetration of water. Each block is leveled and aligned to the mason's line by tapping lightly with the trowel handle. The use of the mason's level between corners is limited to checking the face of each block to keep it lined up with the face of the wall.

Figure 8-11. Adjusting block between corners.

d. *Mortar.* To assure good bond, mortar should not be spread too far ahead of actual laying of the block or it will stiffen and lose its plasticity. As each block is laid, excess mortar extruding from the joints is cut off with the trowel (Figure 8-12) and is thrown back on the mortar board to be reworked into the fresh mortar. Dead mortar that has been picked up from the scaffold or from the floor should not be used.

Figure 8-12. Cutting off excess mortar.

e. *Closure Block.* When installing the closure block, all edges of the opening and all four vertical edges of the closure block are buttered with mortar and the closure block is carefully lowered into place (Figure 8-13). If any of the mortar falls out leaving an open joint, the block should be removed and the procedure repeated.

Figure 8-13. Installing closure block.

f. *Tooling.* Weathertight joints and neat appearance of concrete block walls are dependent on proper tooling. The mortar joints should be tooled after a section of the wall has been laid and the mortar has become "thumb-print" hard. Tooling (Figure 8-14) compacts the mortar and forces it tightly against the masonry on each side of the joint. All joints should be tooled either concave or V-shaped. Horizontal joints (1, Figure 8-14) should be tooled first, followed by striking the vertical joints with a small S-shaped jointer (2, Figure 8-14). Mortar burrs remaining after tooling is completed should be trimmed off flush with the face of the wall with a trowel or removed by rubbing with a burlap bag.

1 Tooling horizontal joints

2 Striking vertical joints

Figure 8-14. Tooling mortar joints.

g. *Anchor Bolts.* Wood plates are fastened to tops of concrete masonry walls by anchor bolts ½ inch in diameter, 18 inches long, and spaced not more than 4 feet apart. The bolts are placed in cores of the top two courses of block with the cores filled with concrete or mortar. Pieces of metal lath placed in the second horizontal mortar joint from the top of the wall and under the cores to be filled (1, Figure 8-15) will hold the concrete or mortar filling in place. The threaded end of the bolt should extend above the top of the wall (2, Figure 8-15).

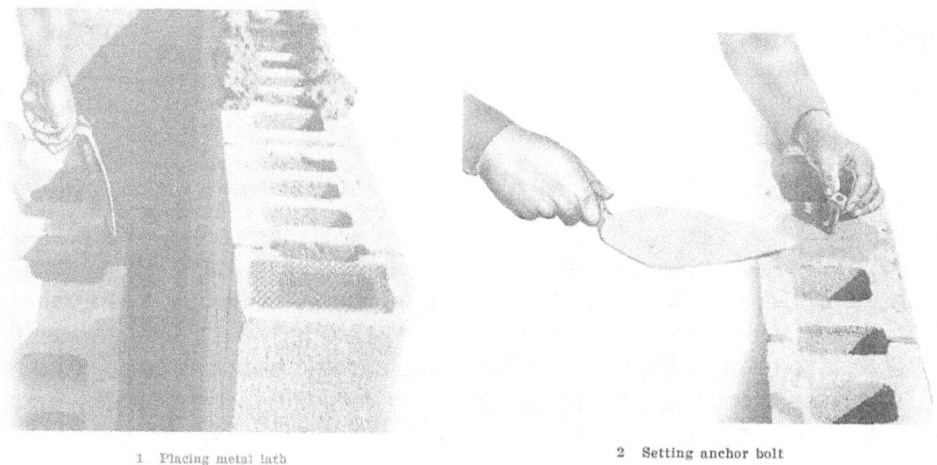

1 Placing metal lath

2 Setting anchor bolt

Figure 8-15. Installing anchor bolts on top of wall.

h. *Control Joints.* Control joints are continuous vertical joints built into concrete masonry walls to control cracking resulting from unusual stresses. The joints are intended to permit slight wall movement without cracking. Control joints should be laid up in mortar just as any other joint. Full- and half-length block are used to form a continuous vertical joint (1, Figure 8-16). If they are exposed to the weather or to view, they should be calked. After the mortar is quite stiff, it should be raked out to a depth of about ¾ inch to provide a recess for the calking material (2, Figure 8-16). A thin, flat calking trowel is used to force the calking compound into the joint. Another type of control joint can be constructed with building paper or roofing felt inserted in the end core of the block and extending the full height of the control joint (Figure 8-17). The paper or felt, cut to convenient lengths and wide enough to extend across the joint, prevents the mortar from bonding on one side of the joint. Sometimes control joint blocks are used if available.

1 Full and half length block for joint

Figure 8-17. Paper or felt used for control joints.

2 Raking mortar from joint

Figure 8-15. Control joint.

8.9 Intersecting Walls

a. *Bearing Walls.* Intersecting concrete block bearing walls should not be tied together in a masonry bond, except at the corners. Instead, one wall should terminate at the face of the other wall with a control joint at the point. Bearing walls are tied together with a metal tiebar ¼ x 1¼ x 28 inches with 2-inch right angle bends on each end (1, Figure 8-18). Tiebars are spaced not over 4 feet apart vertically. Bends at the ends of the tiebars are embedded in cores filled with mortar or concrete (2, Figure 8-18). Pieces of metal lath placed under the cores support the concrete or mortar filling (1, Figure 8-15).

1 Tiebar 2 Filling core with mortar

Figure 8-18. Tieing intersecting bearing walls

b. *Nonbearing Walls.* To tie nonbearing block walls to other walls, strips of metal lath or ¼-inch mesh galvanized hardware cloth are placed across the joint between the two walls (1, Figure 8-19), in alternate courses in the wall. When one wall is constructed first, the metal strips are built into the wall and later tied into the mortar joint of the second wall (2, Figure 19). Control joints are constructed where the two walls meet.

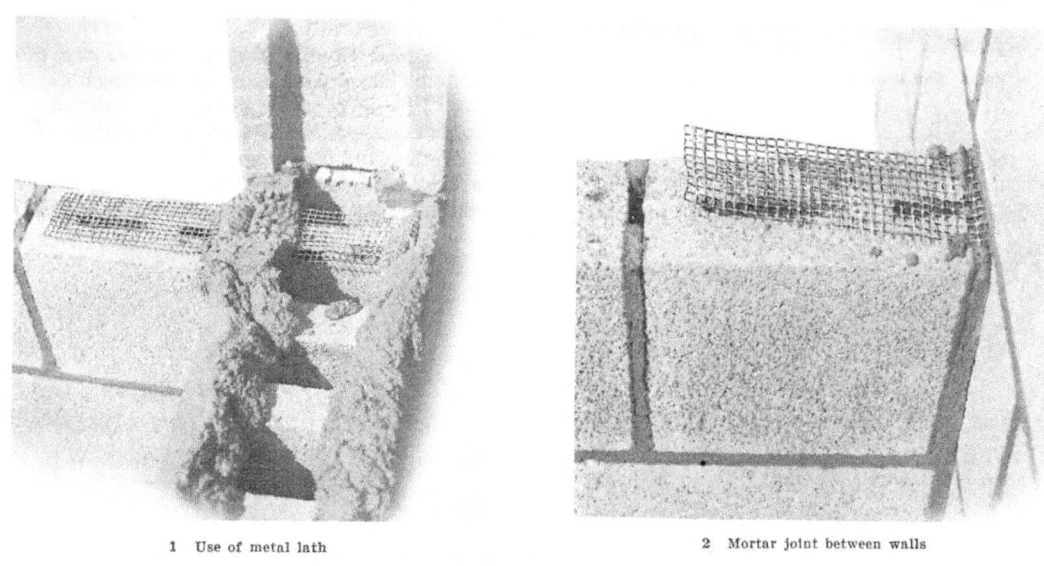

1 Use of metal lath 2 Mortar joint between walls

Figure 8-19. Tieing intersecting nonbearing walls.

8-10 Lintels and Sills

a. *Lintels.* Precast concrete lintels are often used over door and window openings (1, Figure 8-20). Precast concrete lintels are designed with an offset on the underside (2, Figure 20) for modular window and door openings. Steel lintel angles are also used for lintels to support block over openings. They must be installed with an offset on the underside (3, Figure 8-20) to fit modular openings. A non-corroding metal plate placed under the ends of lintels where control joints occur, will permit lintels to slip and the control joints to function properly. A full bed of mortar should be placed over this metal plate to distribute the lintel load uniformly.

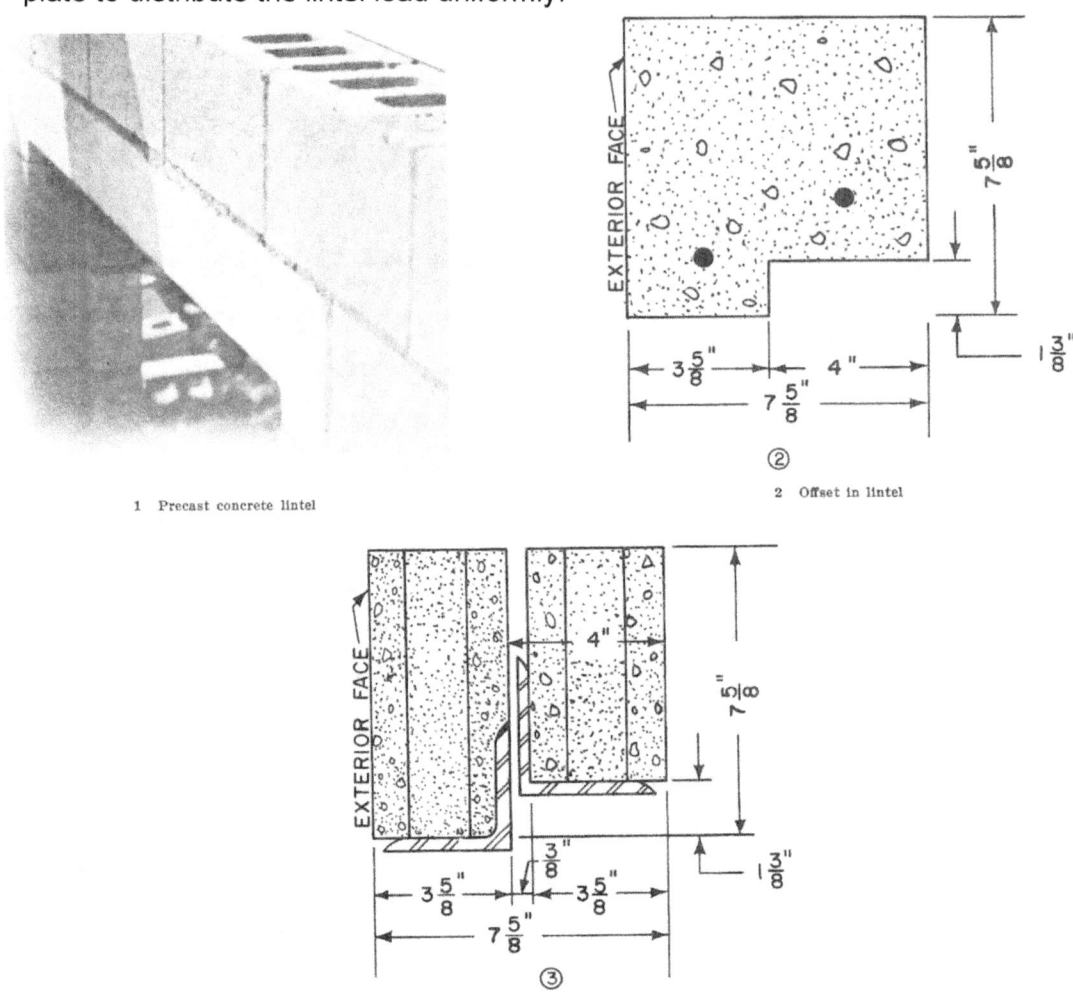

Figure 8-20. Installing precast lintels.

b. *Sills.* Precast concrete sills are usually installed after the masonry walls have been built (Figure 8-21). Joints at the ends of the sills should be tightly filled with mortar or with a calking compound.

Figure 8-21. Installing precast concrete sills.

8-11 Patching and Cleaning Block Walls

a. *Patching.* Any patching of the mortar joints or filling of holes left by nails or line pins should be done with fresh mortar.

b. *Cleaning.* Hardened, embedded mortar smears cannot be removed and paint cannot be depended on to hide smears, so particular care should be taken to prevent smearing mortar into the surface of the block. Concrete block walls should not be cleaned with an acid wash to remove smears or mortar droppings. Mortar droppings that stick to the block wall should be allowed to dry before removal with a trowel (1, Figure 22). Most of the mortar can be removed by rubbing with a small piece of concrete (broken) block after the mortar is dry and hard (2, Figure 8-22). Brushing the rubbed spots will remove practically all of the mortar (3, Figure 8-22).

1 Removing mortar with trowel

2 Using piece of broken block

3 Brushing

Figure 8-22. Patching and cleaning concrete block.

8-12 Duties of Concrete Mason and Helper

a. *Mason.* The mason is responsible for laying out the job so that the finished masonry will be properly done. If the construction involves walls, he must see that the walls are plumb and the courses are level. He is responsible for all the detail work such as cutting and fitting of masonry units, joints, and installation of anchor bolts and ties for intersecting walls.

b. *Mason's Helper.* The mason's helper mixes mortar and carries concrete blocks and mortar to the mason as rapidly as these materials are required. He assists the mason in the layout of the job and at times he may lay out block on an adjacent course to expedite the mason's work. He keeps the mortar tempered as required.

SECTION III. RUBBLE STONE MASONRY

8-13 Uses

Rubble stone masonry such as that shown in Figure 8-23 is used for walls both above and below ground and for bridge abutments. In military construction, it is used when form lumber or masonry units are not available. Rubble masonry may be laid up with or without mortar; if strength and stability are desired, mortar must be used.

1 Random rubble masonry   2 Coursed rubble masonry

Figure 8-23. Rubble stone masonry.

8-14 Types

a. *Random Rubble.* This is the crudest of all types of stonework. Little attention is paid to laying the stone in courses (1, Figure 8-23). Each layer must contain bonding stones that extend through the wall (Figure 8-24). This produces a wall that is well tied together. The bed joints should be horizontal for stability but the "builds" or head joints may run in any direction.

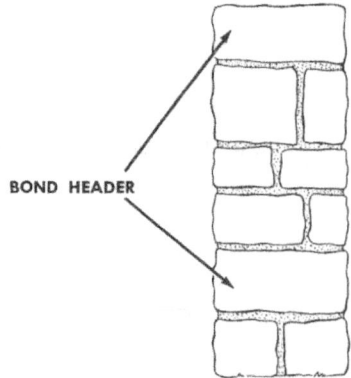

Figure 8-24. Rubble stone masonry wall showing bonding stone.

b. *Coursed Rubble.* Coursed rubble is assembled of roughly squared stones in such a manner as to produce approximately continuous horizontal bed joints (2, Figure 8-23).

8-15 Materials for Use in Random Rubble Stone Masonry

a. *Stone.* The stone for use in random rubble stone masonry should be strong, durable, and cheap. Durability and strength depend upon the chemical composition and physical structure of the stone. Some of the more commonly found stones that are suitable are limestone, sandstone, granite, and slate. Unsquared stones obtained from nearby ledges or quarries or even field stones may be used. The size of the stone should be such that two men can easily handle it. A variety of sizes is necessary in order to avoid using large quantities of mortar.

b. *Mortar.* The mortar for use in random rubble masonry may be composed of portland cement and sand in the proportions of one part cement to three parts sand by volume. Such mortar shrinks excessively and does not work well with the trowel. A better mortar to use is portland-cement-lime mortar. Mortar made with ordinary portland cement will stain most types of stone. If staining must be prevented, nonstaining white portland cement should be used in making the mortar. Lime does not usually stain the stone.

8-16 Laying Rubble Stone Masonry

Workmanship in laying stone masonry affects the economy, durability, and strength of the wall more than any other factor.

a. *Rules for Laying.*
   (1) Each stone should be laid on its broadest face.

   (2) If appearance is to be considered, the larger stones should be placed in the lower courses. The size of the stones should gradually diminish toward the top of the wall.

   (3) Porous stones should be moistened before being placed in mortar in order to prevent the stone from absorbing water from the mortar and thereby weakening the bond between the stone and the mortar.

   (4) The spaces between adjoining stones should be as small as practicable and these spaces should be completely filled with mortar and smaller stones.

   (5) If necessary to remove a stone after it has been placed upon the mortar bed, it should be lifted clear and reset.

b. *Footing.* The footing is larger than the wall itself. The largest stones should be used in it to give the greatest strength and lessen the danger of unequal settlement. The footing stones should be as long as the footing is wide, if possible. The footing stones should be laid in a mortar bed about 2 inches deep and all space between the stones filled with mortar and smaller stones.

c. *Bed Joint.* The thickness of the bed joint will vary, depending upon the stone used. In making the bed joint, enough mortar should be spread on the stone below the one being placed to fill the space between the two stones completely. Care must be taken not to spread the mortar too far ahead of the stonelaying.

d. *Head Joint or Builds.* The head joint is made after three or four stones have been laid. This is done by slushing the small spaces with mortar and filling the larger spaces with small stones and mortar. The head joints should be formed before the mortar in the bed joint has set up.

e. *Bonding.* Bond stones should occur at least once in each 6 to 10 square feet of wall. These stones pass all the way through the wall as shown in Figure 8-24. Each head joint should be offset from adjacent head joints above and below it as much as possible (1, Figure 8-23) to bond the wall together and make it stronger.

f. *Laying the Wall.*
   (1) If the wall need not be exactly plumb and true to line, the level and line will not be used and the wall will be laid by eye. Frequent sighting is necessary.
   (2) If the wall must be exactly plumb and erected to line, corner posts of wood should be erected to serve the purpose of corner leads and the stone laid with a line. No particular attention is paid to laying the stone in level courses. Some parts of the stone will be farther away from the line than other parts.